Transit Life

D1003121

Urban and Industrial Environments

Series editor: Robert Gottlieb, Henry R. Luce Professor of Urban and Environmental Policy, Occidental College

For a complete list of books published in this series, please see the back of the book.

Transit Life

How Commuting Is Transforming Our Cities

David Bissell

The MIT Press
Cambridge, Massachusetts
London, England

© 2018 Massachusetts Institute of Technology

All rights reserved. No part of this book may be reproduced in any form by any electronic or mechanical means (including photocopying, recording, or information storage and retrieval) without permission in writing from the publisher.

This book was set in ITC Stone Sans Std and ITC Stone Serif Std by Toppan Best-set Premedia Limited. Printed and bound in the United States of America.

Library of Congress Cataloging-in-Publication Data

Names: Bissell, David, 1982- author.
Title: Transit life : how commuting is transforming our cities / David Bissell.
Other titles: Urban and industrial environments.
Description: Cambridge, MA : The MIT Press, [2018] | Series: Urban and industrial
    environments | Includes bibliographical references and index.
Identifiers: LCCN 2017027987| ISBN 9780262037563 (hbk : alk. paper) | ISBN
    9780262534963 (pbk : alk. paper)
Subjects: LCSH: Commuting--Social aspects. | Commuters. | Commuters--Time
    management.
Classification: LCC HD5717.2 .B57 2018 | DDC 388.4/132--dc23 LC record
available at https://lccn.loc.gov/2017027987

10 9 8 7 6 5 4 3 2 1

To Pat and Bill, with gratitude

Contents

Acknowledgments

This book came to fruition only with the encouragement, guidance, critique, inspiration, patience, and humor of many people and with the generous support of numerous organizations.

I am grateful to the Australian Research Council, which provided financial support for the project that this book is based on through a Discovery Early Career Researcher Award (DE120102279). I would like to thank acquisitions editor Beth Clevenger at the MIT Press; her assistant, Anthony Zannino; and Robert Gottlieb, editor of the MIT Press Urban and Industrial Environments series, for their support for the project and for their editorial direction and expert guidance. Thank you to Melinda Rankin for her meticulous copy editing, to Deborah Rogers for undertaking such precise transcription, to Karina Pelling for drawing the maps, and to Edgar Daly for providing exemplary research assistance. Three reviewers of the manuscript provided extensive and engaged feedback that was incredibly helpful, and I am grateful to them for their time and encouragement.

The School of Sociology at the Australian National University provided a wonderfully supportive environment for the project. At different times, Cathy Ayres, Rachel Bloul, Darren Halpin, Maria Hynes, Helen Keane, Kaima Negishi, Gavin Smith, Clare Southerton, Emmeline Taylor, Anna Tsalapatanis, and Kevin White made the school an enjoyable and intellectually stimulating place to be. I am also grateful to Karina Bird, Louise Knox, Erin Preston, and Meg Sawtell for their expert assistance with project administration.

I am indebted to so many colleagues in geography and mobilities research who have helped shape the ideas in this book. I deeply value the friendships and collaborations that have enriched my academic life.

Whilst I cannot name everyone here, I would like to thank several friends who have contributed to the book more directly at different points during the project. I would like to thank Tim Edensor for convincing me that I wanted to write this book. I am grateful to J-D Dewsbury for helping me think about habit; to Mitch Rose for helping me think about empirics; and to Donald McNeill for helping me think about time-lapse photography. I would like to thank Ben Anderson, Tomás Errázuriz, Eric Laurier, Paola Jirón, and Elaine Stratford for inviting me to present parts of this book to engaged audiences who provided valuable feedback at different stages of the writing. I would also like to thank Phillip Bissell, Gillian Fuller, Andrew Gorman-Murray, Katie Meehan, Gavin Smith, Peter Thomas, and Vickie Zhang, who kindly read and commented on drafts of different parts of the book.

Looking back, I am grateful to Laurence Mitchell for being such an inspiring geography teacher, and to Jim Duncan, whose third-year undergraduate class in cultural geography was the main reason I decided to continue studying geography. I am grateful to Mike Crang and Paul Harrison, who supervised my doctoral work and nurtured my enthusiasm for mobilities and social theory. In more recent times, Anthony Elliott and John Urry provided me with generous and supportive mentoring, for which I am very grateful. Gillian Fuller is a long-time collaborator and friend whose ideas and life trajectories have firmly grooved my own. I am particularly grateful to Ann Hill for friendship, inspiration, and encouragement, especially while I wrote this book. I am so grateful to Margaret Bissell, Phillip Bissell, Deborah Flüeler-Jones, and Peter Thomas for their love, care, and unwavering support; and to Pat and Bill for the train rides from Stourbridge Junction all those years ago. Finally, I would like to express my heartfelt gratitude to all the commuters and participants in Sydney who were so generous in sharing their transit lives with me.

A few parts of this book draw on ideas that I have published in academic journal articles. I am grateful to the publishers named here for permission to reprint reworked parts of the following articles: "Transforming Commuting Mobilities: The Memory of Practice," *Environment and Planning A 46*, no. 8 (2014): 1946–1965 (SAGE); "Micropolitics of Mobility: Public Transport Commuting and Everyday Encounters with Forces of Enablement and

Constraint," *Annals of the American Association of Geographers* 106, no. 2 (2016): 394–403 (Taylor and Francis); "How Environments Speak: Everyday Mobilities, Impersonal Speech, and the Geographies of Commentary," *Social and Cultural Geography* 16, no. 2 (2015): 146–164 (Taylor and Francis); and "Encountering Stressed Bodies: Slow Creep Transformations and Tipping Points of Commuting Mobilities," *Geoforum* 51, no. 1 (2014): 191–201 (Elsevier).

Introduction: Thinking Commuting Differently

Cities in Transit

"Overslept. So tired. If late. Get fired. Why bother? Why the pain? Just go home. Do it again." These sardonic lines adorn eight low ceiling beams in a dingy underground passageway between the Port Authority and Times Square subway stations in the heart of New York City. "The Commuter's Lament" is an art installation by Norman B. Colp, commissioned by the Metropolitan Transportation Authority in 1991.[1] Its alternative title, "A Close Shave," pays homage to the iconic Burma-Shave adverts on American highways in the mid-twentieth century, which used a series of road signs spaced apart with a line of a poem on each sign to amuse passing drivers.[2] However, it is hard to imagine that the thousands of commuters who pass under the lines of Colp's poem every day are amused or uplifted, as was the intention of the original Burma-Shave ads. Far from providing diversion, these lines zero in on the life situation that many commuters striding beneath them find themselves in day after day. Simultaneously mocking and commiserating, the lines evoke a pessimistic sense of the overtired and overworked life of the commuter.

Few activities that bead our everyday lives have earned such dubious notoriety as commuting. That the words *hell* and *nightmare* are so often invoked to describe journeys to and from work indicates just how disparaged this part of our lives often is.[3] Through popular representations on screen and page, the commute has often been depicted in dystopian terms, as a source of endless slog and drudgery,[4] coming to stand for all that is stressful and wearying about our contemporary daily routines. As one study by psychologist Douglas Kahneman and colleagues found, of all daily activities, commuting was ranked by participants as the least satisfying.[5]

The study suggests that commuting is an activity that many would happily give up in exchange for doing something more pleasurable or rewarding. Nobody, it would seem, likes to commute.

Tidal Restlessness

Commuting is one of the most significant travel practices of our time. As Elwyn Brooks White wrote of New York, "Commuters give the city its tidal restlessness."[6] This twice-daily ebb and flow of people is one of the major rhythms of contemporary urban life. We spend so much of our lives in transit to and from work. A survey in London reported that on average British workers will spend one year and thirty-five days commuting 191,760 miles, or 308,607 kilometers, in their lifetimes.[7] Other studies indicate a similar magnitude, with the average worker in Britain spending 139 hours a year commuting, the equivalent of nineteen standard working days.[8] One in five workers in Britain now travels in excess of one hundred kilometers each way, and one in ten spends over two hours a day traveling to and from work.[9] All this travel is not cheap, either; the same survey found that commuters spend an average of £42,000 on travel over their working lives.[10]

Although it might feel like commuting has always been part of urban life, it is a relatively recent phenomenon. Before the twentieth century, people in many cities tended to live much closer to their places of work. Rewind to the early nineteenth century: People only traveled about fifty meters a day on average.[11] Even at the turn of the twentieth century, studies looking at commuting in Britain reveal that walking was still the main way that people traveled to and from work, especially outside London.[12] Then, as industry and commerce expanded and became increasingly centralized in cities, demand for workers' accommodation grew and cities developed outwards. The construction of vast suburban railway networks in many cities in the early twentieth century helped transport large volumes of people efficiently and relatively cheaply into the city from the new outer suburbs, effectively bringing once-distanced locations closer together.[13] The origin of the word *commute* itself heralds from the late nineteenth-century United States' *commutation ticket*, a reduced price railway season ticket by which the price of multiple daily tickets was "commuted" into a single payment. It was not until the 1960s and 1970s that the car became such a dominant way to commute in many cities.[14] Although the amount of time that people spend in transit has remained relatively stable,[15] the distances that people travel and the number of people traveling have both increased. Today, people travel an average of fifty kilometers a day.[16] Now, over half a million people arrive in central London every day by train.

Bleak Premonitions

Journeys between work and home are a strange, liminal part of our lives. They are curiously suspended between the other activities we undertake at home and work—activities that, for better or worse, give our lives meaning and shape who we are. However, these journeys are often so deeply routinized that we rarely stop to think about them.[17] The blindingly familiar world of traffic and travel has become so deeply grooved into the everyday life of cities that it often goes unremarked upon.

Yet at times, this unexceptional activity becomes exceptional. Commuting periodically pierces our collective attention, sometimes enough to make global headline news. In 2012, a traffic jam in Beijing lasted for an eye-watering twelve days. In São Paolo, there are sometimes traffic jams over two hundred kilometers long. Given that even more people will be living, working and moving around cities than ever before in the twenty-first century,[18] such scenes are bleak premonitions of what intensifying processes of urbanization around the world could potentially lead to.

In Manila, the average length of time spent commuting every day is currently ninety minutes.[19] In Bangkok, it is three hours.[20] In India, massive population growth and associated urbanization have swelled the number of people commuting into city centers. Yet transport infrastructure development has only grown at a fraction of the rate of demand.[21] From Mexico City to Milan, and from Shenzhen to Sydney, transport infrastructures in many large cities around the world are at a breaking point. In Mumbai, for instance, 7.5 million riders travel each day on some of the most overloaded trains in the world. Every day, there are twenty to twenty-five serious accidents and between ten and twelve people are killed. Some stations even employ their own undertakers.[22]

As if these headlines are not evidence enough, from a range of professional perspectives there are many reasons to be concerned about the prevalence of commuting. For transport professionals, the assumption of conventional transport modeling is that the travel time of the commute is wasted time.[23] This is echoed by economists, for whom the commute is economically unproductive time taken away from the ostensibly productive parts of daily life. Such waste is illustrated in statistics that attempt to calculate the economic price of congestion. For instance, the cumulative financial cost of traffic congestion in the United States by 2030 is estimated to reach $2.8 trillion.[24] For environmentalists, this mass daily mobility is a problem viewed in terms of the carbon emissions contributing to human-induced climate change, as well as the detrimental localized effects of air pollution on the health of city dwellers.[25] For public health professionals, commuting means that many people are leading more sedentary lives than before, hemmed into cars or wedged into seats on public transport and thus increasing problems such as back pain and cardiovascular disease.[26]

These multiple problems have prompted multiple solutions. Many of the solutions proposed by transport professionals imagine the problem of commuting in terms of blockages to flows. Drawing on language often associated with human bodies, these solutions are about removing blockages and making flows happen more efficiently to restore a city's healthy "metabolism."[27] Building more road capacity, investing in public transport, spreading the peak morning and evening load more evenly throughout the day, and congestion pricing are just some of these practical solutions.[28] These solutions can be addressed through integrated "transit-oriented" planning, in which convenient public transport and active travel by bike and walking are at the forefront of the development of new homes and businesses, rather than pesky afterthoughts.[29] From this perspective, the solutions to commuting problems are about developing new infrastructures, changing the mode of transport that people use, and changing when people travel and to where.

Knowing Statistics

Much of what we already know about commuting and many proposed solutions are based on statistical knowledge. Commuting is usually understood in terms of the number of people involved, the mode of transport that people use, the time that it takes for people to get to work, and the distances that people travel. Statistical modeling is complex and valuable, providing a composite picture of where people are traveling from and to, as well as trends over time. However—and crucially—this only provides part of the story. A focus on these aggregate statistics obscures the myriad things that are taking place below the radar. As Tom Vanderbilt writes: "Engineers can look at a section of highway and measure its capacity, or model how many cars will pass in an hour. That traffic flow, while it may mathematically seem like a discrete entity, is made up of people who all have their own reasons for going where they are going, for enduring that traffic. Some may have no choice; some may choose."[30] In other words, focusing on statistics and trends overlooks that commuting is a hugely differentiated experience.

In statistical accounts of commuting, a commuter often becomes reduced to a singular axis of identity that obscures the diversity of what might be taking place. To talk about commuters in a generalized way overlooks the countless differences that make up the experience. The experience of commuting for migrant workers might be very different from that of business-class weekenders, whose experiences might be very different from those of long-distance commuters. Furthermore, to talk about *the commute* in a singular way overlooks all kinds of commuting scenarios that exist. For example, many commutes might be "radial" journeys between home and work, but others might involve "trip chaining," with journeys that involve joining many different places together, such as school drop-off, shopping, and other errands.[31]

Statistics also treat transformation in a similarly aggregate way. Commuting statistics only pick up on certain kinds of transformation over time, based on parameters such as mode of transport, distance traveled, and time taken. Consider, for instance, that between 2001 and 2006 in Sydney, the mode of transport that people used to get to and from work was relatively constant, with the proportion of car commuting increasing by just 1.4 percent and public transport decreasing by only 1 percent.[32] We might surmise from such statistics that the activity of commuting is relatively unchanging, yet such aggregate trends hide all manner of subtler transformations that might be taking place.

There is evidence that people's well-being is being significantly compromised by their commutes.[33] Yet alarmingly, aside from these large-scale diagnoses, very little is known about how commuting is transforming urban life. How is commuting affecting the social fabric of urban life, striking to the core of who we are? Would our lives *really* be better without commuting? Is commuting just a means to an end? The question of how our everyday journeys are changing our lives over months, years, and lifetimes is one that has yet to be adequately addressed. This book tackles this challenge head-on by examining commuting from a different perspective. Rather than looking at it in a top-down way, inspecting aggregate patterns and collating numbers of people involved, this book zooms in on the nitty-gritty events and encounters of the commute.

Experiencing Commuting

Our customary understanding of movement is that it is a displacement in time and across space from one point to another, such as between home and work. However, philosopher Erin Manning invites us to think about movement rather differently, encouraging us to consider how movement *creates* space and time, rather than displacing it.[34] She challenges us to overcome our habits of thinking about bodies as if they are fixed and bounded entities that move across the surface of the world. Instead of being an unchanging "essence," Manning's point is that bodies are much more "relational." This requires us to think about bodies in terms of their changing capacities, rather than just as fixed, idealized identities of the sort that are often invoked in transport statistics. What bodies can do, what they can sense, and what they can perceive does not stay fixed but *changes* in relation to movement. It is only through the events and encounters of movement itself that these capacities change.

This book explores how the journey to and from work is an overlooked sphere of everyday life fizzing with all manner of events and encounters. It appreciates that we are not closed off to this world, but open to it and informed by it. All the events that we experience, all the environments that we move through, impress on us and leave their mark. They might increase some capacities while depleting others. Even if we are not conscious of how an event has affected us at the time, we might come to realize, sometimes much later, how forceful that event was. Think of how being in a specific place can catch us off guard by sparking a memory that might be felt with overwhelming intensity. Our capacities to be affected by things and our capacities for action change through the experiences that we have. However, in parallel, our own presence changes the world as well. Think about how we might have left traces on the people that we travel with and on the environments that we travel through. What we experience becomes part of who we are—and who we are comes to be part of the environments that we move through.

This has some profound implications for reimagining the significance of our everyday commutes. For many writers, it is the exceptional experiences of travel associated with touring and vacations that are imagined as being transformative. Recall here the life-changing impetus for the Odyssean classical-era Grand Tour around Europe undertaken by the elite youth of the day.[35] Or, when planning a holiday, think of how we might hope that it will transform our being in some way.[36] This book shows how the everyday journeys that we make to and from work can be transformative in ways that are different, but no less profound.

Capturing the significance of understanding commuting as transformation, Filipino novelist Francisco Sionil José writes: "I am a commuter, not between the city and the village, although I do this frequently; not between the inane idealism of the classroom and the stifling reality beyond it, which I must do for survival and self-respect. I am a commuter between what I am now and what I was and would like to be and it is this commuting at lightning speed, at the oddest hours, that has done havoc to me."[37] Our experiences of moving change the manner in which we move and how we respond to events. As philosopher Levi Bryant says, "Action itself transforms our capacity to be affected by generating new capacities to be affected."[38] What we do changes the choices that we make. In other words, experience itself makes a difference. What matters here is that these changes are not just *internal* to us. They have only happened because of our ongoing experiences of moving through our environments. Therefore, rather than passively transporting us, commuting journeys actively change us.

The Ecology of Commuting

To appreciate the transformations that commuting creates requires us to approach our object of analysis more expansively. Rather than imagining individual commuters as atom-like particles that mechanistically move from one point to another according to unchanging laws, we need to develop an appreciation of the richer suite of forces at play. This book develops an "ecological" approach to exploring transit life. This way of thinking helps us sense how our everyday journeys to and from work are entangled in complex webs of relations with other people, places, times, ideas, and materials. As we will learn, these webs of relations are kaleidoscopic. They are shape-shifting rather than static. This has important implications for the way that we think about the politics of our everyday journeys. Because politics is concerned with relationships of enablement and constraint, this ecological approach provides us with a richer appreciation of the multiple sites of enablement and constraint and the transitional nature of enablements and constraints. There are six aspects to the ecology of commuting that this book navigates, which are explored through its six chapters.

Transit Skills

Chapter 1 explores the skills that might be involved in different ways of commuting. The idea that commuting involves any skill at all might sound rather puzzling. However, this is because for many people commuting is something that happens on autopilot. Yet beneath the threshold of conscious attention lies a whole series of fine-grained experiential knowledges that commuters develop over time, enabling them to traverse urban transport systems with ease. Skill is therefore a vital but often overlooked dimension of commuting that enables us to appreciate its changeability. The understanding of skill developed in this chapter draws on social theories of habit that can assist us in thinking about how habit is an enabling rather than repressive force, in which skills are transitional and open to change rather than a part of our life that inhibits change. Although we might we might conventionally imagine that what moves people around cities are the various technologies of transit themselves, what this idea overlooks are the forward-leaning tendencies that are created through routine action itself. It is these tendencies that form a vital part of our everyday urban mobilities.

Although skills draw our attention to the changing muscular, sensate capacities of bodies themselves, as we will learn, the development of commuting skills can depend on all manner of place-based cues. The significance of specific environments for skill development raises important questions about how people might start out commuting from a new place, how they might draw on previous bodily knowledges or use the new place as an opportunity to attempt a different way of moving about. This also raises important questions about the extent to which bodily knowledges might be transposed between different environments, especially given the significant population movements that happen between different cities. Sometimes, the development of commuting skills might be incremental, occurring below the threshold of conscious attention, registered only in momentary, backward-tracing realizations. At other times, commuters might work more consciously on their mobility skills, perhaps even undergoing specific forms of training to sharpen them. This is an issue that brings training institutions that specialize in the development of mobility skills into the frame.

Analyses of skill typically tend to focus on its developmental dimensions. However, a focus on skill construction comes at the expense of thinking about its destructive aspects. The latter prompts us to consider how commuting skills might break down—perhaps momentarily through unexpected interruptions, or more incrementally over time, such as through bodily fatigue—and how commuters might respond to such breakdowns. Furthermore, how this waxing and waning of skills might become registered in different combinations of bodily sensations such as pleasure, joy, discomfort, or fear is not necessarily clear-cut. Yet such sensations provide a valuable indication of the changing constellations of enablements and constraints experienced by commuters. Ultimately, the concept of skill helps us trace a more transitional politics of commuting in which relations of enablement and constraint change in response to ongoing practices of mobility.

Transit Dispositions

Chapter 2 explores the dispositions that emerge through commuting. During commuting journeys, people are often thrust together, sometimes in very tight proximity. This means that commuting creates a complex social setting, raising a set of important questions about how people relate to and are affected by others in commuting spaces. In exploring the social life of the commute, this chapter spotlights the diversity of social formations that commuting can give rise to and the sorts of dispositions toward others that these social formations might create. Different people's trajectories temporarily coming together in tight spaces can create highly charged social formations. In these settings, there are various subtle gestural communications at play, which might be sensed by others through differing degrees of comprehension and responded to with different forms of involvement or withdrawal.

Rather than diagnosing generalized patterns of behavior, this chapter explores how different intensities of light-touch and forceful events and encounters can change the nature of collectives. Given that people might relate to each other in cars very differently than in the more intimate spaces of public transport, the precise nature of commuting collectives can depend on the technology of transit itself. However, it might also be conditioned by the histories of a specific route or transit space and the precise relations that form between people over time in that space. Rather than attempting to diagnose social relations with broad brushstrokes, this chapter focuses on the events and encounters that take place during the commute in order to examine the different transient collectives that might form and then dissipate through these happenings. It explores how different qualities of unfolding action can create distinctive atmospheres on the move that have different capacities for affecting people. These atmospheres might be intensified by the capsule-like spatialities of the commute.

By developing social theories of micropolitical change that draw attention to the transitional qualities of events and encounters, this chapter helps explain how commuters might be enabled and constrained in minute ways by the encounters they experience while in transit. It considers how the bodily registration of such events and encounters might be situated within complex constellations of social inequality, prompting us to question how certain bodies, owing to their previous experiences, might be more susceptible to being affected than others, tying these dispositions into longer-duration social formations. This draws our attention to how the repetitious nature of commuting might affect how encounters are sensed, with the buildup of little events over time potentially reaching tipping points. Although these issues have important implications for the design and management of commuting spaces in terms of attending to the safety and well-being of commuters, the contingency of such events also alerts us to the limits of governance techniques that can take place in transit spaces. Putting dispositions under the spotlight therefore reveals how the commute is a charged duration that actively shapes attitudes and opinions, changing dispositions in the process.

Transit Times

Chapter 3 explores the temporalities of commuting. The activity of traveling to and from work involves significant amounts of time, which, when measured by the clock, traditionally has been viewed as wasted and unproductive from an economic perspective. However, this chapter highlights a series of other temporal dynamics in the commute that are often masked by clock time. It develops a more qualitative and differentiated understanding of time as created by the activities that are undertaken by commuters, in which different durations can coexist to produce new qualities of experience. Drawing on different social theories of temporality, this chapter explores these multiple temporalities to evaluate how commuting time becomes differently valued.

Commuting time can be intensely managed and organized, bringing into view not only a series of orienting ideals, such as efficiency and productivity, but an intricate network of social relations that might need to be coordinated. Yet commuters' relationships with such techniques might also be fraught and ambivalent, especially when such ideals rub against the thorny contingencies of everyday experience. The spaces of different technologies of transit raise key questions about what it is possible to do while on the move. Relatedly, new technologies can change the parameters of what might be possible to do during the commute, producing new bodily experiences of connection. Highlighting the variability of travel time, this chapter explores how the imperatives of productivity or entertainment sometimes jostle uneasily with the desire to withdraw, indicating how the commute is a malleable transition time between home and work.

Reflecting on the squeezed lives of commuters whose travel time is much longer than average, this chapter explores how commuters differently reflect on the impact of especially long journeys on work, family, and community life. Because both the physical bodily demands and the opportunity costs of commuting might inflect bodily experiences in diverse and sometimes unexpected ways, such lives bring into the frame new ethical questions for commuters about how to go on living. In making such evaluations, spectral pasts and anticipated futures might be brought into the present, indicating the complex bundle of temporal relations that characterize these commuting practices. Some commuters might make radical responses to increasingly unlivable commuting lives. However, although telecommuting or retraining for a new employment field might alleviate some of the stresses of commuting, these resolutions can also give rise to their own prickly challenges.

This chapter helps explain the multitextured, uncertain, and ambiguous times of the daily commute. By linking the duration of commuting journeys to wider circuits of contemporary capitalism and zooming into situations that raise more intimate questions about work–life balance, this chapter highlights how the changing temporalities of commuting can be sensed in different kinds of bodily experience, which might be characterized by mourning, commiseration, and empathy. Exploring how commuters reflect on the temporal relations of their everyday lives helps us sense some of the changing values and aspirations that commuting lives can create.

Transit Spaces

Chapter 4 explores the spaces of commuting. From platforms and footpaths to car parks and bus stops, every commuting journey involves moving through a diverse combination of spaces. However, in contrast with a static understanding of space that would imagine space as an inert playing field that social life unfolds across, this chapter draws on social theories that can help explain how spaces are differently produced and differently affecting. As will be discussed, many agencies that have a stake in the production of commuting spaces are intent on engineering specific bodily experiences into those spaces. These experiences might be based on a variety of different logics. For instance, the ways in which smooth passage is designed into space by transport planners folds through the more seductive designs of advertising agencies, combining to producing unique and situated experiences. The multiple ways that commuters themselves curate their own experiential interruptions in commuting spaces further complicates these engineering logics.

This chapter explores how new digital technologies are potentially transforming the experience of space for some commuters. For instance, the growth of location-aware, real-time journey apps can provide new ways of sensing urban space through their capacity to visualize the precise locations of taxis, buses, and trains. These commuting apps can also potentially make commuting spaces easier to navigate for differently mobile bodies, changing relations of enablement and constraint in the process. Other technologies, such as contactless smartcards, not only change the way that financial dimensions of commuting might be experienced, creating new bodily gestures and sensations in the process, but also connect the city in new ways, making public transport a potentially easier and more attractive journey option.

One of the ambitions of this chapter is to draw out the experiential richness of commuting spaces as a way of illustrating that design imperatives and technological devices do not operate deterministically or in isolation.

Through detailed descriptive vignettes and experiments with photographic practices, this chapter invites consideration of the ways in which commuting experiences are riven with all manner of moving intensities that combine personal biographies with the site-specific memories of place. The memories of different commuting places add multilayered potentials for sensing spaces, which always intrude on the engineering logics of design and operation. What each of these elements indicates is that commuting space is not pregiven; instead, it is the emergent effect of multiple simultaneous processes. This means that though it might be tempting to imagine that commuting spaces only really change when a new transport infrastructure is built or upgraded, doing so overlooks how the activities and happenings that make up these spaces might themselves be transformative.

Transit Voices

Chapter 5 explores different ways of voicing the commute. This chapter surveys how various practices of speaking and writing about commuting have different capacities to change the commuting experience. They are an important but overlooked part of how everyday urban mobilities take shape and gain definition. They are significant, because rather than taken to be passive representations of what is going on in buses and in cars, speaking and writing can be better appreciated as active agents in these commuting experiences themselves. Drawing on social theories of performance and expression, this chapter travels beyond the spaces of the journey itself to explore some of the dispersed sites through which practices of voicing the commute take place.

There are more formal modes of voicing, which might include different forms of "eye-in-the-sky" traffic reporting, transport journalism, and transport blogging. Each of these forms of voicing does more than just relay information to beleaguered commuters. These different modes of expression can change how moving around the city is felt, affecting commuters as much through the expressiveness of their tone as by what the words and sentences might signify. Different forms of expression might provide empathy, reduce feelings of isolation, intensify a sense of community, or even create new passions. Although each mode has a distinctive quality, experiences tangle them together in unforeseen ways. Folded through commuting journeys themselves, a different kind of voicing is taking place, involving the commentaries that we give of our everyday journeys to others at work, at home, and while on the move. Contrasting with more carefully crafted journalism, commuting rants and raves are murkier forms of expression that might be aftereffects of specific events or encounters. Further questioning the conventional notion that speech is something that we intentionally will, everyday journeys are also threaded with the commentary of our inner voices, which can serve to intensify specific bodily feelings while on the move.

One historically significant way of voicing the commute is drive-time radio, a medium that continues to be a significant dimension of many commuters' lives, inflecting the experience of homeward journeys in the afternoon. Often combining music and analysis of current affairs with a talk-back dimension, the drive-time format can entertain commuters through an on-the-pulse narrative that twists and turns in unexpected directions. In this regard, it can imaginatively transport commuters to a place beyond the confined coordinates of their everyday journeys, while potentially giving rise to a distinctive sense of intimacy and companionship. Taken together, these forms of voicing are significant through their different capacities to change the experience of commuting. They give shape to the otherwise more vague and ambient forces that make up commuting. However, the ways that they do this are complex and are by no means determinate. They vary in their spheres of influence, they evidence different degrees of authorial control, and they generate different qualities of relation.

Transit Infrastructures

Chapter 6 explores how commuter infrastructures emerge. The development of new transport infrastructure is often sorely needed to respond to the growing populations of cities. However, the way that infrastructure comes about is by no means straightforward and is often contingent on a delicate interplay of practices undertaken by different institutions and organizations. This chapter explains that we need to expand our understanding of infrastructure to account for the various materials, ideas, practices, and performances of advocacy that unfold in different ways across the city and that aim to transform commuting experiences. In doing so, and developing social theories of infrastructure, this chapter explains that we need to understand infrastructures as transitional and always in formation.

Taking up the concept of waiting, this chapter explores some of the forward-leaning expectations that infrastructure plans create. The extended timescales involved in developing large transport infrastructure projects can create their own effects for commuters, especially in parts of the city where expectations are running high, where transport infrastructures might have been repeatedly promised but have not yet materialized. It explores the kinds of dispositions that reneging on infrastructure plans might lead to and how these dispositions might be sensed and expressed at different sites and with different people. It explores how a sense of being stranded might be expressed through different forms of speech, revealing charged atmospheres. It also considers how transport infrastructure projects attempt to manage these situational dispositions alongside the more construction-based aspects of projects. This chapter examines some of the techniques developed, such as the use of display and demonstration, and how such techniques attempt to foster affinities with infrastructure projects in development.

Waiting for new transport infrastructure to materialize can feel like an endemic condition of urban life. In contrast to large-scale transport infrastructure projects that take a significant time, this book also explores the practices of organizations advocating for more modest infrastructure changes. By reviewing some of the diverse activities undertaken by grass-roots and community organizations, we can appreciate how their tactics for bringing about infrastructure change are rather different. Storying transport experiences can become a valuable dimension of transport advocacy, especially through the capacity to highlight important social justice issues. Taken together, what begins to emerge through these diverse forms of advocacy is a more complicated picture of how transport infrastructures materialize and change. In this way, this chapter emphasizes the indeterminate nature of transport infrastructure developments. This indeterminacy requires an appreciation of how macropolitical decision making manifested through plans and policies always goes hand in hand with more micropolitical transitions that take place through encounters with a range of different materials in different sites, such as media stories, political statements, and demonstration materials.

Thinking Sydney

To explore transit life, this book joins the commute in Sydney, Australia's largest city. Sydney is in the spotlight because it suffers from some

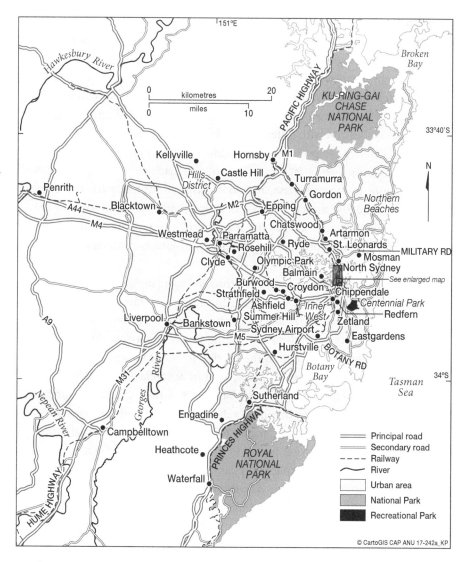

Figure 0.1
Map of Sydney metropolitan area, showing places mentioned in this book. *Source:*
Australian National University CartoGIS.

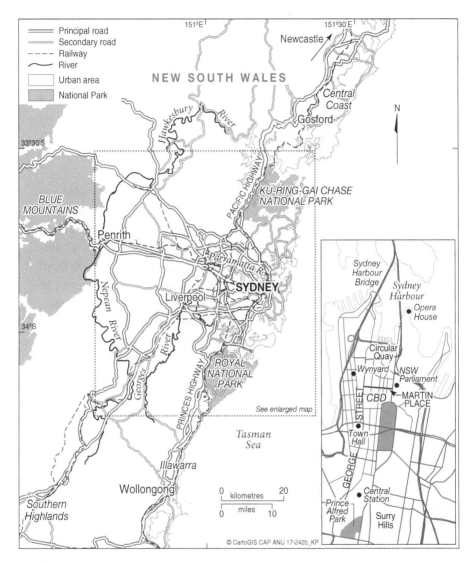

Figure 0.2
Map of Sydney region with Central Business District inset, showing places mentioned in this book. *Source:* Australian National University CartoGIS.

of the most critical transport predicaments that many other large cities in the world face, in which the fantasies of the good life seem perpetually compromised by the challenges of mobility. Sydney is a city that experienced rapid population growth during the second half of the twentieth century, transforming from a provincial postcolonial center into a global city that is now home to just under five million people. Yet sustained economic prosperity has also created uneven social development, skewed settlement patterns, and, most importantly for this book, profound infrastructure stress.[39]

While trying to catch a glimpse of the iconic Sydney Harbour Bridge and Sydney Opera House, a newcomer flying in to Sydney's Kingsford Smith Airport might be taken aback by the sheer extent of the city that unfolds to the western skyline, almost as far as the eye can see. These western suburbs and the dormitory suburbs shimmering in the haze further beyond them are the result of huge speculative residential development that began in the mid-twentieth century. Connected by freeway systems, the construction of which was cemented by powerful road users' lobby groups, this development locked much of the city into car dependency. Fifty percent of Sydney's annual population growth continues to be attracted to the more affordable housing located in these outer western suburbs.[40]

However, since the mid-1980s, the rise of financial, property, and knowledge services and the fall of manufacturing jobs have centralized much employment in an area that spans the Central Business District (CBD), Chatswood, North Sydney, and Parramatta. This centralization has been bolstered by broadly neoliberal sympathies in city planning, which have been particularly concerned with tapping Sydney into global financial and cultural flows, thus lessening dependence on the regional and national economy.[41] The resulting mismatch between where jobs, services, and affordable housing are located has given rise to long commutes for many of the city's inhabitants. Sydneysiders continue to have the longest commutes in Australia, averaging thirty-five minutes each way. With an average commuting distance of fifteen kilometers,[42] they are also the longest distance commutes of any city in Australia. Commuting by private vehicle still currently accounts for over seventy percent of journeys. Public transport, such as buses, trains, trams, and ferries, accounts for just seventeen percent of journeys, with walking and cycling making up only five percent.

In a recent biography of the city, Delia Falconer writes that everything in Sydney has "an extra layer of reflection, of slip beneath the surface."[43] Drawing on her experiences growing up in the city, Falconer reflects on the ghostly absences, concealments, and contradictions that give the city its often menacing undertow, belying its more superficial glitz. Her evocative account serves as a reminder that more functional sweeping histories of a city narrated through the familiar spatial language of center and periphery and peppered with statistics can only ever provide an insulated point of view, as if seen through the sealed window of a plane. Like every city, down below is a much more intricately patterned cityscape, made up of many complex fragments and intersecting histories that do not add up and that certainly cannot be discerned from such a distance. Sydney's cityscape is shaped by countless intersecting happenings. Each area has its own processes of economic growth, population dynamics, and cultural distinctiveness. As our newcomers on the plane are about to touch down, arriving from the south, their plane flies low over Botany Bay within meters of where the Gweagal people were confronted with James Cook in 1770, marking the start of a period of violent colonial dispossession. True to Falconer's evocation of the multilayered nature of the city, many of the roads that commuters use every day in Sydney trace the routes of Aboriginal paths.

From a distance, Sydney consistently scores highly in international rankings that compare the "liveability" of the world's major cities, and it continues to attract tourists from all over the world. Zooming in, behind this sparkly facade is a much more troubling reality for many people who live and work in the city. As a city concerned with improving its global competitiveness, Sydney's most recent metropolitan plan drawn up by the state government emphasizes "efficient transport" as one of its three key measures of a global city standard. However, and crucially for this book, transport is the area in which the plan concedes that Sydney does not meet perceived global city standards.[44] Whereas other "competitor cities" have invested heavily in transport infrastructure, Sydney continues to trail. This is borne out in a study that compared levels of "commuter pain" between different cities worldwide and ranked Sydney as more painful than Los Angeles, New York, and London.[45] Confirming this "accolade," a recent report stated that poor transport is quite simply Sydney's "most fundamental drawback."[46]

Commuting is a global phenomenon, but, as geographer Tim Edensor notes, riding the Tokyo Shinkansen, riding the New York subway, and driving in Kolkata are very different commuting experiences.[47] They each have different histories, different politics, different regimes of surveillance, and different manners and styles of moving. Although every city has its specifics, the processes happening in Sydney provide an ideal setting to explore the richness and complexity of commuting. Connections are made with other cities throughout this book to bring distinctions into focus, but the insights, methods, and analyses developed through engaging with Sydney can enhance our understanding of commuting experiences happening all over the world.

Thinking in Transit

As a child growing up in England, railway journeys provided some of my most meaningful and memorable experiences. The most magical part of holidays to see my grandparents in Birmingham was the short train journey that Nan and Grandad would take my brother and I on from Stourbridge Junction into New Street Station, a line mostly used by commuters. We would go to McDonalds, suck on Teddy Grays boiled sweets, make a slow loop of the Pallasades shopping center, and then return home—but it was the journey itself that I was most entranced by.

Mobilities Thinking

That such ordinary spaces of transit might be meaningful for people is the one of the most important ideas developed in the "new mobilities paradigm," a multidisciplinary academic field that this book draws on and extends.[48] Mobilities thinking takes seriously the previously overlooked patchwork of traveling experiences that form our lifeworlds and explores how these journeys shape who we are and what they enable us to do.[49] It invites us to think about the kaleidoscope of activities that spaces of mobility enable and the quality of social relations that these journeys facilitate. Mobilities thinking also has a powerful political dimension: It directs our attention to how the mobilities of some people can happen at the expense of the mobilities of others. This means that though mobility can alleviate certain forms of social inequality, it can intensify other forms. This book extends and deepens our understanding of the politics of commuting by investigating the enablements and constraints that sculpt this most everyday form of movement.

Mobilities thinking draws our attention to the intricate and varied practices that different people on the move undertake. In doing so, mobilities thinking takes inspiration from social theories of practice that show how an ostensibly singular practice, such as that implied by the blanket label *commuting*, is in fact much more multiple, because it is made up of many diverse practices linked together in time and across different spaces, often involving other people, objects, and technologies.[50] Drawing on this idea, this book expands our understanding of how commuting practices can involve intricate forms of coordination and synchronization with others at work, at home, and while on the move. Furthermore, though commuting journeys have often been understood from a transportation perspective as a displacement from one point to another, theories of practice also help us appreciate how commuting journeys are intricately connected to so many other everyday activities. This means that the influence of the commute can extend well beyond the confines of the actual travel time itself. By capturing this sense of the interconnectedness of commuting practices, the ecological approach of this book charts the links between some of these diverse practices, sites, and people.

Mobilities thinking provides important methodological tools to help us navigate these movements. This book is based on over four years of research conducted in Sydney. I interviewed fifty-three commuters who responded to newspaper advertisements in two of the city's daily publications, my choices based on maximizing the diversity of people's commuting scenarios.[51] Following in the footsteps of mobilities researchers who have shown the benefits of mobile methods,[52] I also undertook journeys around Sydney myself. As I performed more interviews, my own reflexive awareness of the commuting spaces of the city changed. I gradually became attuned to new dimensions that the interview encounters alerted me to. In addition to traveling across the city for interviews, I conducted two "week in the life" experiments, which involved commuting from Castle Hill in the city's northwest and from Wollongong, a city to the south, to the center of Sydney each day by train and bus. In each of these experiments, I reflected on my bodily experience on the go, using my phone to make detailed notes about how the commute was registering in my body at the time. I also undertook a photo experiment at a transport interchange in the central business district of the city. Some of the issues that commuters introduced led me to arrange interviews with a variety of professionals involved in the city's commuting scene. I spoke with journalists, transport advocates, policymakers, politicians, radio presenters, traffic reporters, transport staff, human resources staff, advertising executives, writers, and historians. Taken together, this book develops a rich suite of qualitative techniques for better understanding transit life.

Performative Thinking

My golden memories of riding the commuter train with my grandparents and brother is a reminder of the significance of the sensate dimensions of our transit lives. As a child, I was thoroughly entranced by the colored trackside signals, the soft-flutter change of station destination board panels, the blue diesel train fumes, and the mannerisms of other passengers. Each of these experiential aspects and more taken together gave the experience a special quality that no doubt inspired my own curiosity about transit spaces. The significance of the multisensory dimensions of experience in this book is influenced by *performative thinking*, a diverse field that offers ways of understanding how our lifeworlds are made up of various actors, agents, and forces with different capacities, expanding what counts as both the social and the human.[53]

Performative thinking is suspicious of ways of thinking that are overly preoccupied with trying to figure out the hidden codes, scripts, symbols, and structures—or representations—that often seem to undergird our lives. Thinking about the events and happenings in our lives, both big and small, as just the playing out of fixed structures and already written scripts effectively reduces us to lifeless marionettes, with powers already decided upon in advance of action. Performative theories challenge us to consider that if who we are is in part affected by the qualities of the spaces that we inhabit, the objects that we dwell with, the sounds that we hear, the sights that we witness, and the performances that we enact, then the idea of who *we* are becomes much less fixed.[54] This does not deny the existence of all manner of abysmal inequalities. Performative thinking helps us understand how social and economic disadvantage is perpetuated through repeated bodily experiences. Indeed, our indeterminate capacities may well be reduced by more structural forms of inequality, as traditionally conceived. However, these structural forms of inequality are also registered in and complicated by the open-ended nature of our bodily experiences, meaning that there is always some wiggle room, even in the most seemingly constrained situation.

This book draws on performative thinking to change the way that we think about the transit life of commuting as a complex ecology of open-ended processes. This style of thinking also has important implications for how fieldwork is presented and the status of the claims made. Interviews and observations often have been used as techniques to extract relevant information about a person or a situation to build a coherent picture of what is going on. However, the idea that talking with anyone provides a transparent window into someone else's world is problematic—not just because of the context-dependent nature of talk, but also because the idea that we all share one universal, unchanging form of subjectivity is misguided.[55] Each interview is instead an encounter in its own right, chock-full of awkward pinch points, backward-tracing realizations, and cascading memories, replete with subtle transitions, overbrimming with heart-thumping intensities and felt emotions. When treated as a representation of wider things, the interview might have had its day,[56] but when treated as a creative encounter in itself, the interview offers exciting potential for becoming attuned to the uniqueness of different situations.

Anthropologist Kathleen Stewart urges us to be more sensitive to the complexity and richness that emerges in any research setting. She says that we need to be wary of "strong theory's tendency to beat its objects into submission to its dreamy arguments."[57] Social theorist Raymond Williams also warned of the way in which social analysis can dampen the complexity of the world, writing that "all the known complexities, the experienced tensions, shifts, and uncertainties, the intricate forms of unevenness and confusion, are against the terms of reduction and soon, by extension, against social analysis itself."[58] This is an intrepid tightrope to tread: to control an object just enough to be able to say something about it and to change it enough that new depths of association emerge.[59] My hope is that the narration of the stories in this book allow for such new depths of association to emerge while providing folds of interpretation that are provisional and speculative enough to catalyze this adventure of thinking about transit life differently. Therefore, rather than shoehorning the split-endedness of fieldwork encounters into overly neat and packaged accounts, the presentations in this book attempt to retain some sense of the richness and drama of the encounters while being honest about what each encounter provoked for me. The edges are still bleeding: teetering on the brink of saying something different, meaning something different, feeling something different.

Changing Commuting

Now, when the transport challenges that beset so many of our cities are being felt more acutely than ever before, there is no better time for a refreshed understanding of what our commutes might be doing to life in our cities. Whereas previous analyses of commuting have tended to champion hard infrastructure investment or technological innovations, the events and encounters charted in this book indicate how changes in these domains might be part of the solution to commuting problems, but are not silver bullets. The ecology of commuting woven by the stories in this book shows how commuting intimately connects multiple sites in the city, including workplaces, homes, schools, governments, advocacy organizations, developers, planners, and the media, among many others. Furthermore, too much emphasis on infrastructure investment as a solution presumes that change is only possible at some point in the future, when there is enough political will or finance available. Evaluating the situation according to future ideals means that the present is always falling short and overlooks all the changes currently taking place.

This book does not make any large-scale diagnoses about "what people want" or "what should be done." A generic picture would flatten the richness of transit life, in which the dim vagaries that make life what it is, with its split ends and nonresolutions, are formalized to such an extent that the intensities are blunted. Such an approach would assume that commuting is the same for all people all of the time. As sociologists Monika Büscher and John Urry point out, it is much more interesting to learn about how exactly people make up their journeys than to try to find and define underlying orders, rules and structures.[60] More modestly, the intention of this book is to change how we might think about commuting. Rather than imagining the events and encounters that make up the commute as either the mere playing out of large-scale social processes that have been diagnosed by commentators or as trivialities, the significance of which we should be careful not to overinflate, this book spotlights how the events and encounters of the commute are the very elements that are changing people's lives in this liminal, in-between zone—a zone in which the tensions and contradictions, the diverse influences and desires that *are* our lives come to the fore in ways that are sometimes wonderful, sometimes sobering, but always intriguing.

1   Impression Zones: The Rise and Fall of Traveling Skills

"Circular Quay!" yells the ferry worker as he finishes securing the flimsy gangway between the vessel and the wharf. As he says this, a stream of smartly dressed figures start striding across the gangway, turn left, and pace toward the exit barriers. Smartcards already in hands, they tap the sensor, stopping only momentarily to let the barrier open with a low thud. It is just after 8:40 on a Monday morning in late summer, and the scene is nestled in one of the most instantly recognizable waterfronts in the world, between the spectacles of Sydney's Harbour Bridge and Opera House. The area is bathed in white morning sunlight, made all the more luminous by flecks of silver where the sunlight catches the water.

The smartly dressed figures walk purposefully, confidently, briskly. I am struck by the effortlessness of their movements. There is something debonair about the way that they carry themselves. They bear rucksacks, some on one shoulder, some on both. Others carry sleek leather bags. There are clicking stilettos, brogues, loafers. A few wear more spongey trainers, creating a look that jars a little with the self-conscious refinement of dress above the ankle. Fanning out, they peel away from the wharf, setting a straight-line course to their next waypoint, where they adjust their angle, much like the vessel they have just alighted from. Some head to the train station; others continue to the cluster of skyscrapers that make up Sydney's central business district. Their measured precision is made even more conspicuous here as they push straight through the slower, eddying, and slightly clumsy movements of the tourists who are up early to make the most of their precious time here. A man in dark sunglasses, brown brogues, and a blue suit hops to the right to avoid a tour group, the collective attention of which is immersed somewhere more distant, a little dazzled by the spectacle.

Witnessing a scene such as this, it might be tempting to imagine that commuting is something that happens easily, even automatically, for the people involved. However, this chapter goes behind the scenes to investigate the host of advanced skills that commuting involves. It explores how commuting skills can take time to develop, how they can continue to change over time, and how they are possibly more fragile than we might assume. These details are significant, because commuting is so often taken to be intransigent and resistant to change.[1]

While writing in a very different era, concerned with the more mechanistic understandings of matter in the physical sciences of the time, philosopher Henri Bergson recognized that we need reference points in everyday life. He was concerned, though, that the way we tend to think about activities is too fixated on their apparently stable points,[2] rather than on all the changes that might be occurring. Although the route or duration of someone's commute to work might *appear* to be the same each day, for Bergson this is an example of our tendency to fixate on a spatialized[3] understanding of movement in terms of positions, locations, and orders. The problem is that understanding activities in terms of isolated and observable elements downplays the subtler changes that take place. Tracing some of these changes can help us appreciate how people learn to commute, how people come to make decisions, and how people develop different sorts of competencies and types of expertise related to their commute, which are open to change.

Section 1 explores how commuters begin their commutes. It looks at how people start to acquire the kinds of skills that lead to the sorts of measured movements I witnessed at Circular Quay. Section 2 focuses on a more formal scheme that trains bicycle commuters in how to commute. Here, the discussion is on the relationship between skill and confidence. Section 3 investigates how commuting skills can be fragile. It explores how disruptions can prompt people to change their commuting habits in different ways.

1 Starting Out

Learning to Be a Commuter

Of all the activities that bead together to form everyday life, commuting was never an activity I would have expected to induce the sense of anxiety

I am feeling. It is my first day of fieldwork, at six minutes past seven on a Monday morning in early summer, and I am approaching a group of suited people standing in silence. This is the Castle Hill bus interchange, a gray concrete slab flanked by the occasional palm tree in the middle of a leafy and well-to-do suburb in Sydney's northwest. This part of the city is the result of outward expansion over the past few decades—a product of the "great Australian dream" for so many of owning a detached house with a garden in the face of soaring house prices closer to the center of the city.[4] As I drove into the suburb for the first time yesterday, I could sense this dream in emerald green lawns and electric purple jacaranda trees in full bloom, neatly cut nature strips at the side of the road, and immaculately weeded, brick weave driveways.

Bucolic charm aside, the airplane tracking high overhead provides an indication of just how far I am from where it took off, near the center of Sydney, where many of the people who live here work. Commuting has gained notoriety in this part of the city, and it is this notoriety that has drawn me here. There are no trains here yet; public transport options are limited to buses, and, owing to expansion, roads have become choked during peak commuting hours. Tired crusts of beige bitumen erupting at the edges of the smoothed tire gullies here at the interchange show how commuting has become physically grooved into the very fabric of this place.

It is curious that we know so little about how people begin a new commute. As a new inhabitant of Castle Hill, this is what motivated my first "week in the life" commuting experiment. Part researcher, part commuter, I had spent some time the previous day on the state transit website to find out what sort of ticket I would need. But now, as I walk closer, I notice that there are several loosely formed lines of people along the pavement. Despite my preparation, I have no idea which queue to join. These lines seem held together by their own histories, created by the people performing this routine every day. This realization elevates my sense of being a novice.

Intensities of Starting Out

In his account of the rise of railway travel in the nineteenth century, historian Wolfgang Schivelbusch writes of the shock and disorientation experienced by the first railway passengers.[5] Here, waiting at Castle Hill, his account reminds me that novelty produces specific intensities of experience.

Amid my anxiousness, there is an intensity only felt when experiencing something for the very first time. A few months later, I spoke with someone who has been commuting between Castle Hill and the city center for a few months. Tom, a journalist from the United Kingdom, had moved to Australia less than two years ago. He couldn't find work near his flat in the city, so after receiving a job offer in Castle Hill, he couldn't afford to turn it down. At around an hour each way, this was his longest commute ever, much longer than his short commute in London. What I found so striking about his reminiscences was that he spoke fondly about the initial impression the journey made on him. With a smile, he recounted: "Well, it's the first couple of weeks, you're kind of listening to music and taking the view in. And, you know, I noticed different things each day and, you know, it took me about a week or so: 'Oh, there's the Foxtel building; oh, and there's this, this and this,' and—because there's one part of the motorway that's kind of a rainforesty area and, you know, I was only six months in Australia, so everything was all new to me."

Although my first commute from Castle Hill had a similarly heightened intensity, what is dominant in my recollections is a sense of clumsiness, a sense of my body not quite fitting into this performance that has been so well-rehearsed by others here. This clumsiness brings to mind anthropologist Marc Augé's observations on how novice and expert commuters have different bodily comportments. Writing about travelers on the Paris Metro, Augé says that "the regular traveller on a given line is easily recognized by the elegant and natural economy of his or her way of walking."[6] A "seasoned traveller ... can be recognized in the perfect mastery of his or her movements,"[7] much like "skilled artisans who shape the objects of their craft."[8] Like the proficiencies that are developed by the skilled artisan over time, I began to realize that these virtuosic "body ballets," to use geographer David Seamon's[9] phrase, might take some time to develop.

Finding a Groove

Learning about acquiring commuting skills takes us to the cavernous foyer of a CBD skyscraper. It is lunchtime; suited people—some in small groups, others on their own—are skimming across the beige glassy marble floor with a sense of purpose, to and from the six steel-fronted elevators. I sit with Ethan on an opulent lounge sofa. Ethan works in finance and is one of the many people who have moved out of the Inner West to the far northwest of the city. He moved to a suburb just beyond Castle Hill about two years ago.

I'm taken aback as Ethan admits, with frank honesty, that he and his partner didn't contemplate what would be involved in their commute. He says, with a wry smile, "At the time we bought the house, we even didn't know there's the M2 road works going on. ... We only came to know after we bought the house and when we were traveling to the city."[10] I detect an edge of sheepishness in his voice as he says that even the time taken to travel in came as a surprise. "Then we thought, like, 'Oh, we're taking more than an hour and a half.' So sometimes we ignore some stuff because, when the house ticks all the boxes, that's your dream house, and you forget everything. So we didn't look at what's the commute like."

There is a familiarity to Ethan's confession that I had heard in similar guises from other commuters. Ethan follows this quickly by justifying his fixation on the right house for his family, his hands neatly gesturing as if to emphasize a sense of control. "As a growing family, we want our own space, and the kids they need some kind of a backyard where they can play. That's kind of the things we were weighing up. If you think only of ourselves, we would have bought something smaller. But, you know, we're a growing family." He talks about the steps they took, which led them to the northwest of the city, beginning with determining a budget. Once they had done so, he says, "We saw some but they didn't tick all the boxes. And then, when we found the property, we were weighing the schools and the facilities—and, obviously, the crime rate: that comes first." Ethan was adamant that their priority was getting the house and its neighborhood right. The commute into the city seemed secondary. I sensed that Ethan wanted to give his children a good environment, even at the expense of his own quality of life, as he admitted later: "So we're just sacrificing our time; that's all." His nonchalant delivery contrasted with the gravity of this admission.

"And then we moved to the northwest." Ethan pauses and frowns. "It was a *huge* difference for us," he adds, shaking his head slowly. I take this opportunity to ask how he and his partner started their new commutes. He describes the experience of starting out as being "in an impression zone," a phrase that instantly resonated with my experience of starting out in Castle Hill. He takes me through his thought process: "'Okay, we can go to Blacktown and catch a train and travel here'—and I wouldn't know even how much is the bus ticket at the time," he says, referring to how he was used to catching a train to work from the Inner West. However, this was evidently a short-lived arrangement. He says: "We tried two weeks or so. Then we tried all of the other ways." I am struck by just how experimental Ethan's first few weeks of the commute were. This initial period of starting to commute from near Castle Hill was a malleable time for Ethan and his partner, which contrasts strikingly with the idea that the commute is a fixed and relatively unchanging routine.[11]

Ethan continues: "There's another bus which comes close to where we live. But that bus goes to the next suburb, so we're kind of wasting, again, ten, fifteen minutes inside where we are; so we're not going anywhere. So then we trialed the current one, which we got used to and, most of the time, it's okay now." The idea of meandering around their own neighborhood on a bus was clearly frustrating, but during their bus experiment they discovered that they were saving around twenty-six dollars each week between them, "which we can put it to our mortgage—or child education in the future." He admits that this "came all as a surprise for us, when we started traveling in the bus and saving this much amount of money." In some respects, Ethan is describing how this experimentation involved gradually economizing the range of movements that made up his commute. Geographer Tim Cresswell[12] explains this logic through the example of the mechanized production lines of Taylorist systems, in which movements that become superfluous to the task at hand are excised because they are seen as wasteful.

I press Ethan on how he journeyed to work today. Contrasting with the sense of surprise and uncertainty that runs through his reflections on starting out, I am struck by how his account of today's journey demonstrates fine-grained expertise about the route. He says, "I take the bus from Kellyville Station, one of the stops there, a major one, and people park everywhere. ... And the reason all the people park there is that's where you get the seats from; because, if you go to the next stop, the bus is almost full—and then you have to stand for, you know, God knows; sometimes you take an hour and a half or an hour and forty minutes." What strikes me here is that this sort of detailed knowledge of timing and capacity, together with explanations as to why other people do things, is gained only by performing the commute many times. He says, "Of course, now we know what time we have to leave on time so that if the traffic builds up or there won't be enough parking spots for us and you have to go a bit further to park and then you have to walk from there to the stop—so we know we have to be there by 7:20."

As if to emphasize their previous naivety, he says, "Now we know what time the traffic light turns and what time the traffic builds up before the lights, how many cars will be there, and now we kind of grasp all that stuff." These are intricate knowledges he has developed about his route and how the traffic infrastructure works. He says, "Because from our place we have two traffic lights—because I always want to skip the first traffic lights and go on the lane—like, sideways. There's one big one, which connects to the Windsor Road. So that one—it takes a bit of a long time because they give more time for the main roads, and this is a side road. But we know now, by the time we come to the signal, they're already parking to go to the other side."

Based on the experience that he's built up, Ethan says that he can anticipate what time he will get to work. "So, by the time you're on top, you see the traffic. If it's jam packed, I know I have to text my boss saying, 'I'll be there, like, 8:40 or 8:45 or fifty.' I know—I can even predict—I can tell by the traffic—if it goes smoothly for a few kilometers and then it starts building up, then I can say it'll be 8:40." However, these skills did not come quickly. Later in our conversation, he suggested that it took half a year to figure out all these practical knowledges: "Six months will give you a rough idea."

Persisting Memories

The idea that we start out without skills when we begin a commute is erroneous. People bring with them skills that they have developed on other journeys and during other activities in other places. Our bodies come prepopulated with the knowledges that they have developed through previous experiences. There were so many things unfamiliar to me at Castle Hill interchange, yet I realized that my body intuitively knew many of the skills that this situation required of me, such as the lineup and the social convention of avoiding eye contact with other commuters. Sociologist Anthony Giddens's idea of *tacit knowledge*[13] is a useful reference point that accounts for the taken-for-granted practical bodily knowledges that we bring to situations such as these.[14] Relocations might therefore be better understood as extended periods of transition, rather than clean breaks.[15] After starting a new commute, previous habits still persist. At the same time, new habits take time to develop.

I was reminded of the persistence of my own previous journeys as I waited at the Castle Hill interchange for my first journey into Sydney. After finding the right queue (I ended up asking someone), the quality of that moment transported me back to my bus journeys to college: seven o'clock, deep blue skies, sixteen, standing with a rucksack at the turnout at the top of the High Street in a small town in Norfolk, England, waiting for the number 12 bus. Foggy-headed conversations with two school friends who sometimes caught the same bus were often about dreams for our futures and the people we might become. Standing next to the older woman with the beige fabric bag who always carried more books than was probably good for her back, I overheard her once telling someone else that her daughter had become religious, moved away. She never hears from her.

I felt the significance of how previous journeys can persist into our commute sharply when I talked with Mike later in the project. In his late twenties, and like many people his age in Sydney, Mike lives with his parents. He works as an engineer in a suburb just north of the harbor, but lives in the far northwest of the city, just a little further out than Castle Hill. He spends three hours each day commuting. He describes his routine to me: "Get up around quarter past six, get myself ready, and I drive to the bus stop—which is about fifteen, twenty minutes by car—at Castle Hill. I park there and catch a bus into North Sydney from there; it goes up the M2, which is normally pretty bad. And then I get off at St. Leonards and walk up to work." He pauses before saying: "It's the same routine I've been doing since year seven. It's the same bus!" I find the thought of taking the same route for over fifteen years, through different life transitions, dizzying. He continues: "It just depends whether I'm going to high school, going to uni, or going to work. ... It's the same routine; different stops for different places, but it's the same routine." I sense sadness in his voice when he reminisces about previous journeys: "When I went to school and even when I went to uni, there was mates on the bus or there were girls from the other school that would talk to you. So, when I was at school, we sat up the back and mucked about and we had a great time on the bus. Now that I'm working, I don't talk to anybody on the bus, you know. They don't talk to me. We don't make eye contact."[16]

Traveling Propensities

Like myself, some of the people that I talked to during the project were not originally from Sydney. I met Anton one evening after work in his deserted open-plan office in the city center. Anton has lived in Eastern Europe for most of his life, but moved to Australia about a year ago. He lives in the eastern suburbs of the city; relative to Castle Hill, he is quite close to the city center. Because of his proximity to work, he cycles into the city from his apartment. He tells me that he'd only been cycling for a year before he arrived here. He says, "Before, I didn't ride bicycle. In my country, it's extremely dangerous. Yeah. I had a bicycle, but I ride it, like, five times in all because, when you go to the road, you actually have a risk to be dead and no one will actually do anything about this. On the roads, we don't have any space for bicycles. So, you need to ride directly in a stream and people ride a bit crazy. We have some people there cycling, but it's pretty ... like, extreme sport or something." We laugh. I'm a little perplexed that he took to cycling as his first choice here, so I ask how he got into it. He tells me: "The year before, I had an opportunity to live two months in Netherlands and that actually changed everything—absolutely—for me because it's just heaven for cycling." His face lights up as he tells me about the joy of riding a bike in the Netherlands, because "just everyone rides there." He tells me that when he moved to Sydney, he thought, "'Mmm; people are cycling here.' So I saw some cycling roads, cycling paths, and I thought, 'So I must have a bicycle here; why not?' because, actually, it saves a lot of money and a lot of time for me."

However, Anton says that there were some significant differences when cycling in Sydney that he did not expect. He says, "At first, I was just riding almost all the time on the footpaths and then I got some knowledge about riding here, in Sydney, because it actually differs from the place I come from. So it's all right to ride with cars and to take a normal road. But it's legal and it's what you should actually do." He also says that when he started cycling in Sydney, he didn't realize the legal requirement to wear a cycling helmet. This was something that he learned about in a more happenstance way, through a TV news snippet he caught accidentally, in which police were stopping cyclists in the suburb of Surry Hills. For Anton, it was not just the formal road rules that caught him by surprise, but also the place-specific informal conventions of cycling in Sydney, "like some smaller things—how to ride exactly in Sydney in the city," even though he had already developed his cycling skills in the Netherlands.

Significant here are the propensities for moving in particular ways that Anton has brought with him to Australia. One way of understanding this can be gained from sociologists who have written on social practices.[17] These researchers are interested in learning about how people become "recruited" into particular practices. Part of this recruitment draws on the array of skills we already have. Social theorists Cecily Maller and Yolande Strengers' study of Australian migrants, for instance, looked at how migrants carry certain habits and routines with them, through what they call "practice memory."[18] However, they also point out that practices are tweaked and adjusted in new settings, just as Anton's account demonstrates.

2   Building Skills

It is a little past nine o'clock on a cold, drizzly Sunday morning in late April, and I am seated in a dimly lit room in a low-rise building at the edge of Centennial Park. I'm here to find out how the Cycling in the City course helps people learn how to commute by bike. Anton recommended I take this course and told me how much he had benefitted from it. Given the inclement weather, I'm not surprised that there are just two of us here today. Elsa is the other participant, and she says that she is here to learn to be more confident on the road so that she can eventually bike to and from work. Aside from my academic interest, I'm here to dampen my anxiety about cycling in Sydney, which developed after a friend had a cycling accident in the city. Gavin and Ben are our instructors, and they begin the session by making sure that our understanding of the basic road rules are up to snuff with the aid of a whiteboard. Off-white smudges all over the board are a testament to the many other sessions that have taken place here.

There are many ways that people learn how to commute, as section 1 demonstrates. However, in this section, I zoom in on cycling to examine how commuting skills can be developed. This is significant, because, as geographer Kim Kullman rightly points out while writing about urban transport, "the practices whereby mobilities are taught and learned have received [little] interest."[19] In the literature, there has been a focus on how people's movements, particularly children's, are disciplined through techniques that are designed to make them conform to a predefined standard.[20] Geographer Peter Merriman's[21] historical study of the M1 motorway in the United Kingdom is a good example of how this logic can operate in the name of safety and efficiency. He shows that different direct and indirect techniques were used to discipline drivers new to motorway driving in order to reduce accidents and improve flow. However, in contrast to this understanding of learning as disciplining, I follow Kullman by suggesting that learning can also be thought of as an inventive activity. This is where learning is less about the "simple reproduction of existing skills and knowledges" and more a "creative practice that may inspire people to think about mobility ... in new ways."[22]

City Revelations

A few months before attending the cycling course, I met up with Rob—appropriately, on the morning of Bike to Work Day. I feel guilty taking up his time today; he was up since the very early hours of the morning handing out free hot drinks and breakfast snacks at bike stations in the inner city to cyclists on their way into work. For late October, the weather was unseasonably cool. A dim gray blanket of cloud was sitting like a lid over the city, and it had been raining on and off all morning. Rob works for a cycling company, the business of which is about helping people realize that cycling is an option for commuting to work. Bike to Work Day is part of this, helping encourage people to journey to work differently for the first time. However, probably owing to the inclement weather, Rob tells me that the people he chatted with this morning were mainly seasoned riders, persevering despite the weather. This event was part of the Sydney Rides festival, a month-long span of bike-related events designed to enhance the prominence of cycling in the city. Sheltering from the rain that had started to fall again in the comfort of a bright bakery in Chippendale, I chatted with Rob over a coffee to learn how his company helps people begin cycling in the city.

The start of our conversation took me back to the northwest of Sydney, but to a time before it was swallowed by the new suburbs that are now the Hills District. Rob tells me that it was in this countryside that he grew up. Like many children there, he rode his bike on the dirt roads that have since been paved for housing construction. He rode to school until he was sixteen, but after he moved to the inner city and changed schools, his cycling experience ended. "Having to ride through the inner city, it was like, 'Well, hang on; this is a different experience!'" It was only a decade later that his partner decided that she wanted to start cycling, so they signed up for one of the City of Sydney's Cycling in the City courses. His face lit up: "It really made a massive difference to my life, coming on the course and then starting to ride again. I'd actually kind of grown sick of Sydney and was pretty keen to get out of here. ... I'd had my fill of it." In fact, it made such a difference in Rob's life that in the five years since then he has become an instructor and now directs the company.

For me, the very idea of cycling in Sydney seems, frankly, terrifying.[23] Rob laughs like a man who has heard this too many times before. "It's a bit of a Sydney problem," he admits. "It seems like, in Sydney, a lot of people are really in a big rush to get where they're going and have a very—I don't know if *selfish* is the right word, but it seems like there's a very self-centered, entitled view about, you know, 'I have a right to get where I'm going and I'm going to get there as quickly as possible.'" Then, his tone changes. "A lot of people will talk about a war on the roads. ... There's an extensive narrative about animosity and conflicts. And it's really easy that, if you go out of the house thinking, 'I'm about to engage in a war on the roads,' you start interpreting things that happen out there as part of this war. You interpret someone, you know, passing you a little too close as being some sort of aggressive action towards you or you interpret people's mistakes as maliciousness, and you then get angry; and then you ride around in this angry head space and you create situations of conflict yourself, and it just spirals out from there. If you ride around angry, you make mistakes."

Rob continues: "And so, for me, the big change, kind of pre- and post-course, was this concept, which BikeWise teaches, which is called *cycle graciously*." Rob is quick to point out that this is not about being deferential to cars or about being polite, but about cultivating a specific disposition. With measured precision, he says: "It's about maintaining a coolness within yourself and a calmness so that you can make the best decisions for yourself and your own safety." He tells me that gracious cycling is a very different philosophy from those of other cycling education courses, which focus on developing defensive riding techniques—which can actually create conflict. "Whereas the way we teach, we apply a set of principles: see and be seen, communicate with others, be predictable, cycle graciously." Although Rob admits that there are lots of "hard" infrastructure changes that he would like to see happen to make cycling easier, what was so empowering about the course was that he realized "so much of that conflict was something that I could control, and to minimize it through my choices. ... I think a lot of cyclists aren't really aware of how much changing their own perspective about what they're doing and how they go about things can have a really positive impact on their experience as a cyclist." He suggests that the best way to understand this is by taking the course myself.

Drilling Confident Habits

Back in drizzly Centennial Park, theory over, and our capacity for rote learning about to be tested, Elsa and I head outside and pick up our bikes. Gavin and Ben direct us to a large concrete area. The next part of the course is all about checking our basic bike control, focusing on braking, pedal control, and hand signaling. While Ben provides verbal commentary, Gavin shows a practical demonstration on his bike of exactly when hand signaling and looking back over our shoulder should happen. Demonstration quickly over, it's now our turn. I've ridden a bike all my life, yet I find the exercise taxing. I'm not braking with my pedal in the correct position and feel frustrated. Ben tells me to try it again. And again. Feeling somewhat sheepish, only on my fourth attempt do I manage to get the signaling, breaking and pedal control as instructed.

Rob had emphasized the significance of these drills in our interview. He pointed out that although this is about teaching people new skills, it is also about developing people's existing skills. Rob emphasized quite early on that he "never asks anyone to do something that they haven't already demonstrated." He said: "The things that we drill and are relentless on are, whenever somebody's riding around in a group with us or by themselves, they've got two fingers hovered over the brake lever so they can pull up and stop. They'll never be surprised. If someone consistently doesn't do that while we're in the control skill session, we won't take them out and they will get drilled at. ... By the time we've got them out on the road, they've heard it about a hundred times from us."

As we do something again and again, things are changing, however slightly. Every time I performed this drill, it felt a little different. This logic could be extended to whole journeys. Did you really take *exactly* the same journey today as you did yesterday? Could this ever be possible? What, exactly, has changed? These minute changes were something that fascinated nineteenth-century philosopher Félix Ravaisson. He was interested in the minute changes that mean something that once required conscious effort from us becomes automatic and second nature over time. He explains this though a *double law* in which, on the one hand, any action becomes stronger and more precise through repetition. On the other hand, any sensation becomes weaker the same way and we feel it much less acutely.[24] What this means is that over time, any repeated action becomes more automatic, requiring less conscious effort to perform, and the accompanying sensations, especially of pain, decrease. The gradual changes that happened for me with each drill are a testament to this. This, for Ravaisson, is *habit*.

What is so novel about this idea is that in contrast with how habit has often been understood as unchanging, mechanical repetition of the same action, habit here is what allows for transformation. Habits change our capacities such that our previous experiences work to help us anticipate what is required of us in future situations. In short, they create tendencies to act.[25] It is these same habits, then, that are the bedrock competencies from which we can devote our conscious effort to other tasks, providing room to fashion new stimulations.[26]

It is finally time to leave the somewhat artificial sanctuary of the cycling center and hit the very real streets of inner-city Sydney. I'm excited—and a little nervous, as I am aware that my bike handling will be under constant scrutiny from a watchful Gavin and Ben. We cycle in a single-file line along a quiet back street. After about ten minutes of cycling, Ben indicates to pull over to the side of the road and dismount. This is our first road drill site. Elsa and I stand by our bikes in this tree-lined street. This drill is all about learning to deal with traffic confidently. "Part of this is about choosing the right lane position," Ben says, but another part is about projecting confidence to other road users, which is about making sure that we check around us for traffic. Elsa and I watch Gavin complete the maneuver. Echoing Ben's description and sitting up straight on his bike, Gavin is a picture of debonair poise, making the task look simple. It's now my turn, and I feel exposed as all eyes are on me. I'm focused on maintaining my central lane positioning and can hear a car approaching my tail. Feeling flustered, I move to the curb but turn my head around much too hesitantly at the same time. I've been a cycle commuter in my home city for six years, but here in this new setting, and armed with new knowledge about how to act, I am finding my old cycling habits hard to break.

Earlier, when I interviewed Rob, he indicated that confidence is central to the development of commuting skills. "If you project confidence," he said, "people are going to be confident in you. If I'm out there riding around, looking around, making a few signals, everyone around me goes, 'Okay, that guy knows what he's doing. I don't to have worry about him. He's turning right; excellent'; whereas the person kind of wobbling in the corner, everyone looks at them and goes, 'I am afraid for you,' 'You're concerned for your safety; I'm concerned for your safety. I just want to get around you and leave you behind me, so I don't to have worry about you anymore.' And so then those people will find: 'Oh, there's all these cars; they're always in a rush to get past me, and I don't see them because I'm not looking back,' and it spirals into this situation where they're feeling really out of control."

Remembering this conversation, the subtle change in comportment that this drill site is teaching us is designed to change our perceptions of how we interact with others on the road. I can see now how the drills are designed to show us how an activity previously perceived to be dangerous can be much less risky. As Rob noted, people are saying, "'Look what happens when I commute with people; that person gives way and I can turn'; they see: 'Actually, hang on a second; this perception of a chaotic world with people out to get you disappears and there's actually a world in which I've got a lot of control.'" Demonstration is key here, as Rob attested to earlier when he mentioned that "when the group is riding as a group, they're just mimicking the lane positioning of the first person." He says that "one of the things we tell people is that you need to 'fake it till you make it.'"

Rob explains that confidence minimizes discomfort on the road. "I think the vast majority of anger between motorists and cyclists comes about when people are made to feel uncomfortable," he says. This is a situational discomfort rather than anger directed at a person. "It's because that cyclist was acting in a way which made them feel like the cyclist was unaware of their presence or acted in a way that wasn't particularly predictable because they weren't looking around and making eye contact and making signals, and so they got surprised. And you get people like: 'Oh, you surprised me and you shocked me and now I'm going to get angry at you for surprising me.' When you stop surprising motorists and you start giving very clear instructions about what you're doing and what you'd like them to do, you immediately become treated differently."

With the first drill site behind us, the four of us continue further into the city in single file, crossing Prince Alfred Park. This is the second drill site. Even though it is Sunday, the traffic is heavy. This maneuver is all about turning left onto a side road and then turning back out. Ben makes this maneuver look easy as he shows us what to do. However, because the traffic here is heavier, when I'm called to take my turn, I feel much more nervous. I remember the instructions: Make eye contact with drivers, because, as Rob said to me, "until you show them your face, you're basically an object and something in their way, an obstruction. You turn around and you become a human being." As I approach the side road, I look around before giving my hand signal. My eyes lock with the man who is driving the white taxi behind me. As I do, he nods and gives me an extra two meters of room. I'm quietly impressed.

We do the drill twice, but the drizzle that has been falling intermittently since we left the cycle center has now turned into rain—an east coast low rolling in from the Pacific. Ben suggests that we head back now. As the drops become heavier, I feel my cotton shorts and canvas shoes become sodden. Yet as we retrace our route, I become aware that this creeping discomfort is offset by a new sense of confidence. I'm reminded of anthropologist Tim Ingold's writing on skill, which questions the conventional idea that a skill is simply a technique that individual bodies develop. He argues that we need to think of skill "not as an attribute of the individual body in isolation but of the whole system of relations constituted by the presence of the artisan in his or her environment."[27] What this means is that the development of skills such as this cycling course is not just about "intravenously" taking up a set of predefined ideas, but is much more about changing the *living relationship* between people and their surrounding environment.[28]

As we experience something again and again, over time and through repetition, habit is the change in the relationship between us and our environment. Participating in the cycling course made me appreciate that these opportunities are powerful ways to kick-start new habits that might, over time and with practice, change people's capacities to react and respond to their surroundings differently,[29] creating a "knowledge in the hands," to use philosopher Maurice Merleau-Ponty's phrase.[30] Indeed, habit is what enables people to undertake commuting journeys every day without expiring.[31] Imagine just how exhausting it would be if we had to consciously think through how we get to work every single day? More than this, confidence is about developing a belief in this relationship of body and environment: a belief that our bodies will be able to do something. Philosopher David Lapoujade argues that belief is the root of confidence. We "believe in order to be confident."[32] It is belief that changes our relationship with our worlds. As geographers J-D Dewsbury and Paul Cloke describe, belief is a powerful force, because it makes people "experience very real and specific feelings."[33] Belief makes "certain things happen that would not otherwise."[34] When we are confident, when we have a belief in something—in this case, the belief that we *can* ride to work through difficult traffic, for instance—it is belief that helps us achieve this end.

3   Maintaining Skills

There is a tendency to think that when we've mastered a skill, it's ours for keeps. In a rather different context, philosopher Hubert Dreyfus takes the example of learning jazz piano. He argues there is a five-stage progression in learning a skill, passing from novice to expert.[35] However, this assumes that once a skill has been mastered it remains there, ready for us to call on whenever we need it. The bodily habits that make up skills are understood here as *at hand* resources in that they spring to our assistance whenever a situation requires them. Habits here are assumed to be held in a kind of anticipatory readiness. In this section, I question this assumption by exploring three different situations that suggest commuting skills are much less assured than we might presume.

Fragile Confidence

I meet Brian at his workplace, a large medical facility near the center of the city. The bodily vulnerability that the hospital lobby so powerfully evoked turned out to be highly prescient in the context of the conversation that we would have. Brian bikes to work from the North Shore of the city, cycling across the Sydney Harbour Bridge every day to and from work. He and his wife chose their location based on it being within a ten-kilometer radius of his workplace. He describes his route step by step and with pinpoint precision. He describes himself as an "aggressive cyclist": "I will take up a whole lane and I want people to see me. And I don't mind people being annoyed, because I know they've seen me, you know. So I sit at the front of the cars and make myself really visible." I smile, aware that this is exactly the sort of antagonistic manner that the cycling course described earlier frowns on. What I'm most struck by here, however, is how Brian self-identifies as a "confident road cyclist." Even so, he says that there are "still bits of it that, you know, sort of—I feel uncomfortable with." I'm keen to learn more.

Brian clearly enjoys cycling, which is evident from the outset; he begins our conversation by telling me excitedly over a double shot of espresso that he's currently training for a long road challenge. He reflects on the many benefits that cycling to work provides, especially the cost and the time saved in getting to work. In addition to these more systematized rationales given for cycling, what is evident to me in his reflections is the pleasure he gets from cycling. There is a rather lovely moment when he turns to me and says, "And, you know, there's a small boy inside me that just loves that 'wheee, it's raining,' you know, kind of road spray and stuff like that." At this moment, I try to imagine his euphoria while experiencing wheels on wet tarmac, pushing through sheets of warm Sydney rain.

He stops and shrugs his shoulders. "Having said that, there'll be once every three or four weeks that I'll have a really unpleasant experience." His displeasure is accentuated by his furrowed brow. "And it's funny, actually; I'm a really confident rider, but if something happens to me and it exposes my vulnerability, I just lose confidence and then I just feel really uncomfortable for the next—I don't know—sometimes up to a week." I'm quite taken aback by this admission, particularly from a rider who professed earlier in the interview to be "part of a Lycra-clad gang," a type of ultra-confident cyclist that Rob had warned me about.[36]

Slightly hesitantly, and without wishing for him to relive potentially traumatic memories, I ask him whether he can recount one of these moments. "Yeah, sure," he says somewhat sanguinely. "There are a couple of times that I've been cut off by cars turning left. I was coming up West Street and the cyclist in front of me—I was sitting really close to him; you know, we were just sort of going together—he indicated to turn left; that was fine. But I wasn't turning left and the car turned left right across me and I slammed on the brakes and did a bit of shoutiness. And he got out of his car"—he interrupts himself—"It's funny: When people, I think, are in a car and they've made a mistake, they generally respond with aggression. He was just shouting at me." As he says this, my mind is taken back to unpleasant biking encounters that I have had, and can empathize with his sense of frustration. He tells me that these sorts of encounters make him feel like a guest on the road. "I could drive a car, but I choose to ride a bicycle, and that doesn't make me any less of a person or with any less rights," he says, echoing Ben and Gavin's point earlier about the power of eye contact to humanize an encounter.

If we can take from this that confidence can be fragile, I'm interested in learning what he does to regain his confidence. He says: "I consciously find other cyclists and sit with them and I just feel a little bit secure again." He tells me that sometimes he chooses to ride with a *cycling bus*, a group of cyclists that keeps to a fixed route at a fixed time. The one he joins is called, appropriately enough, the *Easy Riders*. "They cycle from Hornsby, some of them, and then they just cycle down through the south end of the bridge, where they stop and get coffee. And they just pick people up along the way. And, by the time it gets to Artarmon, it's about thirty riders. ... But, when you do, you ride with thirty other people and, I mean, it's much safer, you know." As for the confidence gain after this, Brian says that "slowly, it comes back and then you just go again. But it'll be just—just—there still a little."

What this conversation brings to our attention is that even for someone so experienced, the bodily skills that are developed through commuting journeys can be fragile and liable to break down. Whereas a sense of confidence can change the way that we feel the surrounding traffic pressing in on us, so too, as Brian's reminiscences suggest, can temporary breakdowns to this confidence require repair work to bring that feeling back.[37] This repair work might involve developing new journey arrangements, such as cycling with other people. Even when this confidence returns, the trace of these incidents still has a presence, inflecting Brian's journey "still a little." Furthermore, Brian's story reinforces how a sense of confidence relates to belief. In this instance, it is an unsettling event that jeopardizes the belief necessary for Brian to cycle in the way he did before.

Interrupted Habits

On the other hand, too much confidence in our habits also can lead to problems. Adam lives in a small town on the Central Coast, eighty kilometers north of Sydney, with his wife and two teenaged children. He moved there seventeen years ago from Sydney's Inner West just before starting a family and commutes by car to an industrial area west of the city center. He is a technical manager for a major corporation and works a combination of twelve-hour day and night shifts for just over three weeks each month, with two or three days off to transition between day and night shifts. Feeling my own capacities creaking under the strain of my very early morning start, I met him at an airy coffee shop in his home town early one morning on one of his days off after working night shifts.

I was excited about meeting Adam, because he indicated in his participant form that his shift work means that he must change routines regularly. I begin the interview by asking him to talk me through his most recent commute, for the night shift. "Ah, that's a biggie," he notes, smiling. He briefly runs me through his half-hour preparation, often after only three or four hours of sleep, because during the day "there's always life going on." He says straight away how much he enjoys driving because it's "my time of solace; it's my serenity from home life to work life." Straight after that he tells me how much he enjoys freeway driving because "it's that calming, that droning sound of the road."

I sense that after taking this journey for eighteen years, Adam is a very confident driver. He notes: "If I'm in with other commuters, the guys that drive day in, day out, there are times when I've gone to work and I didn't—I cannot remember driving to work." He goes on to describe the style of driving that comes with this experience: "I'm not an aggressive driver; I'm a fast driver, which—a lot of people, I think, misconstrue that as being aggressive. But, for me to get out the front—and what I was getting to is the fact that, if I'm in the car with my wife, I've been driving all these years on average at 130–140 ks. ... But, when I've been with my wife, the fact that I have had to slow down to accommodate her feelings, it's thrown me out in regards to where I can fit, where I can't fit. And the speed of other people who are still travelling at that 130. So, as a commuter, you can see a distinct difference with the guys that commute. There is—we can all sit in the fast lane, all sit tailgating on 130, no brake lights. It's just—it's a weave—it's a nice drive."[38] He contrasts with this with noncommuters making the occasional journey: "You'll see a wife that's taking her kid to the school sports, the swimming carnival or whatever, and she's jumped in and having to commute in that time but wants to sit in the fast lane at 110; and you see all the brake lights coming up. And then I have to wake up."

Adam's reflections indicate how his commute is a thoroughly habitual action, taking place below the threshold of consciousness.[39] His description of a *weave* is suggestive of the sort of flowing action that philosopher Maxine

Sheets-Johnstone describes as being an immersive form of movement that does not require conscious attention.[40] Adam's use of the term *waking up* here indicates that driving alongside more cautious noncommuters interrupts his commuting habits, forcing driving back to his conscious attention, rather than subconscious autopilot. However, this is not Adam's only interruption.

Adam then describes something that formed a refrain throughout the interview: "With the driving, I still find it easy to do. If it's after night shift, a hard night shift, I've trained myself to pull over on the side of the road on the freeway and get a thirty-minute kip, this micro—microsleep; I've learned by experience that it's very real. And, a couple of times, I've had some rock walls facing me that have just scared the bejesus out of me." "What happens?" I ask, perhaps somewhat quickly. His previously cheerful demeanor turns more sober. "Oh, look; just to—goose bump." He points to his arms. The silvery hairs on his thick bronzed arm are raised and arcing out, and the surface of his skin has suddenly erupted into thousands of tightly packed nodules. He swallows, frowns, and looks out of the window momentarily. He turns back and looks at me, his brow now furrowed, and takes a deep breath. "It just scares the life out of you. Immediate anger: 'Why did I let myself get to this just for the sake of fucking work?'"

Later, Adam's train of thought returns to microsleep. He reflects on how his physical capacities have changed since he moved to the Central Coast. "Normally I'm pretty fit and I can—I think it's that sleeping, that need to sleep; whereas, when I was commuting, what, say twenty years ago—at the age of only thirty-one, thirty-two, I was unstoppable. So you could still go and party 'til four o'clock in the morning and not feel the—I can't do that anymore; I can, but it's very difficult to recover." Reflecting on his ability to cope with his commute, he says, "I always thought, 'Yeah, piece of cake.'" Again, his affable demeanor turns slightly colder, and he looks at me with a steely gaze. "It's not so much a piece of cake, because I'm concerned about the falling asleep—just accidents. I do think that I'm an accident waiting to happen; whereas, years ago, I used to commute on a motor bike at times— invincible." He pauses, and I try not to interrupt. "And, again, shit, imagine ending up in a wheelchair—the burden on my family, the kids—or, you know, if I was to be killed or something ... and that's that anger that I was talking about, like: 'Jesus, don't.'" He describes the conditions that can cause microsleeping: "You do know when I'm feeling too much and then, if it's a sunny day, the sun generally comes in on this [he gestures] side of the car because I'm driving north. If I'm feeling comfortable, I just—yeah; I don't know. You're sort of always thinking, 'I'll be right; I'll be right.' And then, again, I don't know; I think it's that—why? Is that a conscious effort? I know why it occurred the other day: because I pushed myself to be here. Why it hasn't happened for so long is probably because I've taken steps before—like, I've been at work—or even the fact of having a cup of coffee."

The habits that we develop and come to rely on to support us through everyday life might be less forthcoming under certain conditions. Adam's thread here concerns the effects that shift work has on his capacities to drive safely. Although habit provides the stabilizing forces[41] that help Adam drive, what we can take from this is that in exhaustion, certain habits that are usually second nature are less easy to summon. Specifically, the concentration and alertness required for him to drive safely can fall away.[42] Although the interruption of habit he described feeling earlier when he is traveling with his wife is felt as an effort ("it throws me out"), the more sudden breakdown of habitual action in exhaustion is felt much more forcefully, as the gravity of the unfolding situation becomes very palpable. Like the traces of Brian's uncomfortable cycling experiences that remained after the event itself, the way that Adam reacts with such anger to recollections of this event in our interview may be a testament to its ongoing effects.

Throughout Adam's recollections, what is particularly striking are the tensions between his confidence in his habits ("I'll be right") and the welling up of the fright of what happens when his attention slackens in a microsleep. Noticeably, Adam has become increasingly alert to the conditions that cause microsleeping, such as sunlight and warmth. This enables him to change some of these conditions through tactics such as drinking coffee. More than just highlighting exhaustion, though, what this recollection brings to the fore is how other processes of bodily change inflect Adam's commuting experience. He reminisces about how when he was younger, it was easier for him to recover from tiring events than it is now ("I do think I'm an accident waiting to happen")—although I sense that his felt vulnerability is intensified by his family responsibilities.

Weary Habits

The perennial debate about increasing the retirement age often prompts questions about people's capacities to do what their job requires of them. Yet often absent from these debates are questions about people's capacities to travel to and from their jobs. Adam's recollections about how his capacities have changed over time suggest that this is not an insignificant issue. Although the complex relationships between mobility and well-being in later life have gained some scholarly attention,[43] life just before retirement has received much less. Jenny is in her mid-fifties and, in the context of research on mobility and aging, hardly qualifies as old. Yet it was during her interview that issues about the bodily processes of aging really came to the fore.

I meet Jenny in her inner-city apartment one muggy afternoon. All the windows in the apartment are open, and I can feel the air, heavy with moisture, pleasantly wafting through. She has been living in this apartment in the Inner West of Sydney for nineteen years. She works at Westmead, just over twenty kilometers to the west, and has had this commute for seventeen years.

Jenny drives into work four days out of five. I'm particularly struck by the experience developed over the many years of her commute, as revealed when she describes the variation in her route based on her changing feelings: "Now, the good thing is that it—well, I sort of—I take a bit of a back route. I've tried over the years various different routes, but I go—I sort of more or less hug the railway line on some back streets I know down through—so Summer Hill, Ashfield, Croydon, Burwood. And now—the latest one—because they were putting up some—what I thought were apartments, but it turns out they're office blocks right along the railway line at Burwood, and there started to be a lot of, you know, the men with the stop signs. And I mean, the buildings are between the road and the railway line and it just feels as though—I mean, they're multi-multi-story—it feels as though you're sort of going into a tunnel. And I just thought, 'I don't like going along there anymore.' So I turn up, I cross the railway line and turn up Shaftsbury Avenue, I think it's called, down past Burwood Westfield, and then I get onto Parramatta Road."

However, early in our conversation, it is the physical demands of her journey that become prominent. In describing her morning routine, before she heads down to her car, she says with a wry smile, "At the moment I've got a bit of an issue with a muscle in my sort of buttock area, so I've got this whole bloody list of exercises I'm supposed to do. So I sort of try and fit some of them in—so I've got my little sort of exercise corner down here." She points to the corner of her small lounge. I can sense her weariness as she says, speedily and with mild contempt, "Try and fit those in, you know; sort of rush, rush, rush, and do a few exercises."

Given that Jenny has had this commute for so many years, I'm somewhat surprised at why she has decided to stay living here. She says that she bought her apartment when her workplace was located very close by. She says, "I think I knew, when I bought this place, that the hospital was going to move, but I sort of go, 'Oh, yeah, well, that's a bit of a drag, but'— you know—'whatever.' But, you know, until you've actually started doing it and—I don't remember it being such a stress in the early days." She sits back in her chair, glances out of the window and looks a little hassled. I'm worried that I've touched on something that she'd prefer not to talk about. But she continues: "I think it's definitely been a cumulative thing for me and I think also as I've aged. ... I just really, I just put it down to, you know, that you just don't want to do these things as you get older and as you've done them for so many years, and you sort of think, 'Well, I've done that'—you know—'Someone else can do it.'" Her tone suddenly becomes warmer. "And I think I really have turned into one of those grumpy old women—have you ever seen that TV show where it's kind of whinge about everything and people's mobile phones?" I laugh and nod a little nervously. She says, with some frustration, "I really feel that I've sort of got into that mindset where everything just seems like, you know, a stress and sort of an annoyance. ... But I think, yeah—the seventeen years, I think, definitely have taken their toll and just thinking, 'Why do I keep'—you know, the more I do it, I think, 'Why am I doing this?'" Her tone becomes more agitated, and she returns to the subject of the location of her house. "Why do I live twenty-two kilometers from where I work?" she asks, rhetorically. "It's just so stupid!'"

I'm suddenly feeling very concerned that asking these questions might have magnified Jenny's discontents. Were they previously safely repressed, I wonder? What if drawing attention to these tensions makes her more anxious? Jenny relieves some of these concerns. She says, "In a way, I'm sort of almost grateful to the commuting hassles; they've been the catalyst to get me thinking about moving." Her tone is now much more resolute.

"Well, anyway, now I've decided I am going to move out there. ... There's the stress of—the cumulative stress, I'd say, of the drive, of the commute, and the increase in traffic, I'm sure, over that time. ... I could walk to work. And that is just looking so attractive to me at the moment that it's more or less, you know, the main incentive to have a—and I think, 'Well, no; in some ways, I still don't really want to live out there, but'—you know— 'what do I really want?'" She holds both her hands up and shrugs, and I can sense that she is still wrestling with many tensions in this decision. "Do I sort of want to keep doing *this*?'—because I'm fifty-five and I plan to retire at sixty. ... So, I think, in four more sort of full years plus, you know, some other months—and, you know, if I just look at it that I'll live out there till I retire and I can always move back here or live somewhere else after I've retired—and it doesn't seem very long; it just seems like it's quite doable." "So potentially, you have only a month and a half left of actually having to do a commute that you've done for seventeen years," I exclaim. She smiles, and her face lights up excitably. "Yeah, I know! And, now I've decided, I'm finding it even harder!"

Conclusion

Our daily commutes might so often seem like the repetition of the same journey. We might take the same route, leave home at the same time, glance at the same sights, and rub shoulders with the same people on the way. Social historian Joe Moran admits that it is difficult to think of everyday life in any other way, and this is because so often "daily life seems to exist outside historical change."[44] However, this illusion is an effect of our habit of focusing on similarities. Topographically speaking, we might well be undertaking the same journey—but as this chapter has shown, our experience of that journey and the bodies that we are and our relationships with the environments that we pass through undergo very real changes over time. The strangeness of starting a new journey and how this journey becomes overlaid with the memory of other journeys reminds us that the commute is anything but repetition of the same. Geographer Yi-Fu Tuan describes how our very sense of place comes about through repeated journeys. He says: "As a result of habitual use the path itself acquires a density of meaning and stability that are characteristic traits of place."[45] Although Tuan draws attention to the stability that repetition produces, the encounters and reflections in this chapter reveal the many kinds of change happening.

Commuting requires many different skills that can take time to develop. These include navigation, timing, and control of vehicles and bikes, and they can involve finely honed reflexes for making split-second decisions. Once developed, these skills continue to change, which makes the experience of commuting different over time. What has this chapter taught us about skills development? The word *skill* conventionally refers to something active—the ability to do something well, for instance. However, its etymological history suggests that it was previously a much more passive concept, formed of a combination of the Danish term for *separation* and the Low German for *to differ*. Skill here is much more about *discernment*, or an ability to make something out, than it is about the ability to carry out an activity. Guided by this alternative emphasis, we might ask how we can improve our discernment of how our commutes are changing us? Philosopher Michel Foucault's idea of *technologies of the self* offers some guidance here. These are the self-techniques through which individuals work on their bodies in all kinds of ways, the "reflective and voluntary practices by which [people] not only set themselves rules of conduct, but seek to transform themselves."[46] What is important for our purposes is the how technologies of the self involve reflection on what works and what doesn't work for people.

Foucault tends to emphasize the activity involved in self-techniques, but this comes at the expense of the passivity involved. To this end, a vital but often overlooked part of skill development might be about paying closer attention to our sensations, or how we feel the world pressing on us. So how can we enhance our skills not necessarily for activity, but for heightening a discernment of how these commutes are transforming us in different ways? It takes one understanding of skill—the active understanding—to master the physical movements involved in commuting. But it takes a rather different understanding of skill—the more passive understanding—to evaluate what these commutes are doing to us as individuals, to discern what they are enhancing or diminishing. Each of the interviews in this chapter are little moments of reflection in which people evaluate what their commutes are doing to them. Maybe these encounters will have prompted some people to make a change, to do things just a bit differently.

"Balmain East, Darling Harbour service!" shouts a young ferry worker to the small crowd of passengers waiting on the covered pontoon to board. It is late afternoon on Friday at the end of my first week of interviews with commuters. I'm back here at Circular Quay, about to head home. The sky is a deep blue and the golden sun is catching the tops of the buildings on the quayside, casting long shadows that provide some cooler hollows from the heat. There is a palpable sense of relief that the end of the working week has finally arrived for many. Top buttons of shirts are undone and ties have been removed. Although I feel privileged that I have a short but stunning ferry commute home, I feel tired after a week of intense fieldwork. Setting suns prompt backward reflection. I reflect on how my own interviewing skills have changed over the week: fewer nerves and more confidence to leave my set of prompts. Most of all, I feel overwhelmed by the generosity that people have shown me by sharing the unexpected twists and turns of their transit lives.

2 Fizzing Intensities: Strange Dramas of Capsular Collectives

"Sardine express: Welcome to the peak hour commute on Sydney Trains," announces a Channel 9 news report.[1] This well-worn epithet draws our attention to how the commute forms a space in which bodies press against other bodies. This particular epithet is well-earned, given that some trains in Sydney run at 167 percent capacity, with around 187 people sandwiched into every carriage.[2] Yet the percentages used to express crowding on public transport in cities worldwide tell us very little about what it is like to travel in close proximity to other people every day. This chapter takes up this challenge by exploring the social relations of the commute.

Quite understandably, the question of how people relate to each other while on the move became particularly prominent during the mid-nineteenth century. Mass passenger transportation through the rise of the railway created a strange social situation in which unacquainted people were thrust together in close proximity for lengthy periods of time. In this unfamiliar social arrangement, geographer Nigel Thrift describes how the sheer awkwardness of having to sit, face to face, opposite a stranger created intense anxiety: "Each of these bodies passively avoided others."[3] Although today it might be rather difficult to imagine the novelty of a social setting that is now so ubiquitous, that transit spaces feature so consistently in films and television dramas as places where danger lurks just below the surface is a reminder that these spaces remain highly charged.[4]

From the evocative lyricism of Paul Theroux[5] to the perfunctory wit of Jenny Diski,[6] contemporary travel narratives often derive their spark from the encounters with others that take place in transit spaces during unfamiliar journeys. With this in mind, the commute might seem utterly banal in comparison. However, just as geographer Tim Edensor reminds us that we often overlook the more ordinary dimensions of our "extraordinary" journeys,[7] this chapter explores how daily commutes are fizzing with all manner of intensities between people. These are clearly of a different nature than one-off adventures, but they render the everyday a little more strange and unpredictable than we might otherwise imagine. From subtle gestures to dramatic outbursts, commutes are beaded with events and encounters that demand our attention.

The commute is a time during which people experience myriad forms of social difference. Nigel Thrift writes that "cities bring people and things together in manifold combinations,"[8] and the commute is arguably an opportunity for this bringing together to happen particularly intensely, as the statistics on public transport overcrowding indicate. A commute can be an experience in which we rub shoulder to shoulder against many different people. For example, geographer Helen Wilson and cultural theorist Greg Noble remind us that the commute is a key site of difference in the multicultural city.[9] However, it is not just a diversity of people that commuting brings together. The spaces of the commute themselves powerfully influence our experience of these social relations and the events and encounters that happen. The differently designed capsular spaces of trains, buses, and cars can induce very different sensations of being with other people. Understanding the joys and frustrations of commuting requires us to grasp precisely these kinds of transient sociabilities.

This chapter explains how events and encounters with others in the commute are changing commuters' dispositions in subtle yet powerful ways. Some encounters have a light touch; others are more forceful. First, in section 1, we join a mid-morning bus commute through the inner south of Sydney, in a dreamy atmosphere formed of the split-ended conversations unfolding between people sitting close to me. Ramping up the intensity, section 2 thrusts us into a more volatile train commute between Sydney and Wollongong, where a heated encounter changes relations of enablement and constraint within the carriage. Section 3 charts an interview encounter with one bus commuter, who testifies to the many intense encounters that she has experienced during her long commuting career. Focusing in on a single testimonial permits us to sense more of the complexity of this experience of being affected.

1   Fleeting Atmospheres

Dreamlike Worlds

Two ladies wearing red face each other as the 310 thunders along Botany Road shortly after 9:00 a.m. They have kindly wrinkles that arc out from their eyes, lines that trace the laughter of times past. "Whaddya gaan a taan fowa?" asks the one on the left. She is looking at the man sitting in front of me. There is a long silence. Does she know him, I wonder? "Goin' a see the parole officer," he murmurs, his voice soft and faintly apologetic. "Oh! Ya dun summit baaad then?" she asks eagerly, addressing the rest of the bus as much as him. "It was a while ago," he murmurs back hazily. The other woman in red is grinning airily. A man's voice behind me croaks, "You've gotta catch me first," or at least I think this is what he said. She answers him back, "It's bad, double days now," still grinning. Her voice is gravelly and only produces one volume, however near or far away her interlocutor is. The dull formalities of turn-taking are forgone as the exchange continues. Incoherent counterpoint rides above the growl of the bus's acceleration. It is pleasantly dreamlike in both its envelopment of me and its lack of demands of me.

There is something irreducibly situational about who the woman in red addresses that keeps me from meeting her eyes. Her head turns to her left to a woman who sits facing her. "Crop tops are they?" She looks over at another woman who is wearing red. "Like a bra?" "Where d'ya get that?" She answers too softly for me to hear. "Twelve?" There is a long pause. "That's too much." I hear the man's voice behind me again. "Who you talkin' to?" she asks, looking behind me and smiling. "No one but your-self!" She turns back to the foreground, addressing no one in particular: "Tight. It's gotta be tight." A moment or two later, a woman behind me asks, "Are yah getting' picked up?" although it's not clear who this is directed at, because no one responds. The woman in red looks up behind me again: "Yah got no brains!" She grins. "Sawdust for brains!" She turns back. "Don't worry, it's just my son in law!" The white-shirted man next to me looks up from his notepad scribbling and smiles at her. "Where you from?" she asks him. "I'm from South Africa," he says. She turns back to the lady facing her. "I'm havin' a knee operation on Monday; going in Sunday, havin' it done on Monday." "I've had an operation," the South African guy says to her, eagerly. "Fourteen of them, on my knee." Her enthusiasm hasn't lasted with him, though, and she answers, "Yeah, mine's bad." As she does, the bus grinds to a halt and I leave.

Multiple Trajectories

Geographer Doreen Massey[10] warns that to imagine places as bounded, homogenous, and unchanging is a dangerous fiction. She instead invites us to consider how places are formed of the entanglement of multiple trajectories. Through our commutes, we might glimpse some of these multiple trajectories. The route diagram for the 310 that I sighted at the bus stop depicted a single line that strung together different places on the way from Eastgardens to City, yet the simplicity of a single line overlooks how this journey is made of many different lines that each person on the bus is weaving. My trajectory this mid-morning involves going to a library, but witnessing these conversations telescopes into view a host of other trajectories: a man about to visit a parole officer, a woman anticipating knee surgery. For the duration of this commute, these multiple trajectories are brought together.

If pressed to identify the most recurrent theme that commuters raised with me in interviews, grievance-causing behaviors would gain a prominent position. Stinky food, feet on seats, clipping toenails, and loud conversations: This inventory grew exponentially. In the scene presented here, some elements, such as the loud conversation, do seem to push at the limits of what geographers Eric Laurier and Chris Philo call *light touch* forms of sociality, in which the presence of others is acknowledged, but people's right to be left alone in public is also respected.[11] Although sociologists especially have been interested in diagnosing breaches of social etiquette,[12] limiting our interest to the extent to which interactions display conformity with an ideal is restricting. For a start, we shouldn't presume that all people traveling on the 310 embody the same ideals; there might be different ideals at different times of the day or week.[13] More significantly, focusing on how an event has congruence according to an ideal ignores what is unique about every situation. This event might be characteristic of traveling at this time on this route, but it is also resolutely singular. This configuration of trajectories will never happen in this way again.

Vagueness

Although seemingly inconsequential, the events that happen during each commute matter in part because they contribute to distinctive situated *atmospheres*. As geographers Ben Anderson and James Ash write, atmospheres "have effects and are effects."[14] This means that atmospheres are the effects of encounters such as these, but at the same time they are also agents that change the way encounters unfold and how they are felt. As the conversation at the start of this section unfolds, a distinctive atmosphere emerges that envelops the bus interior. This idea of envelopment is captured by philosopher Gernot Böhme, who suggests that atmospheres "seem to fill the space with a certain tone of feeling like a haze."[15] There is possibly something convivial about the atmosphere on the 310 at that moment. However, Anderson and Ash caution us not to stabilize something that is, by its very nature, "ephemeral, seemingly vague and diffuse."[16] Naming an atmosphere as this or that contributes to such stabilization and "potentially denies the coexistence of multiple 'minor' atmospheres."[17] Thus, to say that the atmosphere on the bus commute is convivial overrides a sense of vagueness—a more faithful description of the sense of being caught in an act.

Just as there are trajectories of individuals on the bus and their own daily routines, at another level each utterance also has its own trajectory. Each remark has a life of its own. "Sawdust for brains!" is a barb that suddenly slices through the convivial atmosphere with the potential to provoke and enrage, for instance. There is a volatility of being caught in the act at this very moment. Pause here and we might sense ambiguity about what the next moment will be. While our forward-leaning anticipations might provide comfort at this moment—we might hope that it probably won't get out of hand—we just don't know what will happen next. In this context, the woman's jibe—"Don't worry, it's just my son in law"—eases the tension slightly, but its overtones of shame seem to curdle the atmosphere further.

Reminiscent of geographer Allan Pred's description of a dock worker's daily commute through the streets of Stockholm, formed of fleeting glimpses, transient perceptions, and a sense of vagueness,[18] this scene reminds us that atmospheres of commuting are always in transition. As Anderson says, "Atmospheres are perpetually forming and deforming, appearing and disappearing, as bodies enter into relation with one another.

They are never finished, static or at rest."[19] Even the scripting of this event from my scrappy notes polishes the split-endedness of the unfolding atmosphere. It anchors it in ways that further defuse the instability of the event, while at the same time inflecting it with my own bodily judgments and habits of observation.

Withdrawal

Even in the most public of places, there is often a degree of wiggle room in how we respond to the atmospheres that bubble up. While there might be occasions when we become dragged into an unfolding event, as the previous section shows, there is a degree of freedom over whether we become engaged with or withdraw from what is going on around us. Sociologist Erving Goffman writes about *involvement shields*,[20] strategies that indicate disengagement from unfolding action in public, such as reading. This idea has been developed by media theorist Michael Bull, who describes how people use portable music players to create their own individualized soundscapes to manage their experience of the city, effectively tuning out the surrounding environment.[21] However, at other times, our freedom to zone out might have less to do with technological supports and much more with the weariness of the day's demands, as I was to learn on my return commute.[22]

On taking a seat near the back of the 310 bus later that afternoon, I find myself glancing at the other side of the road where I got off the bus this morning. Something about the site transports me back to this morning's commute. I find myself airily musing about the man's meeting with his parole officer. I find myself mouthing the phrase *sawdust for brains*. I wonder how the woman is feeling about her knee operation, drawing ever nearer. I wonder where their days have led them; their trajectories will have become entangled with so many others since I saw them. After a while, fatigue has blunted my enthusiasm to make sense of any encounters happening around me, as the chug of the engine induces a pleasant state of dreaminess. I'm faintly aware of two schoolgirls sitting behind me, having a disagreement over whether a certain teacher is kind or not ("She totally hates me!" "Yes, but she's so nice!") which transforms into a discussion about how to spend the next hour at home, whether to watch TV or watch a DVD, which transforms into a discussion about the merits of Ben and Jerry's ice cream ("But it's so expensive!"), which transforms into a discussion about whether you can ever be too old for Tae Kwon-do ("Dad *is* too old.").

2 Enablement and Constraint

Sneer

"GOLD DIGGERS! Look at them!" shouts a sneering teenage boy, swaying from a yellow pole. From his "stage" at the end of the packed, double-deck train carriage, his accusation spears the placid atmosphere, addressing no one in particular, but startling everyone. "I can see he is!" the boy grins, wagging his finger knowingly at a man in a white shirt sitting near to him, as if to expose his ruse. The man refuses to look at him, his eyes trained on some distant point. The boy's eyes casually scan the carriage. "She isn't!" This time, I can't see who his target is. There are three other boys with him, and one of them sniggers; this choice must be similarly condescending. Facing the passengers downstairs in the carriage, who are all seated facing him, one of the other boys pipes up: "It's all about the money, money, money!" "MONEY, MONEY, MONEY!" chimes another, this time more provocatively, holding both hands out as he says it, rubbing his thumbs against his fingers to emphasize the sentiment. The first boy laughs.

As geographer Peter Adey writes, people on the move are differently enabled and constrained by their experience of travel.[23] The architects and planners responsible for airports and railway stations often design in enablements and constraints, especially when there are groups of people willing to pay more for a faster or more comfortable journey.[24] However, sometimes enablements and constraints are less intentional, such as in environments in which only certain sorts of bodies can move faster or more comfortably.[25] In this section, we join a late afternoon train commute to explore how the events and encounters that take place during commuting journeys can change relationships of enablement and constraint.

Until the boy shouts, the soporific roar of the air conditioning smothered the train carriage: white noise to lull tired bodies. It is well past five o'clock, and many people in the carriage have finished their paid working day. Foreheads are gleaming. It will be a while before they are home, though. Many people in this carriage live in the Illawarra region, over sixty kilometers to the south of Sydney. This is Australia's busiest commuting corridor. Twenty thousand people (out of a workforce of eighty-one thousand residents) travel from Illawarra to Sydney every day. Around fifteen percent of these people take the train. Many commuters are from Wollongong, the region's main city.[26] The journey from Sydney to Wollongong takes an hour and thirty-five minutes.[27]

On this late afternoon in early summer, the atmosphere in the below-ground station at Redfern, close to the city center, is fuggy. I board the front "quiet" carriage, go upstairs, and find one of the few remaining seats. The feel of air conditioning is quite beautiful, a relief from the humidity outside. This is my penultimate journey back to Wollongong from Sydney. I have been engaging in participant observation on this line for the past week, leaving Wollongong on the 6:56 a.m. train and returning on the 5:07 p.m. from Redfern, two of the busiest services. I have been using a notepad app on my mobile phone to inconspicuously make brief notes of happenings during each journey.

Fake Eyelashes

"Do you think they're fake eyelashes?" one of the boys quips at a woman, turning back to the more intimate vestibule area between the upper and lower decks. A dozen or so passengers are sitting side on to the direction of travel, facing inwards toward the boys, who have resumed their swinging around the yellow pole in the center of the carriage. One is holding onto the yellow ceiling grab rails, lifting himself and straining. Their captive audience looks unenthused, but the boys continue their jibing unperturbed. "Do you laaaiyke ma haircut?" a boy in a white top rhetorically asks the vestibule, drawling *like* into almost two syllables and flashing a wide smile. His eyes dart between the two rows of faces doing well to suppress a reaction. "A dirty mullet?" he adds, as if to both preempt his audience and mark himself as different from them. "A dirty mullet!" "A dirty mullet!" he repeats, dropping the final *t*, each time a little slower than the last, nodding calmly. An overly cheery recorded voice relieves the scene: "This train will stop at Hurstville." One of the women in the vestibule stands to leave and others follow. The automatic doors close tightly again. I feel a twinge of panic, worrying that the four boys will come upstairs to where I'm sitting. I contemplate changing carriages, but it's quiet for the moment. The air conditioning roar provides reassuring comfort, broken suddenly by laughter. A woman enters the vestibule from downstairs. "You don't have to run away!" one of the boys call to her. "I've been sitting in an office chair all day, that's alright," she says back, sounding nonplussed and tired. More laughter.

It might be tempting to shrug off this unfolding event as merely another skirmish on public transport. However, this event is anything but inconsequential. Rather than aspects of design, different forces of the action itself are working together to actively change the sense of place in the carriage. These forces include the sound of the boys' jeering intonation and their timbre of voice, alternations of silence and noise, and the repetition of phrases.[28] They include the gestures of swinging and circling around the pole, the action of the opening and closing of doors, the juxtapositions of the heat of the boys' taunts and the cool automatic announcements, the fatigue in the woman's retort. Each of these elements, and more, contributes to the in situ enablements and constraints created by this event. Each of these unscripted elements builds on and combines with one another.

What are these enablements and constraints? The concept of *micropolitics* addresses the barely perceived transitions in power that occur in and through situated encounters. This makes it an ideal concept from which to think about how this event might transform relations of enablement and constraint. For our purposes here, an instructive understanding of micropolitics comes from philosopher Gilles Deleuze's interpretations of the writings of Spinoza.[29] The key point that I draw from Deleuze is that every encounter a body has increases or decreases its capacities to perform actions and register sensations. This observation has some important implications for our understanding of the bodies involved in this event. First, a body becomes understood in terms of its capacities to perform actions and register sensations. Second, if a body's capacities to perform and sense are changed by the encounters that it has, then rather than understanding these passengers as self-contained entities that are being displaced through space by the train, bodies are always transforming, however subtly, in relation to what is happening around them.

Different qualities of an encounter have different effects. Some encounters are constructive and enhance a body's capacity to act, which Spinoza calls *joyful encounters*. Others are destructive and diminish its capacity to act, which Spinoza terms *sorrowful*. What this means is that encounters are not innately good or bad according to a predetermined logic. Rather, a body's power—understood here in terms of its changing capacities to perform and sense—depends on the exact unfolding of the event itself. Each encounter, however big or small, is therefore a recomposition of the capacities of those involved.

The concept of micropolitics therefore helps us appreciate that multiple forces are creating these subjects here and now. For example, the space itself alters bodily capacities to perform actions and register sensations. As the carriage doors close at Hurstville Station, the space becomes a sealed capsule with little escape. This potentially transforms how the unfolding events are sensed, heightening the capacity to sense anxiety. Therefore, it is not just the boys' actions that have power here, but the way that their performances become heightened by the enclosure of the carriage itself. The performativity of the space becomes intensified by the boys' actions. Most commuters in this carriage are returning from a day at work in the city. Faces are etched with signs of tiredness. For one person, this event was the final straw, a body affected that pushed a tolerance threshold to its breaking point.

Toy Gun

"BOYS!" roars a man's voice from downstairs. "IF YOU WANT TO TALK, FUCK OFF!" The surface tension has broken. There is a momentary drawn out silence; it's hard to imagine what will happen next. "Fuck off!" one of the boys stammers back to him, somewhat clumsily, as if taken aback and still processing this unanticipated response. Following his lead, the others join in taking turns, and the downstairs carriage erupts into a volatile zone of choppy, overlapping, scatter-gunned obscenities. "You fucking pommy cunts!" "You dirty fucking dog mate!" "You faggot!" The older man sitting next to me, who has gazed through the window until this point as if lost in thought, turns his head very slowly, looks straight ahead, and with wearied sarcasm says, "You're really smart guys," raising his eyebrows. My heart is racing. It occurs to me that they might come upstairs and start on us. "YOU in the glasses! You DOG!" one of them shouts. "DOG!" "Daaaawg!" "Daaaawg!" "I'll break your jaw!" another shouts. "Yeah, yeah everyone's looking now." "Wait 'til my brother comes to get me at the train station at North Wollongong." "Why are you recording us?" "You fucking pedo!" "Let's steal his iPhone." The recorded voice, oddly indifferent to this onslaught, optimistically announces: "This train will stop at Sutherland." Upstairs, a man sitting across from me answers his ringing phone softly. "Yep, carriage oh-dee-six-nine-two-four. Just coming into Sutherland. Yep, four boys." A young woman sitting adjacent to me smiles at him weakly. "Yes ... I can't really ... I didn't see their faces." The shouting continues downstairs. "Get a haircut you dreadlocked cunt." The train doors open at Sutherland and a man with glasses in a crisp white shirt, perhaps the man who lost it with the boys, steps onto the platform, takes a deep breath, waits, and is met by two guards, who have walked down to this end of the train. The four boys step onto the platform, turn to the left, and nonchalantly walk away. The man gives a business card to the train guard. The train guard is holding a translucent purple plastic toy gun.

Micropolitical transitions are taking place at this moment. The heady mix of expressive forces is affecting bodies here and now. The anger and frustration in the volume of the man's yell startled the boys, momentarily constraining them, but the momentary incapacity seemed to agitate them further, the transition in their capacities palpably felt through the newfound excitability and resentment in the boys' razor-sharp profanities. At the same time, the volatility of this event created new constraints for others in the train carriage, unsure about how to respond, perhaps intensifying a sense of claustrophobia—but it also created capacities for other people in the carriage to reach out. It enabled consolation between me and the older man next to me, as he turned to me to express his weariness. It enabled an intimacy between the man on the phone and the woman adjacent who smiled at him. Witnessing the purple toy gun at the end intensifies the surrealism of this strange drama, pushing the limits of my capacities to fathom what is going on. It is in this event's precise unfolding that relations of enablement and constraint are transforming.

In a discussion on the collective dimensions of an event, philosopher Brian Massumi reminds us that different bodies have different tendencies and capacities. What this means for us is that people "will be responding differently together" as inhabitants of the same environment.[30] In short, the same event will have different impacts on different bodies because of the different trajectories that have carried them to this moment. Being on this journey as a researcher invariably altered my capacities to sense the event. Because of the unique way that events are sensed by individuals, different commuters' capacities will be affected by the stream of previous encounters that have led up to this moment. It would be therefore be inappropriate to make bold inferences about how everyone else is feeling, even if they are based on well-meaning attempts to read body language.

Lorikeets

The train is now deep into the Royal National Park (*Nasho*, as it is known in these parts), the vast tract of coastal heathland and littoral rainforest between Sydney and the Illawarra. The sun is now much lower in the sky and the eucalypti next to the track are creating a chiaroscuro effect in the carriage. Did the boys get back on the train? Their destination, North Wollongong, is still to come. The train stops at Engadine, and through the twittering of rainbow lorikeets I hear police sirens on the freeway parallel to the railway. Are they coming for the train? Will they stop at Heathcote? A rabbit scurries to safety as we stop. As we pull out from Waterfall Station, I'm still feeling a bit shaken. I fantasize about what I might have done if I was sitting next to the man in glasses and whether I would have confronted the boys. A compendium of much too late retorts darts across my mind. At Helensburgh, the man who called the police gets up and walks down the carriage. I nod to him, slightly unexpectedly. The lady adjacent to me resumes her Flight Centre careers quiz. I notice that she must link landmarks with countries. The binder announces: "Training for a career that will take you places." The woman next to her is playing Bejeweled on her phone.

This event dissipated as obscenities faded into the familiarity of background noises that I had come to expect after making this journey for several days. The temporariness of my journeying on the Illawarra line might have heightened my senses to things that more regular commuters might overlook, but I was a temporary witness; tomorrow would be my final day commuting on the line. How might these events have been differently enabling and constraining for commuters who have been traveling on the line for years? In section 3, we turn to an interview with a commuter to explore how repeated exposure to intense events might effect rather different transformations.

3   Losing It

Tense Encounters

One of the things that makes fieldwork so tantalizing is that you never know how an encounter will unfold. After completing a dozen interviews, I was learning that the indifferent metadata commuters submitted through my online form gave little warning of the sometimes overwhelming intensities that would later slice through face-to-face meetings. Claire is a case in point: bus commuter, Inner West to Eastern Suburbs, eight years—seemingly benign, tightly packed word objects that conceal any explosive powers well. That's all I know as I wait, eagle-eyed, heart racing, on a street corner in her suburb. My eyes lock with the gaze of a woman with blonde hair. Is it her? She walks over. "David, right?" We buy coffees from a nearby café, but the noise inside is deafening. "Well you don't *look* like a knife-wielding murderer, so let's talk at my house," she suggests. Having conducted all previous interviews in public places, I am a little nervous, but her compliment—though glib—makes me feel strangely comforted.

The lounge room in this cozy sandstone federation-style house is cool and dark. It takes my eyes some time to adjust from the dazzling morning sun outside. As I begin rather formulaically talking about the project, Claire walks to her fridge and removes a piece of paper that has been affixed with a magnet. "May I ask, for what purpose, eventually?" she asks pointedly, catching me off guard as she walks back to the sofa. I have not been asked this question before; I state that I will be doing some academic writing, but that ultimately "I hope that it will do some good.'" She nods, although I feel a little more daunted now. She holds the piece of paper in her hand and I can see numbers along the side, with extensive scribbles next to each. I hope that the encounter will do justice to her preparation.

As in all previous interviews, I begin by asking Claire to describe her commute yesterday. "Well, I have different schedules on different days," she says. "So, a bus down to the post office, had a cup of coffee, walked half a block up, another bus comes up. I get that bus to Central—and I go down the escalator, down the little tunnel, and up again to what I call the 'island of doom.'" My caricatured mental image of a storm-ravaged tropical island fuses with Claire's description of a place that would form a refrain throughout our interview.

Yesterday, she was lucky; a bus came in two minutes. However, she adds, "If I had missed that, then I would have sat there for maybe twenty minutes, which doesn't seem like a long time. But, when you've got your lunch in your bag ... I have a chicken sitting in a plastic box with the sun pouring down on me because some smart person decided to build it with glass." Claire's recollections of the inhospitable environment are cutting. "They also decided to provide us with metal seats," she says, sarcastically, "so that on a forty-two-degree [Celsius] day you cannot sit on them." She frowns.

"The alternative are these two pipes, and you're supposed to lean on that, and, for a woman in a dress, you just slide off them immediately. They're useless and they're made of metal and they're hot as well. So, you know—and the glass is always quite grimy and nasty and stained and it's very unpleasant." She interrupts herself. "But, if you wouldn't mind me saying so, this is what I wanted to say." I swallow, abruptly sensing the weight of anticipation. "The 'island of doom' is a terrible place to wait. Twenty minutes is not a long time but, if you are being harassed, it can be a very long time."

The atmosphere in the room suddenly feels tenser. "A few people use it as a begging spot. There is one woman and she has an old-style cane pram with a small dog in it wrapped in a blanket," she says pointedly. "And she begs money and I say no and, when I say no, she harangues me for about fifteen minutes very loudly, in a very perverse and unpleasant way, and she does it *repeatedly*," drawing out the last word as if to emphasize the unpleasantness. "Last time," she says, "I happened to be eating a fruit salad and she told me that she hoped I died choking on my food and that I had no idea of what she was going through and that she had to sleep rough every night and that she gets raped and she could be murdered and that was all my fault." Claire looks a little hassled. "When she'd finally finished and walked off, we [she and the man next to her] just looked at each other and I said, 'What an incredibly unpleasant way to start the day; I feel really shaken.'" Her voice becomes a little calmer. "Luckily, two older ladies were down the footpath and they came over to me and they said, 'It's okay, love; you just keep going on your way to work'—and I thought, 'Oh, I'm glad somebody realizes that I'm on my way to work and I don't need this.'"

"That was one of the reasons I wanted to talk to you," she says, "because I ran into her a few weeks ago." I brace myself for what might follow. "There was an elderly woman next to me, and she started yelling at somebody and I was a bit protective of this older woman, so I said, 'Look, I think we might get yelled at, so why don't we get up and move that way?' and she said, 'Okay.' So we got up and we were standing there and looking a bit awkward, waiting for her to move on." She stops and smiles weakly. "And I think she recognized me." My heart sinks for her. "'You don't have to move because of me!'" Claire mimics. Her tone becomes more exasperated: "And the older lady—her bus came, so I'm left there and pram lady started to yell at me. I was really fed up," she says. "So I said, 'The next time you harangue me, I'm going to call the police.' Well, little did I know that she had an arsenal of small rocks in the pram and she started to hurl them at me, and, luckily, the bus came and the doors opened and I just heard the spatter of pellets."

"Seriously?" I ask, taken aback by the drama of Claire's recollection. "Seriously," she replies. Her tone changes, becoming lighter. "I have noticed people are very kind, actually. I've seen this same woman with the pram with the dog on the bus, and everyone just ignored her, you know? Nobody tackles her. We're so used to mad people on buses that we just go, 'Okay, no eye contact; don't go there and it'll be fine.' And it's this communion that we've made as commuters that we just say, 'Okay, this happens and we're just going to ignore it.'"

"There was another incident," Claire says, as if the telling of this story has ignited other memories. "I was on the bus coming from the city to home and I ran into a friend at the bus stop and he and I got on the bus and the only seat available was right at the back. Dan and I kept talking and suddenly this woman put her head on my shoulder, and I didn't quite know what to do. And I said, 'Could you take your head?' 'Oh, no; I like it here; this is nice.'" Claire recalls that after a while another seat became free. "And so I said, 'I'm getting up,' and I got up and he and I went and sat down, and she started yelling at me." She tells me that she was worried about being followed when she gets off the bus. "So we sort of concocted a plan that I would get off at [a different stop] instead of my regular stop beforehand and I would go into the supermarket. So Dan got off and said, 'Good luck,' because she's still yelling, and I stood up to get off the bus. Well, she really went for it, and the whole bus—you know, in front of all these people she's yelling, 'YOU FAT UGLY SLAG; you're just a fat slag. That dress is just disgusting. Look at that belly on you.'" Again, her eyes look glassy. "It was personal, it was offensive in the extreme, it was scary. And, you know, I'm just standing there, praying that the doors will open quickly so I can just get off. I could still hear her when the doors shut. She stayed on. I was so grateful."

I'm taken aback by the effect of presenting these incidents in succession. A few moments later, her attention returns to this incident. "Because it was physical," she says, "I think that really upset me and, because it was a public embarrassment, even though I'm never going to see any of those people again, and what she said was so personal, I felt really humiliated and frightened, and those two together had a really quite a profound effect on me." I nod. She recounts how this incident continued to affect her—even now in retelling. "The following day at work I was still very upset—I was not in a happy mood—and I remember talking to my supervisor and saying, 'Look, this happened on the bus,' and she said, 'Look, it wasn't personal; this woman was stoned'—you know. But I knew all of that, but at the same time it had a residual effect. And here I am telling you about it because it's still with me." After presenting such harrowing testimony, as if to justify why she continues to commute in the way that she does, Claire comments that the benefits of living where she does are "overwhelming" and that these incidents have taught her to be more wary. "If I see someone on the bus that looks a bit odd," she says, "I might put myself in a situation where I'm not in their sightline or I'm a bit harder to get to. There are safer seats on the bus."

Then, in a declaratory tone, she says, "I'm actually going to tell you now why I contacted you." I'm taken aback at this admission, as if the previous two recollections were mere staging points. I'm on the edge of my seat to learn what prompted Claire to respond to the newspaper ad. The scene has been set, and I sense that drama is about to unfold.

"It was a few weeks ago," she says, poised. "I finished work at about four and caught the 373, which ended up in the city. I walked down and turned the corner into George Street and there was a very light rain falling. Now, that bus stop on George Street, a lot of buses come up it and they often have to queue." I nod, trying to visualize the scene. "So you have to be really on your toes trying and see what the number of the bus four buses down is," she adds. "So, as I walk around the corner, one bus that I could get is just leaving, which is always a frustration; but one lives with that," she adds philosophically. "So, it's starting to rain a little bit harder," she says, "and I'm fixed on the buses and I notice that there aren't very many people around. And it starts to rain a bit harder and I look down and I see my dream bus: the L39. And I run down and, of course, he's pulled, oh, two centimeters out?" her rising intonation implying this slightness. "So he goes"—Claire wags her finger left and right. "So I run back to the head of the three buses, and he pulls out and takes off and doesn't stop at the stop, which is intentionally frustrating," she says, the intensity building further. "So I see another one and the same thing happens."

"And so I lost it," she says, shaking her head. "I really lost it. I sounded like a very salty sailor at the top of my voice," she admits sheepishly, "because he was about as far away as you are but behind glass, and I'm giving him the bird. I'm doing every—and I just *screamed* obscenities at him in the middle of George Street," she says, smiling a little. "Well, the thing was that I'd registered that I was alone. But what I'd failed to realize was that, when it started to rain more heavily, about 150 people were sheltering in the awnings behind me and I hadn't seen them. So I had a huge audience," she says stretching her arm out to her left. "I turned around and saw the people, and that shut me up good and proper." "Oh god, how awful," I reply. "What happened?" I ask. "I sat down next to a woman on the seat and I said, 'Oh boy, I really lost my temper,' and she said, 'Don't worry, love; that's how I feel too,'" she says, her voice much softer. "And I'm shaking and I just couldn't even turn around and look at those people. I wanted to go over and say, 'Look, I'm really sorry about that.' But I just sat there, hoping that nobody would notice me. It was horrible."

Following such a dramatic narration, Claire regains composure. "Anyway," she says more pensively, distancing herself from the event. "I came home, I rang a couple of friends, I told them the story, and they laughed like crazy. They just thought it was hilarious that this middle-aged woman just lost it." She tells me that though she has a temper, the idea of losing it in public was foreign to her and reflects on why this might have happened. "I think it's a cumulative problem," she suggests. "We've got the residual effect of multiple small incidents and some not so small and then this ongoing frustration with the lack of a system that I think that you or I could probably figure out a better way of doing this. And, yeah, I think it's justifiable rage." Interestingly, her emotional response to the event has changed, even in recounting to me. "I'm not going to get embarrassed about it," she says. "Well, I was embarrassed, but I'm not anymore; I think it's quite funny. And probably letting off a bit of steam now and then it's better to just let it go," she adds.

Through the remainder of our interview, we discuss rude, macho bus drivers, wayfinding problems, and transport infrastructure funding. "Golly, I am having a big gripe, aren't I?" she says with a giggle. Yet the preceding event continues to resonate, haunting our discussion. Later, she returns to the topic explicitly. "I think what happened when I lost it in George Street was building up for a very long time, you see, because I was very tired," she suggests. She links this to the intensive nature of her contract work. "If I do three of those weeks in a row, I find that I am extremely tired and I'm just tired to the point of real exhaustion, real fatigue, and I put it down to this cumulative, repetitive, frustrating experience that I cannot avoid." Emphatically, she adds, "It's the bus; it's the bus. You know it's the bus!," the repetition here intensifying her conviction.

"Is there anything else that you want to talk about?" I ask. "Yes. I'm just looking at my list ... I've covered pram lady. Underneath that, I've got junky girl, overdose, psychotic episode, yes," she says, followed by a quick comment on rail trackwork at the weekends. "Just to finish, I have two positive comments," she adds. "The first one is that you do get bus drivers ... I've noticed that if the driver's attitude is friendly and cooperative, the whole atmosphere of the bus changes." She links this to a suggestion. "So I think they need some training because that could really, you know, de-escalate some of the pain that we're all going through and particularly among women." In a parallel gesture of de-escalation, she says, "I would really like to maintain a positive attitude in life, but it can be hard, and so I decided this year that, when something really special and sweet happens, I'm going to write it down."

She reaches for a jar. "I've only got one slip of paper: '7 January, bus driver opened door in George Street and let me get on; first time I got home in time for the 7pm news'—because he had actually started to pull out and he saw me," she adds, arcing back to the incident where she lost it. "That's really unusual—but he stopped and because he could see me sort of huffing and puffing like this [she demonstrates] and he smiled. And I got on and I said, 'Thank you so much,' because it was an L [express] and I got home and I got to watch the news." She admits, "If you start to get overwhelmed by all this negative stuff, that can be really very bad for you and it can manifest itself in all sorts of ways." I agree. "So I want to thank you," she adds, "actually, because I've actually unloaded it all. I can rip this up." As she says this, she tears the piece of paper again and again and again.

Cracks

The "lightning rod" events that punctuate the preceding interview encounter have an intensity that contrasts dramatically with the vague, almost dreamlike encounters narrated in section 1. From the subtly affecting moments of being witness to strange conversations, the affectivity of listening to Claire's story is differently profound. Unlike the single train carriage event that I witnessed in section 2, Claire's story is one testament to the effects of the repetitious quality of commuting. Rather than excising a few unmoored sentences as evidence, reenacting the interview encounter draws attention to the intensities of her recollections and how they spark each other.

Although Anderson and Ash point out that naming an atmosphere has the potential to reduce the richness and complexity of an event, when tensions are running as high as they are here, the temptation is almost impossible to resist. Recollections of abusive encounters evidence fear. This is a powerful emotion because, as literary theorist Philip Fisher points out, in fear "we are overwhelmed by something outside ourselves or by something that we believe may damage or destroy us."[31] They also evidence shame, which feminist theorist Sara Ahmed describes as when "one's body seems to burn up with the negation that is perceived; and shame impresses upon the skin, as an intense feeling of the subject 'being against itself.'"[32]

Yet in other respects, Claire's self-description of "losing it" is the culmination of these experiences. What is lost in losing it is a sense of self-possession. Her confession suggests becoming out of control in a way that socialized expectations would frown upon. In a more consolatory vein, however, we could think of this loss of control in terms of Nigel Thrift's observation that anger is an inevitable undertow of living cities. He notes that "a certain amount of dislike of one's fellow citizens is, given the social-cum-biological-cum-technological make-up of human beings, inescapable: the ubiquity of aggression is an inevitable by-product of living in cities."[33] Certainly, there is an anger evident in Claire's account, which is expressed toward specific people that have abused her. Yet Claire's anger feels less directed at fellow citizens and much more contingent on her cumulative experiences of public transport commuting.

The intensity of this encounter was an almost overwhelming experience: eight years of commuting dissatisfactions telescoped into a ninety-minute encounter. Recounting each incident with such technicolor luminosity indicated just how profoundly these events affected her. Scripted by her bullet point checklist of dissatisfactions, my encounter with Claire felt like a pressure buildup, as recollections of one event became superseded by the telling of another event. Each iteration set the tone through which I experienced the next. Her recollection of losing it late in the interview was, in some sense, the culmination of many other recollections that were marked by traces of fear, shame, and pain. This effect mirrors Claire's own diagnosis of her "rage" as being the cumulative effect of "multiple small incidents."

Returning to the earlier discussion of trajectories, Deleuze says that we ourselves are made up of many sorts of line. There are *rigid lines*; for example, Claire is a home owner, is a bus commuter, and travels to a job, where she takes on another identity. However, Deleuze says that there are also *molecular lines*, lines that are much more supple and lay beneath these apparent fixities. He is particularly interested in what he refers to as the "secret, imperceptible" cracks, "micro-cracks," which happen on the more supple molecular lines and do not necessarily coincide with rigid, segmentary lines.[34] Think of those times when "you can no longer stand what you put up with before, even yesterday": For Deleuze, these times show how "the distribution of desires has changed in us."[35] Claire's commuting dispositions could, in this light, be understood in terms of cracks that form along these supple, molecular lines, causing her capacities to shift in subtle ways and, crucially, potentially reach tipping points.

Deleuze says that "silent" cracks along supple, molecular lines become apparent "only at a distance and when it is too late."[36] Echoing cultural theorists Billy Ehn and Orvar Löfgren's point that we only become aware of our habits when they become disrupted,[37] it might be that the moment of Claire losing it was the disruption she needed to sense how thresholds of bearability along her molecular lines had indeed been reached. Claire's desire to participate in the interview, her preparation, her palpable catharsis that I felt at the end of the interview could demonstrate that a threshold of bearability has been reached.

Conclusion

Commuting spaces are curious sites of communion—yet the label *commuters* implies a uniformity that masks all manner of differences. Education theorist Colin Symes, for instance, points out that student commuters form closed *microcommunities* that engage in different practices from those of nonstudent commuters on Sydney's trains.[38] Geographers Ainsley Hughes, Kathleen Mee, and Adam Tyndall draw attention to the different dispositions that longer- and shorter-distance commuters demonstrate within the same carriage.[39] The social dynamics of commuting certainly have patterned qualities. Commuting can feel intensely choreographed, especially at key moments, such as when boarding and alighting public transport.[40] So much so, in fact, that we might begin to recognize what Symes describes as a "positional calculus of social segmentation and integration."[41]

Tim Cresswell emphasizes that mobilities are always socially segmented in terms of who and what they enable and constrain.[42] As such, mobilities can work to reproduce entrenched social inequalities. The events in this chapter might point to complex constellations of classed and gendered social inequality at play. Consider how both the encounter with the boys on the train and the abusive incidents that Claire sustained indicate a clash of (relatively) privileged and disenfranchised bodies. For instance, recall how the boys' term *gold diggers* and the perceived financial greed implied could be interpreted as a reflection on their own economic and political disenfranchisement. Conversely, Claire's disparaging remarks about the "island of doom" suggests that she has no choice but to take two buses to work and wait in a place where she sometimes fears for her safety.

However, as this chapter has demonstrated, there are also more transitional forms of social difference at play that inflect and complicate more entrenched forms of inequality. This relates to our "indeterminate sociality," understood as our "capacities, our relationships, connections and ways of life in the making."[43] All manner of attractions and repulsions bubble up through the accounts in this chapter, creating new formations in the process. As geographers David Conradson and Alan Latham suggest, "Within a collective, affect may … work to align and mobilize individuals into certain formations."[44] Reflecting on Claire's story, we can discern how events during the commute might forge new alignments. For example, as Claire describes the experience of wanting to be unnoticeable after having lost it with the bus driver, she recalls the consoling gesture from the lady she sat next to. This creates an alignment of sorts—however delicate, however fleeting—which might relieve Claire of the burden of shame.[45]

That our dispositions to an event on one journey might be vastly different from those to an (apparently) similar event the following day indicates that changing configurations of forces shape experience. Recall Claire's description of the repetition of missing her bus, one after the other, which gave rise to a point at which she lost it. That she draws other dimensions of her life into this recollection hints at the configuration of forces acting on her, such as the fatigue induced by the demands of her contract work. What we also witness in her account is a sensitivity to the precise material conditions of the moment: intensifying rain, noticing a lack of people around her, the dream bus missed. This unique configuration of forces gave rise to the event. These transitional qualities of commuting render any blanket diagnosis insensitive to its ongoing variations. Although Claire's prompt sheet was replete with grievances, folded through are moments that testify to generosity, beauty, and grace, which are clearly also dimensions of her commute.

In the early days of public transport, the delightfully named *Railway Traveler's Handy Book* published in 1862 provided uninitiated travelers with a series of helpful hints and tips for interacting with other passengers during their journeys.[46] Today, it might seem quaint that dispositions were ever prescribed like this—but take the Beastly Behaviors campaign developed by Sydney's transport authority. This poster campaign features a cast of cute yet hedonistic cartoon characters that each distill an apparently unsociable quality. "The Yeller," for instance, is captioned: "You told us these beasts bug you by talking really, really loudly on their phone and to their friends (which apparently includes everyone within fifty metres). The worst part is, the more boring the conversation, the louder they yell it." Through its folksy wit, this caricatured description attempts to be instantly recognizable to commuters. Furthermore, the line "You told us" gives the cartoon its authenticity, implying that its authority is derived through its ability to speak on behalf of all (respectable) commuters.

The objects and narratives spun through such campaigns are examples of what sociologists Steve Woolgar and Daniel Neyland have called "mundane governance."[47] In contrast with high-level governing, *mundane governance* refers to the forms of regulation and control that take place through ordinary objects and technologies. The instigation of quiet carriages on trains is another example. Signage and announcements remind passengers of the etiquette particular to these carriages, attempting to make the carriages self-regulating. This collective self-regulation is reminiscent of Claire's point that in the face of potentially volatile bus passengers, people do not attempt to provoke: "It's this communion that we've made as commuters."

However, if we agree with Thrift's idea that certain kinds of aggression are just a part of city life, then the idea that particular kinds of dispositions can be designed out might be misplaced.[48] Dealing better with this diversity of commuting dispositions might therefore involve becoming more attuned to the specificity of each present moment, as section 1 tries to emulate: a strategy in which we might snatch a glimmer of the vertiginous, unstable, and fizzing aspects of an event that might otherwise bore or tire. Or dealing better with this diversity of dispositions might, as Claire suggests, involve becoming more attuned to specific events that uplift us, letting their duration extend a little longer than they otherwise might.

3   Squeezed Transitions: Traveling Times, Lost and Found

Few transport statistics are more sobering than the cumulative time a person spends commuting. In Australia's largest cities, the average weekly commute for full-time workers is five hours and forty-five minutes.[1] This equates to just over eleven and a half days of commuting every year. At around thirty-five minutes for each journey, Sydneysiders have the longest average commutes in Australia. These powerful statistics allow comparisons between different years and between different cities.[2] When measured across different parts of a city, such statistics even have the power to affect house prices in those areas. Implicit in these statistics is that commuting time is negatively correlated with well-being: The longer the commute, the lower our subjective level of well-being.[3] However, though they can be powerful, there is something restricting about these measurements.

"The minute-to-minute reckoning, the thing I feel in cities. It's all embedded, the hours and minutes, words and numbers everywhere, he said, trains stations, bus routes, taxi meters, surveillance cameras. It's all about time, dimwit time, inferior time, people checking watches and other devices, other reminders. This is time draining out of our lives. Cities were built to measure time, to remove time from nature. There's an endless counting down."[4] At this point in Don DeLillo's novella *Point Omega*, a woman recounts her father's critical reflections on his experience of time in cities from the perspective-giving distance of a desert in the American Southwest, where time is felt in a very different way. Striking here is how this evaluation invokes transport areas as sites where the endless ticking of clocks obscures any other relationship with time.

Commuting time is clock time—something to be measured. On dashboards, mobile phones, platforms, and wrists, everyday life in the city seems to pulse to the advancing of digits. We might even feel that the pace of life is speeding up, enslaving us even more to the ticking clock. Sociologist Harmut Rosa calls this *social acceleration*, the idea that developments in technology have quickened the pace of life and made time a scarcer resource.[5] Although this theory has widespread support,[6] such generalized diagnoses about the sped-up nature of contemporary life often turn out to be hyperbolic,[7] not least because commuting times in many cities are increasing.[8] More importantly, such blanket theories can hide a more complicated picture of our relationships with time, which are not necessarily beating to the incessant *blink, blink* of the separator that divides the hour digits from the minutes on digital clocks.

Rather than understanding commuting time as a container or a resource that can be measured, filled with activities, or exchanged for other things, this chapter invites us to consider time as something actively created through our experiences. Contrasting with our more familiar *extensive* understanding of measurable time, this chapter draws our attention to the *intensive* dynamics of time by which different times coexist to produce new experiences.[9] For example, different cycles relating to seasons, day-to-day jobs, career stages, and lifecourses[10] might overlap in complex ways to create unique bodily experiences. These dynamics are borne out in commuters' stories of their traveling experiences. Sometimes alluding to generalities and other times referring to specific events, the interviews themselves poke holes in the smooth veneer of clock time by ducking and diving into different times. As they do, they gather different pasts and different futures into the present.[11] Taken together, what these stories suggest then is that the time of the commute is not necessarily the clock-driven "dimwit" time that DeLillo's protagonist bemoans finding in the city, but instead is something a little more unstable.

Through the presentation of fieldwork encounters, this chapter draws attention to the multiple, overlapping temporalities threaded through commuting. Section 1 explores how commuters manage time, revealing a spectrum of orientations to routines in which rigidity or flexibility are differently prized and in which travel time becomes differently valued. Section 2 pinches the map and zooms out of the city to explore the trials and tribulations of *supercommuters*, whose much longer journeys highlight a different set of temporal relationships and strategies for surviving. Section 3 visits commuters who have exited their commutes to reclaim "lost" time, exploring diverse scenarios in which commuters have attempted to reduce their commutes.

1 Time Managed

Organizing Time

Commuting can be an impressive organizational accomplishment.[12] Take Kay's pared-down description of her morning commute to her office: "I get up at 6:51 and I leave the house by 6:57. And then I walk up to Rosehill train station, which is a seven-minute walk, and then hop on the train there. So the train I get on at 7:11 is actually an express into Central, but it goes to Clyde Station and sits there for five minutes. So another train arrives, but I switch platforms and go on to that one because it arrives three minutes early—and then I train in." Kay's perfunctory account is described through the language of clock time. Her tight timing is remarkable. Minutes clearly matter: Saving three minutes is worth the effort of alighting from one train and boarding another. With streamlined precision, she does not approximate. She gets up at 6:51, not 6:50. With some envy, I remark that her efficiency is impressive. "Yeah, it is," she concurs. "I have all my stuff ready the day before. I like sleep." Kay implies that no conscious decisions are needed; her knowledge is thoroughly bodily, developed over two years.[13]

Yet our relationship to routines can be more fraught. For two years, Vida has commuted an hour each way to her place of work between the Inner West and Parramatta. Early in our interview, she admits, "I generally don't like routine, so I don't wake up with the mission of knowing what train I'm going to catch." In contrast to Kay's tight schedule, Vida tells me, "I need to just wake up slowly and, when *I'm* ready, I leave for work." Such is the benefit of living on a frequently served train line—but clearly, something isn't working. She says, "This New Year's resolution is to try and add a bit of routine, because I think that might help me; but I haven't actually decided whether it does or not. So I have been aiming for the same train, but I haven't had much luck." I ask her why she's trying to make this change. "I just thought the routine would help me make my day more efficient," she says. "By catching the same train, I just would add a little efficiency to my life. I don't know why I don't like routine," she muses, before conceding,

"I don't like being dictated by my work, in terms of how I should live my day."

Communication theorist James Carey suggests that the standardization of time is a key regulatory tool through which state and corporate capitalism can extend its grip on everyday life.[14] Although this tension might account for some of Vida's ambivalence about work dictating her routine, for others, synchronization is more enabling. Kim manages a team of public servants in the CBD. She also has two children, aged 11 and 13. She tells me, "Our morning commute is a tripartite exercise. I usually get up, get dressed, and then I get them up and we all have breakfast and pack lunches and we all leave together." This sounds simple enough, but then things become more complex. "What varies is what time we leave home and which station we actually go to, depending on the time of the day of the week, depending on which activities the children have. So Mondays, for example, I drive my son to sports training—he has to be at school by 7:30—and then drive back, park the car, go to Turramurra Station and catch a train in, and then walk from Wynyard to the office. There's variations on that. On Wednesdays, my daughter has to be at school by 7:15 for band practice, so I drop my son to Turramurra Station; then I drive down to Gordon Station and drop her at school, park at Gordon Station, and then I get on the train and come in."

However, this variation does not mean waking at different times each day. Echoing Vida's comments about efficiency, she says, "No. It's all got so complicated and my poor little brain was overloaded. So I've decided that it's easier just to set the alarm for six and not worry. It's easier just to stay in the routine because it gets too complicated. And at six in the morning trying to remember who's got to go where, when, and why and whether I actually have to race out of bed or not is just too much of a decision to make." Significant here is how the coordination of Kim's commute needs to be synchronized with her children's activities.[15] This variability over the course of the week is accommodated by standardizing her waking time so that she can maintain her routine without too much conscious effort. This is helped by the flexibility afforded by her car.[16]

Producing Time

While the clock clicks loudly through reflections on commuters' routine organization, a different set of time relationships emerges when we turn to the journey. As Chen recounts, with a mixture of bafflement and acceptance: "You sit on the bus and you're looking at everyone and going, 'What would we do without phones and iPads?' Everyone does have something. A few have got laptops, and you can tell they're last minute presentations. A few will have massive sheets of paper that they're going through and pages are going all over the place. It's just amazing." A few days earlier, while waiting for a train at Martin Place Station in the evening rush hour, I glanced along the platform lined with hundreds of people, and every single face was lit by a blue pool of light from a mobile phone.

Transport economists typically understand travel time in financial terms, with savings in travel time given a monetary value.[17] Yet the scene just described indicates that travel time is not necessarily wasted time. The ubiquity of personal mobile devices has altered the parameters of what can be done in transit, which has transformed how the time of the commute is experienced.[18] Take Benji, for instance. He works in law and takes a bus and then the train from his home in the south of the city to his workplace north of the harbor. What stuck out for me during his recollections of his routine are the morning "phone rituals" he describes. He says that when he boards the bus, he usually first checks his weather app, which tells him about rain potential over the course of the day. "Today it was forty percent rain from 2:00 p.m.," he confidently assures me. Through a twist of volition and compulsion, he then describes the set of websites that he "has to look through," carousel-like, before getting off the bus.

Through his idea of the *taskscape*, anthropologist Tim Ingold describes how the specificity of a place emerges through the practical activities we are engaged in, rather than being something that is pregiven.[19] Mobile devices have changed the taskscape of the commute through the various ways they have become folded through people's traveling routines, producing new perceptions of time.[20] Mick is an engineer who takes the train for twenty-three minutes between his home in the north of the city and the city center. Early in our interview, he gives a clear sense of how he values this travel time. This is "essentially an hour and a half where I could be doing other things," he says disparagingly, echoing earlier thinking on how travel time is wasted time. "Other things are arguably more important to my immediate life. You do need to use time wisely." Given this self-discipline, I was interested in Mick's travel-time reflections. "In the early days, I used to play games and I found that not particularly productive and useful," he says, distancing himself from such implied frippery.

Such variation in routine indicates how Mick's perception of travel time has changed; time-stilling experiences of boredom prompt him to experiment with something new.[21] "The routine changes every three to six months, give or take," he says, "when I get bored with certain things." It changed in December. "I was missing out on news, so that bothered me. So what I then started doing is podcasts or read my Twitter news feed. So I actually try to look at things that actually interest me from a socioeconomic background, be it religion versus science." For Mick, this connects the time of the commute with his quest "to answer the big questions in life," as he puts it.[22]

Writing from a Marxist perspective, and critical of the rapid suburbanization that he witnessed in postwar France, philosopher Henri Lefebvre was concerned that commuting time was eating into people's free time at home. Referring to commuting time as *compulsive time*, which he describes as "the various demands other than work," the commute becomes another example of how time is pressed into the service of capital.[23] Yet some commuters reflected on their working practices in a much less critical manner. Some described how traveling by public transport presented opportunities to do work that would otherwise need to be done at home, such as grading tests and papers. Media theorist Melissa Gregg describes mobile technologies creating a *presence bleed*, blurring the boundaries between home and work,[24] but in some cases the commute might instead help people keep their work separate from their homes.

Michelle, an executive for a telecom company in the city, is a case in point. She drives ten minutes to her nearest station and then rides the train for fifty minutes. She tells me that she catches up with her most urgent work during her train ride, work that would otherwise need to be done at home. The way that she uses the train to create a semiprivate environment reflects this, turning this traveling space into a mobile office. She says, "The seat where I sit is in a position where it's private and nobody can look over my shoulder, and that's quite important." She describes how this seat is ideal because the sun doesn't glare on her tablet screen.

Michelle draws our attention to how the material environments of the commute shape the activities that produce travel time.[25] Some commuters voiced frustration that their commute wasn't conducive enough for working; such was the annoyance of mobile phone signal blackout spots along the route, for instance. However, for others, the resistances to work were about the materiality of the vehicle itself. Lauren, who commutes by bus between her home in the northwest of the city to North Sydney, tells me that when she started this commute she anticipated that she would be able to put this time to work. "I had great plans!" she exclaims. "There was stuff I was going to get done on that commute. That was my justification for: 'Okay; North Sydney's not that bad, because I'll have this time.'" For the first six months, she says, "I tried just planning for the day ahead, doing some notes, doing my emails on the bus with the iPad, tried the laptop. But there's just not enough space and with the stop-start, you're going to hit it against the chair in front." She says that after months of trying to work, she gave up. "I can't do anything on the bus! The number of times I've hit my head against the seat in front!" she says, exasperatedly. There are a couple of bus drivers renowned for their erratic driving, she says. "There's one guy that wears one of those Greek fishing hats; and it's like, 'Oh, I'll wait for the next bus.'" To draw on psychologist James Gibson's idea of an *affordance*,[26] the idea that environments hold the potential for actions and perceptions, different commuting environments *afford* different possibilities for action, which create different perceptions of time.

Transitioning Time

Sociologist Christena Nippert-Eng indicates that commuting is a liminal time, because it acts as a bridge between the spheres of home and work, thereby giving rise to a range of *transitional activities*.[27] Liz's reflections provide a lucid sense of how transitional activities reorient her sense of time, both over the course of journeys themselves and over longer durations. Liz is a teacher, and though she has lived in the Inner West for over two decades, she has taught in schools in different parts of the city over this time, necessitating commutes of very different lengths. At different times, she's taken the train, driven, and walked. What I find most intriguing from our conversation is how her journey choices have been shaped by her changing experiences of travel time.

Currently, she takes the train to her school in North Sydney. "Probably one thing that I do is I spend the first ten minutes of the train journey meditating; so I time myself using my watch," she says, looking down at her wrist. Implying the subtle power of this practice to transition her into a calmer place, Liz asks, rhetorically: "The question is for me: Do I miss that ten minutes when I don't do it because I've traveled another way? And the answer is yes." She recalls a time when this meditation helped her recalibrate after being rushed. "One day I'd run for the train, and you've panted, you've made it. By the end of that ten minutes, your heart rate, everything, had gone back to normal, or lower, and you just thought, 'Oh, wow; isn't that interesting that that same routine has created that—that rush of the morning has all gone and now I'm back here again at this point.'"

"After I've had my ten minutes, then I'm allowed to start on the crossword," she notes, hinting at the often-stubborn bargains that we make with ourselves. Whereas meditation is a journey transition, the crossword marks transitions between different days of the week. Commutes over the course of the week can have a different tonality, and what helps mark out these different tones are the activities that we engage in. "Today is a Thursday," Liz announces, "so I have to do the cryptic crossword on a Thursday. It *feels* like a Thursday because I've got the crossword. We're such creatures of habit," she adds, joking: "Thursday's doable, that's why! Wednesday, Monday: I've got no idea. Friday: Maybe I'll just play a game on my phone because there's nothing left in the tank." Liz interrupts herself: "Always make sure you look up when you go over the bridge," she says, as if reminding herself. "Because it's a beautiful city and there's nothing like experiencing that moment: It's the sunrise; it's just gorgeous." At this moment, I picture the scene as the train suddenly emerges from the dank city tunnels to cross the Sydney Harbour Bridge. The unsympathetic gray light of fluorescent tubes is extinguished by the searing amber dazzle through the right-hand windows; the warm glare silhouettes the instantly recognizable shape of the Sydney Opera House below. "I always have a look around and see if anyone else has noticed it," Liz says. "Even when it's really quiet, there'll always be some people there that have just taken a moment, and you catch each other's eye."

Philosopher Michel de Certeau writes rather disparagingly about train travel as a form of "traveling incarceration" that offers little escape.[28] However, far from being shackled by both the disciplining effects of clock time and the material constraints of the carriage, Liz's reflections show how her train commute is made up of multiple overlapping temporalities that are created by experiences of meditation, crosswords, and sublime views. She contrasts these experiences with the times that she drives to work when she needs to be in early. "When I drive, you don't get your time to yourself," she says unequivocally. Referring to the journey home, she says, "By catching public transport, by the time I get home my head has processed the day, and then you're home and the work day is behind you. When I drive, I need to then still take another fifteen minutes, when I get home, to let the day go."

Liz says that for eight years she drove to a school in the far west of the city. "That's quite intense because it's freeway driving and then it's really heavy on Parramatta Road," a road that for most Sydneysiders conjures an image of bumper-to-bumper traffic. She had a car-share arrangement with a colleague ("We're still good friends," she reassures me) and so this time was good for the "bitching and debrief of the day," as she puts it. But when her colleague changed jobs, after driving on her own for one more year she said, "'I can't do this; this is killing me. It's too far; it was too much, so that's when I gave it up. I ended up tired. And coming home and you're late. I mean, it only took half an hour, but it was a tiring drive. Cars weaving around, you just don't know what's going to happen, where the next attack is coming from. You could never turn off," she says, as she mimes holding a steering wheel tightly while staring doggedly ahead. "I would get to work; I would sit there and have to have a cup of tea before I could do anything because I felt like I needed to come down into the day." Offering qualification, she adds: "I can only vaguely remember it; but I do remember that I didn't enjoy it."

Liz clearly had reached a tipping point. "I'd started catching public transport. It took me an hour and forty minutes," which seemed quite staggering when compared with her thirty-minute drive. "Part of that was a forty-minute walk, but I had to do it, because the school was nowhere near public transport." Her motivations perplexed me. "I did that because I wanted to read the Harry Potter books for nothing. How else was I going to get an hour and a half?" she says, with a deadpan expression. She tells me that she was living on her own, and therefore "time wasn't an issue." Sensing my surprise, she says, "I've been known to make some weird calls in my life," echoing transport researcher Glenn Lyons's point that travel behavior is often far from rational and cost-optimising.[29] She tells me that the commute was a big part of her decision to find another job. "So I went and got a job in a school where I could walk to." Yet this decision had its own surprises, perhaps showing that her transition time was more important than she had previously thought. "It rained and I drove one day and I thought, 'I'm not ready to be at work yet' because it took two minutes and I was at work. So, I sat in the car for a while and I thought, 'No'—anyway. You just haven't woken up, and obviously part of the commute is waking up."

2 Time Squeezed

The impact that transport infrastructures have had on our everyday routines is dramatically captured by a key statistic: Just over two hundred years ago, people in the United States on average moved fifty meters a day, mostly by foot. Now, they move fifty kilometers a day, mostly by car and plane,[30] indicating that our everyday lives are becoming more spread out.[31] In Australia, long-distance commuting of over one hundred kilometers each way is increasing.[32] Similar upward trends have been documented in Europe and North America.[33]

Polemic diagnoses are often made about how the disconnects between the most distant outer suburbs and inner city are pushing cities to the breaking point.[34] That far-flung dormitory towns are somehow "pathogenic" to social cohesion is not a new assertion.[35] Indeed, there are important social inequality issues at stake here. Increases in fuel prices can disproportionately affect those people who live further away from their places of work.[36] As Katharina Manderscheid explains, mobilities "constitute a significant stratifying force through which unequal life chances are being continuously reproduced."[37]

However, generalized diagnoses about the negative effects of longer commutes can obscure the complexity of how supercommuters are being affected by their different situations. In response, section 2 traces the forces narrated by three supercommuters, to glimpse some of the transformations that supercommuting journeys are giving rise to. These miniature portraits, mainly composed of quotes, are painted in an impressionistic manner to draw out some of the intensities and ambivalences that beaded the interviews themselves while also highlighting the different temporalities narrated.

Portrait 1: Paradise Found (on the Weekend)
For centuries, in the deep, cool eucalyptus forests of the Southern Highlands, 150 kilometers south of Sydney, the kookaburra's alarm call has been

the first to announce the morning. Just before first light, its hacking laughter shatters the silence, as if to signal the relief of having survived the hour of the wolf. But now, the kookaburra is no longer the first harbinger of the new day. In a large, four-bedroom house on a remote acreage, a shrieking alarm call knifes through a woman's split-ended dreaming. Often, Diane wakes a few minutes before: 3:58 a.m. It is as though her body is anticipating the pain that the sound of the alarm brings. The blinking luminous colon is unsympathetic to her sluggish neurons. She must not think. There are no alternatives. Heave torso while swinging both legs out of bed. This is the only way to overcome the fuggy force of the heavy blanket and heavier eyelids. The dream—it is still dancing faintly—is extinguished by the first dull thoughts of the day, the final ember from a magical masquerade.

Walking by flashlight to the car, the black gum and white-topped box forests sag with nighttime dew. With handbag on shoulder, large coffee in left hand, flashlight in right, she opens the car door and scours for spiders. Still a little scarred from past encounters, a surge of adrenaline wakes her up. She returns for her wheelie suitcase. The car ignition startles a wombat crossing the driveway, unexpectedly dazzled by the headlights. Before the highway, a blanket of thick fog crosses the road, headlights illuminating the cloud from within: dry ice for stadium rock, with the radio set to Triple M. Much later, on the highway, a barely perceptible band of azure blue glows low on the horizon, definitely there, silhouetting the distant treetops. Silently, its gradients become richer; cool greens are added, then flamingo pinks, then peaches, then golds. As the tones brighten, the landscape gains features and depth, rippling out on all sides to the furthest horizon. The tunnel etched by the headlights dissolves. Diane reaches into her handbag and gropes around for her necklace, earrings, and breakfast.

By the city limit at Campbelltown, one of Sydney's furthest tentacles, she is accompanied by a flotilla of pickup trucks racing to service the city's construction boom. These concreters and builders start early to beat the city's unbearable late afternoon heat. On some days, one of these trucks might be her partner's. "Ships in the night," she says they are. This week, she won't see him until Friday. She's staying with friends in the city. She doesn't want to drive back every night. Sometimes, if he can get an hour's break, she will meet him for a cup of tea in the city during the week. She turns off the highway at Fairfield Road to avoid the worst of the M5 tunnel buildup. Here, the high noise barriers along the highway fall away to reveal a more riotous streetscape: single-story brick houses, red roofs, tangled transmission wires, weatherboard fences, and wheelie bins. These give way intermittently to fast food joints and gas stations and little rows of shops that are still slumbering. Just before Ryde, there is a brief queue, the first of her journey, before she arrives at Chatswood, two and a half hours after she set off. .

She is upbeat about her commute. She has always had a long commute to a job that she enjoys. She loves driving. She has had this one for twelve years. "It takes a certain type of person," she says. She is a manager for an IT company, but there is no such work in the Highlands. Weekends home are sacrosanct. They don't see a soul, just gang-gangs and yellow-tailed cocka-toos; they have built no relationships with people there. Diane's daughter has just moved out. Like her partner, she used to only see her on weekends. "She could have done with having me around," she says. But when they were together, she made sure that it was always quality time. "This is the price I pay for living in paradise," she says.

On first glimpse, it might be tempting to evaluate Diane's experience through the figure of the "tree changer." This is a rather new phenomenon in Australia in which relatively wealthy city dwellers move out of the city in search of an idealized rural "refuge."[38] Certainly, Diane's managerial eco-nomic capital combined with the social capital of having accommodating friends to stay with on some weeknights help sustain this lifestyle choice. Yet given that the forces of traffic and commuting are reportedly two of the key motivations for tree changers,[39] Diane's portrait clearly bucks these assertions.

Diane has never lived in Sydney; her working life has always been shaped by supercommuting. In this respect, we could imagine that her body has become accustomed to a commuting rhythm that for others would be inconceivable—so accustomed that her body anticipates her morning alarm. As Félix Ravaisson's understanding of habit suggests, the more that we do something, the easier it becomes; the less it impresses on sensation; and the more sharpened our perceptions of that activity become.[40] Such sharpening is certainly evident from Diane's detailed attention to the plea-surable transitions of her morning journey from the world of the Southern Highlands to the center of the largest city in Australia.

Yet what is distinctive about Diane's portrait is the temporal rhythm that her supercommute has carved out between weekends and weekdays. Her relationships with her partner and daughter resemble a new form of household that some have called *living apart together*,[41] and thus weekends are fiercely preserved as important quality time for the family. As though compensating for the hypermobility that characterizes her week, weekends are resolutely sedentary, spent in the solitude of the bush.

Portrait 2: Life on Hold

Wind chimes sound at 4:50 a.m. Over 200 kilometers away from the Southern Highlands, another woman wakes to a mobile phone alarm on her bedside table in a small house in a Central Coast town. Kelly changes the alarm sound every few weeks; each sound, however mellow to begin with, soon grows spikes and turns sour as it becomes intimately coupled to her interrupted sleep. Her fingers are desperate to hit snooze, but, with just enough willpower, she relents. She creeps out of bed to avoid waking her partner, although perhaps not as quietly as she might. After all, he will sleep for another two and a half hours (she will text him later when she arrives at work: "Up you get: wakey-wakey!"). This four-year, well-oiled routine means that she can shower, dress, and be out the door at 5:20.

Kelly drives twenty-five minutes to Gosford, the main station in her part of the world, where all the trains stop. The lot that you can only find a parking space in before 7:00 a.m. is a small consolation that the early start provides. Winters here are hard: drenched from head to foot between the car and the train, even with an umbrella, waiting for the traffic lights to change. She wishes she could drive all the way. Her colleagues drive. She even has a car parking space at work. The 1980s business park where she works in administration in North Sydney was built for the car. Filling the tank every two and a half days is far too expensive, especially as she now has a mortgage. At the station, she has ten minutes to talk, sometimes more (the 5:57 train never leaves on time), with the other morning people who stand at the same place on the platform, to board the same carriage (number 3), to sit in the same seats. She knows what they do, where they live, what they do on the weekend. The afternoon people are different, somehow.

The 5:57 train is for sleepers. You certainly don't talk (it's one of those unspoken rules). The new train seats look nice, but they're not practical for sleeping. The angle is slightly different from that of the seats in the old "tin cans," which had cushioned green leather you could just sink into. These seats are hard and uncomfortable. "The person who designed them clearly didn't sit in them for four hours a day!" There are some tall people Kelly knows who avoid catching the new trains. She wakes up just before Epping. Most times, wind chimes are not needed. Sometimes, a man who sits near her will tap her on the shoulder. Carriage number three always makes sure that no one has slept through.

Kelly hardly sees her husband, save on the weekend (he is a "lucky person," with his fifteen-minute commute and his ability to sidestep household chores). There is no quality time at the end of the day. "Once you've said hello, talked about your day, discussed dinner, made dinner, cleaned up, and made lunches, it's already bedtime: maybe a quick crash on the couch with a little mindless telly, and then you're done." Weeks go by when Kelly won't do anything when she gets home. She can't be bothered. A quick ten-minute meal will have to do again; certainly, there's no energy to exercise. She never gets a full night's sleep; there just isn't time. She goes to bed early but can't sleep: mind still whirring, so much still going on. Weekends are luxury time, even though they are spent catching up with the rest of life that has been put on hold until then: groceries, housework. You don't move more than you absolutely need to.

"*It's not going to be forever.*" That's what Kelly keeps telling herself. "You can't do it forever! It'll kill you! It's a chore. It's a struggle. You don't do it for fun." These words soothe, taking heat away from the four years that she has already "done." She says she'll do it for another year. Then, she'll take a pay cut and work on the coast. She worked out the other week that she's away from home for sixty-four hours a week. She doesn't get paid for sixty-four hours a week! Half of her day is getting to work and back. Eventually, Kelly will get home at a decent hour, without the uncomfortable afternoon commute in carriage number three—chitter-chatterers who haven't been up since the early hours; without missing the connecting train by one minute yet again. "Eventually, I will take care of myself," she says.

Compared to Diane's, Kelly's portrait indicates a rather different temporal orientation for the supercommute. The gendered nature of temporality, or what sociologist Arlie Hochschild refers to as women's *second shift*,[42] is more acutely evident here. The inequity between Kelly's supercommute and her partner's relatively short commute is exacerbated by her assertion, tinged with overtones of resentment, that he shirks on housework that she ends up having to do either in the little time she has when she arrives home or on the weekend. Palpable in her portrait is the "time squeeze"[43] that she experiences through the succession of chores that leave precious little free time for her, even on weekends. Her commute becomes part of this unpaid laboring activity.

Contrasting with Diane's greater material privilege, the financial pressures that Kelly narrates through her mortgage commitments, her inability to drive, and the implied envy she feels for her colleagues bring into view how the long commute is acutely mediated by the demands of capital. This again seems to underscore Lefebvre's concerns about the time of capital encroaching on free time. Yet, as Kelly implies, it is not only that time commuting takes away from her free time, but also that the momentum of her succession of chores cannot be easily subdued; her mind still races as she tries to sleep.

Yet perhaps most striking about Kelly's portrait is how she describes that her own ethical obligations to her self-care effectively have been deferred until a future time. Indeed, paradoxically, it is this anticipation of a future that does not involve supercommuting that makes the commute (just about) bearable. A spectral future life on the coast is brought into the present as a way of coping with the material discomforts that she narrates.[44] Until then, there are small consolations that sustain her: the transient community that exists in carriage number three, the small gestures of generosity at Epping.

Portrait 3: Oscillations

Another alarm sounds later still at 5:30 a.m. in the Blue Mountains, over one hundred kilometers west of Sydney. Mike drags himself out of bed. He enters the day slowly. He drives ten minutes to the station to catch the 6:49 train, to get a bus, to be at work five minutes early. There are no buffers here. Thirty seconds' delay can add thirty minutes. He says, "You're on edge all the time." Five hours in transit every day is already enough. The other day the train didn't come. "Just didn't come. There was no announcement. You ring and try and find information, and they say, 'Yeah, we can put you through to complaints.' You don't want to complain; you just want the bloody train."

Mike tries driving every so often, especially when he has become frustrated with the train—but the car is exhausting. When you get to the M4, the traffic just stops. You must contain yourself. How long is it going to be? It's a little better now that they have indicator signs up at Penrith: *CUMBERLAND HWY 15 MIN.* He got there once and it was fifty minutes. At least by knowing that it's fifty minutes, you can relax more. However, people still don't like that—but it's nothing compared with how people feel when they're faced with something that they don't know. The consolation is important. You read about the state the transport system is in. A response like "Look, we're sorry" works. It changes things. It does make a difference.

Transitioning between train and car is only short-term relief. It's the same sort of stress that you have on the train. It just happens in cars a little bit differently. Mike says, "It's these waves. You maybe swap from train to car, and something happens, and the next night something happens. You're just sick of it. And then you swap back to the train—and it seems to be OK for a while, and then something happens, and you stick to it a bit longer, and then you drop back to the car."

Mike left Sydney ten years ago. He just wanted to get away. "Certain things happened." He says he didn't really think it through. So, the commute was there—but if someone told him he'd be doing it in ten years ... ! The pinnacle came a few years ago, when it was just too much. The whole thing fell apart. Mike had a car accident. He fell asleep at the wheel. He says he was just tired, or exhausted. "Everything became just too much and too stressful." He says then those times when the train is late take on a whole new meaning and make you much more anxious. Until a year ago, it seemed to be endless. He says, "Oh my God. I bet I'm going to be doing this for the rest of my life." Banal frustration curdling through vertiginous existential angst.

He says, "You can't look at commutes without looking at everything else. They interact with everything, even though you have the same commute. You can't package the commute and the home." Some people might be able to do that, but he can't. He says that during good times, the commute is really good, and you can cope with everything. He says that right now, he's not in a state in which he just wants out of it. He says it's probably the only way he has during the day to have his own time—"even though it isn't," he adds. That comes and goes, according to what else is going on.

Mike says, "If you're not getting enough sleep at home, you're cranky, and everything just snowballs. The commute then becomes a persecutory object. It's as though the train has something against you. The system is conspiring to add to the misery of your life and this restlessness—and the restlessness, which is ongoing, is very much like a train on the tracks. You feel that you're losing control, especially if in other parts of your life you just don't have control. You're at everybody else's whim all the time. All of a sudden (well, not all of a sudden), you're just out of control. You're part of this relentless sort of conspiring system that's just going to keep you, wherever you are, for the rest of your life."

People look at Mike aghast when he says where he comes from and where he works. He needs to put a lot of stuff off. He needs to give it to other people to do, because he doesn't get time in either place. Things like the doctor and dentists: "You really need to think ten times before you make an appointment, because it means taking time off from work or leaving work early and having to struggle with that." He says there are parent-teacher nights coming up in two weeks. He's now going to have to plan two weeks ahead to try and get away half an hour earlier so he can make it up there.

Mike says he finds himself a little bit low: nothing deeply traumatic, just a dull shade of Payne's grey. He'll soon have been in this town in the Blue Mountains for thirteen years, and he still feels that he's not part of it because of this back and forth, back and forth. He's a bit disconnected from the whole community. Part of that is his personality. He says, "I'm not a community person even at the best of times." He says that he should be more connected than he is and he's realizing that he's not. He's finding it hard to be. He says, "I'm a little bit all over the place." Mike's partner is based in the Blue Mountains and she's more involved in the community, so he must balance it out. He tries very hard to plan something for the weekends. He says that must be a bit more forced. "It's not necessarily such a pleasurable thing."

Whereas Diane's portrait evokes a strong sense of sovereignty freighted with the term *lifestyle choice*,[45] a self-assured trope often associated with supercommuting,[46] Mike's more melancholic portrait provides a much more hesitant, even stuttering, rationale for his supercommuting circumstances. Although he implies that he needed to distance himself from a difficult situation, he plays his cards close to his chest.

Yet even with this ambiguity, a car accident serves as the punctum of his portrait, piercing and spreading out. His reflections on the exhaustion that gave rise to this event resonates with literary theorist Lauren Berlant's concept of *slow death*, the condition of "the physical wearing out of a population and the deterioration of people in that population."[47] The concept is useful here given that it refers to "temporal environments whose qualities and whose contours in time and space are often identified with the presentness of ordinariness itself, that domain of living on."[48] Crucially, and pertaining to Mike's account, slow death happens "where life building and the attrition of human life are indistinguishable."[49] Such a tension seems to resonate with Mike's life pressures well, especially those moments in which he teeters on the brink of spiraling out of control.

Life building and life attrition seem to alternate for Mike. If the temporality of Kelly's portrait is characterized by deferral, Mike's portrait evokes oscillations. His access to both train and car commuting allows him to switch between the two modes, yet this switch is less a result of his active choice and more brought about by the tipping points that his ongoing frustrations lead to. In his portrait, he poignantly captures how the affectivity of his commute is irreducibly contingent on what else is going on in his life. An ostensibly similar happening can be sensed very differently depending on his present circumstances—or whether the transport company provides a gesture of consolation. This differential sensing can redraw his experience of time such that the commute can be endless—or not. Particularly striking is how his commute is both the only time that he gets to himself and, conversely, an object of persecution. The productive ambiguity in his portrait stems from these seemingly inconsistent dispositions being held together in tension. Similar tensions mark his glum reflections on not being part of his "home" community while at the same time accepting that such a disposition does not necessarily suit him.

3   Time Reclaimed

The supercommuter portraits illuminate the different sorts of pressures that lengthy commutes can create. Each portrait hints at temporal strategies that supercommuters develop to survive these pressures. The lure of the weekend, the anticipation of an end to commuting, and changing modes of transport each promise survival of sorts. This section attempts to slow down, by turning to some of the more radical solutions that commuters develop to reduce—or even eliminate—the time that they previously spent commuting. Yet, as will be illustrated, though these solutions might reclaim lost time, they can create their own unexpected challenges.

Reducing the Commute

At many of Sydney's busiest intersections, where traffic lights seem to stay red for much longer than anywhere else, tatty signs hurriedly taped to these signals invite escape from the repetitive scene. *Earn $50/hour. Work from home. Call now.* The lure of homeworking—or *telecommuting*, to use a term that hints at its mildly dated provenance—is one response to the temporal pressures of a commuting life. Ahead, interview encounters with Kim and Eva indicate how two managers' complex orientations to telecommuting are framed by their experiences of reducing their commutes.

Kim manages a large team of public servants in central Sydney. What particularly struck me on meeting her was her sensitivity to her team's commuting pressures. For a start, her own manager commutes each day from the South Coast, far south of Wollongong. He spends four hours each day working on the train, such that his commuting practices fold through the day-to-day operation of the organization. "We give him stuff to read in the afternoon," she says, "and he brings it back the next day; and he's had four hours on a train to read it. And you can tell when he's got on the train because the emails and the text messages on the BlackBerry start." In terms of the management of her own team, Kim tells me that public sector flexible working arrangements mean that people can start between 7:30 and 9:30 and, in theory, finish anywhere from 3:30 to 6:30. She says that she has developed a knowledge of people's working habits so that she knows who she can call on, especially during specific times. "If the shit hits the fan and I need advice or help or information from one of my team, I need to know whether I'm going to be able to find them or not," she says. "Jim's my morning man, you know. Bob, on the other hand, usually doesn't leave until six."

She tells me that when her children were young, she worked from home for about five years. She should have known what she was in for, she says, as her undergraduate thesis was about telecommuting! "It's *very* lonely," she says.[50] "And I ended up [doing volunteer work] because I needed somebody to talk to." She implies that this experience has sensitized her to her staff's commuting pressures. "Having worked from home, I try to be sensitive to people's commitments" by being accommodating. "I've got two team members whose kids started school for the first time this year," she says. "So you try to be aware of if they've got school events or things that they've got to get done." Reflecting on one particularly affecting moment, she says, "I've got another staff member who travels down from the Central Coast. And the opportunity came up to work in the Central Coast office and, when I asked him if would he be interested, his face lit up and he said to me, 'Oh, that would mean I would get home before my two little boys were asleep at night,' and it nearly broke my heart." He now has a seven-minute door-to-door journey, instead of two hours. She shakes her head as the enormity of this life change seems to resonate more intensely. "And, you know, I mean, as a mother, it broke my heart when he said that."

Eva's situation is different. She commuted by train between Wollongong and Sydney every weekday for three years. "It took me two days to get over the commute; so it took me all weekend to get over it because it makes a very long day," she says. What she missed out on in family and community life dominates her reflections. "My eldest son started school, and I missed out on that integration at the school. Easter hat parades and all these kind of little momentous things that are happening. You miss out on integrating with all the mums, so you don't get to meet the parents of your kids' friends. You can't invite the friends to come over after school for a play," she says. Her reflections are sobering, and from the tone of her voice, I sense that these lost opportunities still have a spectral presence in her life. I am suddenly aware of two mothers with children sitting at an adjacent table in the café; their conviviality perhaps intensifies the sense of sadness that Eva expresses here.

Eventually, Eva stopped commuting. She now runs her own business from home, helping organizations instigate change. She is particularly concerned about how organizational habits prevent people from working more flexibly, including from home. She tells me that organizational cultures around telecommuting seem to remain wedded to what she calls a "factory-office mentality." Referring to the shift in the mode of production that has been taking place from the manufacturing economy to the knowledge economy,[51] she says that the latter tends to be more challenging to manage. "It is taking people out of their comfort zone; a lot of people won't go into it willingly," she says. "From a manager's perspective, suddenly you have an office with only half of the people out here and the other half of the people you have to contact by phone."[52] Even "communalizing" office space through hot-desking arrangements is difficult, she says, because people are reluctant to give up their claim to a space of their own.

Flexible working arrangements such as telecommuting can have the perverse effect of intensifying working practices, sometimes requiring an even greater degree of self-discipline from workers,[53] yet Eva talks enthusiastically about how stopping commuting has freed up three and a half hours to put to other ends, including studying for a degree. However, despite Eva's enthusiasm for more flexible working arrangements to accommodate commuters, she warns me that telecommuting is most effective if it is part-time. "People still want to feel connected to the workplace," she says. "You still need to be able to build relationships, and the best way to do that is still face to face," echoing John Urry's assertion about the significance of face-to-face proximity in creating trusting relationships.[54] "Let's face it, when you're removed and you're in your own space, why would you want to care about the workplace culture?" Eva says that allegiance to such a culture is an important part of creating a positive workplace atmosphere.[55] "A good workplace has the ability to motivate you, to get your passions going, and it's much harder when you're on your own."

This sensitivity to the dynamic of workplace environments contrasted markedly with the vibe from a technology company manager I had spoken to a few months earlier about telecommuting. "Get rid of the fear and get rid of the threats, get rid of the trust; just put it all on KPIs [key performance indicators]," she said, somewhat frustrated. Indicating her preference for evaluating staff performance through metrics, she adds, "I mean, to me, it's very black and white; it's very easily managed."

Exiting the Commute

The very idea of stopping a commute that has shaped a person's life so markedly was a proposition that many commuters with whom I talked anticipated but had not experienced. Liz was different. She stopped commuting a week before Christmas after twenty years of traveling for four hours every day by train into Sydney. Sitting at her kitchen table in her home nestled between placid Brisbane Water and the eucalyptus ridge reserves, she tells me that she and her husband moved to this part of the Central Coast when they got married. She would have lived in Sydney if she could have afforded it, but it was just after the 1987 property bust and interest rates at seventeen percent blunted the possibility. Friends suggested that she should come and live here on the coast. "It's like going on holiday every day!" they told her. Outside, the fire-red banksia cones nod in the breeze.

It is 3:30 in the afternoon. Three months ago at this time of day, Liz would have just been leaving her workplace in the city for the two-hour train journey back home. She worked for a planning business that was flexible, willing to accommodate her even further. However, the thought of commuting for the same number of hours that she worked each day became too oppressive. She wanted to strengthen her relationship with her son once he started high school. Until now, he depended on before-school care, after-school care and, when he was very young, day care. With a palpable mixture of regret and sadness, Liz says that he was in care from 7:00 a.m. until 6:00 p.m. "If you didn't make it back by 6:00 p.m., you'd be charged fifty dollars every five minutes," she adds.

On cue, a young boy opens the fly screen and flashes a smile at his mother. "Carl, say 'hi.' This is David. He wants to know how we coped," she says, emphasizing the past-tense nature of this word. "Commuting," I offer, sensing his confusion. "Commuting." She nods. "Commuting," Carl says flatly, looking to a distant point in the room, as if in saying it, he registers how this word has torpedoed itself through his entire biography. He walks over to where Liz is sitting, and she puts her arm around his waist and kisses his cheek. He pulls his head away slightly. Still tightly hugging his waist, Liz tells me that on her last day of work, Carl accompanied her on her final commute. "We just said goodbye to everybody," she says, flatly. A ceremonial journey to mark the end of two decades of travel. She couldn't believe that it had come around. "Go and get your afternoon tea, it's in the fridge," she says, patting him on the back.

"This is the age that you want to be around," she says. "You want to be there. You're always worried Carl's going to get sick and you've got to come home early." She says that they have no other family here and only a few friends. She looks around to check that he is out of earshot. "He needs pushing to do homework," she says softly. She says that the tipping point came toward the end of last year. Carl would ring her at 3:30 wanting to tell her all about his day. It made it even harder. "It shapes relationships from an early age," she says. "Some of my friends, they really didn't cope well." Her husband has been doing the same four-hour commute to and from the city for twenty-four years. When Carl was younger, he hardly ever saw his father during the week. After a full fourteen-hour day, he was ready for bed. She says that their schedules have really affected their relationships with Carl. "It made us closer, I think, and them not so close."

Not doing the journey now, "I'm loving it," she says, more optimistically. Having previously woken at 6:00 a.m. every day, it's good to know you can sleep in. "I'm not missing it." But she corrects herself: "In the morning, I used to put on my earphones, closed my eyes, and listened to my music. So that's what I miss now," she says. This was not time lost. For the first ten years, she worked on an economics degree on the train—distance learning by going the distance.

However, her tone changes. "I'm working harder now for less money, I can tell you. You look in the paper and there's very little work for someone who's got an admin background." She's tried applying for all the office jobs that she could find on the Central Coast, but most people don't get back to her. Elder care, child care, and retail form the trinity of opportunities here. It was her close relationship to her grandmothers that drew her to the first option. No one commutes to this job. She's doing this so that she can be at home in the afternoon. Even though she arrives home at 2:30 p.m., for four days each week she gets up at 5:00 a.m. to start her 6:00 a.m. shift, earlier than when she was commuting. "It's not like I've got loads of time to do whatever I want," she adds. "The twenty years of commuting is easier than one day in the nursing home," she says flatly. "It's a lot of work and you forget about the outside world. There's not a lot of joy in it, I have to say."

As I walked to the bus stop after leaving, the affectivity of seeing Liz's face as Carl arrived home from school continued to resonate. I couldn't help but be moved by witnessing her love for her son. It was such an ordinary moment, yet framed by her recollections, this moment was the frame through which I sensed and sympathized with some of the tensions in her recollections, adding to its intensity. Her palpable joy about finishing a commuting life seemed to sit uneasily with her new earlier starts and the time squeeze that she continues to experience, albeit perhaps less intensely. Forfeiting her career in financial administration, for which she had studied for an economics degree, seemed to sit uneasily with her current retraining for a job that she finds harder, less enjoyable, and less financially rewarding.

Conclusion

Commuting time has often been expressed rather straightforwardly in terms of the hours and minutes of clock time. For economists, the hours and minutes of commuting are lost time that could be better used, economically speaking. Yet a narrow economic perspective neglects how commuting time is lived, perceived, and managed by commuters, generating various opportunities and challenges. Travel time is something produced through the practices that people undertake. This means that the lived experience of travel time is much more variable, and commuters themselves can have a considerable degree of wiggle room in terms of how they experience this time. This might involve trying out different routines or experimenting with different activities during the commute that change how that time is valued and perceived. In doing so, other temporal rhythms come into view, perhaps based on the seasons, on family life, or even on something as seemingly inconsequential as the difficulty levels of the daily crossword over the course of a week.

However, painting an overly optimistic view of the value of commuting time is insensitive to how hours in transit can be transformative in other ways. The concept of *precarity* is useful here, drawing attention to working experiences characterized by insecurity, temporariness, and low pay owing to neoliberal employment policies. Although the participants in this chapter undertake a wide range of occupations, what is important here is that precarious labor is not just about the job itself but is intertwined with other areas of life.[56] Others have suggested that household dynamics and welfare provision are some of these other areas,[57] but what some of the stories here reveal is that commuting can play an important but overlooked part in contributing to a precarious life. Reflecting on the supercommutes undertaken by Kelly and Mike, their accounts invoke a series of bodily vulnerabilities generated through their commutes. These are lives that seem pushed to their limits by commuting, teetering on the brink of what is just about bearable. This is where the commute turns into a chore for Kelly, or perhaps more intensely for Mike, an object of persecution. Although some have indicated that precariousness is characterized by an inability to predict one's fate,[58] for Mike especially, it feels like it is his inability to *escape* a commuting fate that pushes him to the edge.

Yet to make a firm diagnosis of what, exactly, commuting time is doing to us would overlook the nuances that bead these interview encounters. For some, it is not the travel time itself that is unbearable, but the opportunities lost to travel time. These absent presences ebb and flow, materializing in the most ordinary of moments. For Liz, we sense how the significance of receiving a call from her son as he left school one afternoon subtly inflected her desires to spend more time with him and ultimately to find an exit to her commuting life. A firm diagnosis is also insensitive to the changeability of these experiences. As Mike suggests, there are times when the commute becomes "too much," but there are also times that the commute is "really good." Recovering from the commute might involve radically changing a person's working life, such as retraining for a new career, but it might also involve more incremental routine changes. It is through these subtle changes and becoming attuned to how they are working on us that we might become better equipped to cope with commuting times.

4 Experimental Interruptions: Curating Sensing Spaces

In the commute, space can be in short supply. Photographer Michael Wolf's series *Toyko Compression* is a poignant reminder of this fact.[1] Wolf's compositions show commuters squished together so tightly in Tokyo's train carriages that they barely have space to breathe, let alone move. Downcast faces pushed against windows haloed by dripping condensation offer a stark visualization of this constriction of personal space. On the other side of the Pacific, caught in a traffic jam on a Los Angeles freeway, Michael Douglas's character at the beginning of the movie *Falling Down* is pushed to his limits. Here, cars are bumper to bumper with no space to move. These examples illustrate how overcrowding and congestion—two of the most ubiquitous commuting problems—relate to a shortage of space. The policy response is typically about creating *more* space—by increasing the number of trains and buses, and by widening or constructing more roads. Although there are certainly instances in which such "hard" infrastructural interventions are necessary, commuting spaces are changing in many other ways.

Imagining commuting space as a container that can accommodate more or fewer people or vehicles provides a rather static understanding. In *The Production of Space*, philosopher Henri Lefebvre explains that space is much more complex. Lefebvre says that space can be understood as simultaneously physical, mental, and social.[2] In other words, it is real, imagined, and lived. What is significant about this is that a road or a railway carriage is designed and built by policy makers and transport institutions, but the space itself is transformed as it is perceived and lived by social actors and groups.[3] This is exciting, because it suggests that commuting spaces are much more changeable than a container concept could illustrate.

The very idea of commuting "spaces" might seem confusing, given that commuting is ostensibly about moving through or between spaces, rather than being in specific spaces.[4] Yet space is an important concept for understanding commuting, because it draws our attention to the diversity of different spaces that make up the commute. It also helps us identify and trace some of the diverse agencies at play, which transform those spaces. Scholarly engagement with commuting spaces has often been technocratic, focusing on harder-edged issues of design and management. Only more recently have how people relate to infrastructures, how they shape them, and how they are in turn affected by them been taken more seriously.[5] While this chapter spotlights some of the different authorities involved in transforming commuting spaces, it also explores how commuting spaces are potentially much more volatile than such design imperatives imply. Railway platforms and pedestrian crossings might be some of the most banal and apparently uneventful spaces of urban life, but these most overlooked of spaces can be profoundly affecting.

This chapter is split into three sections. Section 1 explores how and the extent to which different sorts of experiences can be "engineered" into commuting spaces. Through interview encounters with a transport worker and people who work in advertising, it describes how commuting spaces are expressions of tensions between different imperatives.

Section 2 investigates how different commuting spaces are becoming more connected through technologies that attempt to create seamless journeys and how this potentially changes the experience of commuting. Based on interviews with a software developer who has expertise in developing a real-time transport app, a partially sighted commuter who relies on such apps, and a travel smartcard designer, we see how smoothness is becoming hardwired into the journey experience, creating new senses of connectivity for some.

Section 3 explores how commuting spaces become differently sensed by commuters. Through an experiment with time-lapse photography and two interview encounters that reflect on how the "past lives" of spaces can live on in powerful ways, this section considers how the changeability of commuting spaces is an effect of a shifting kaleidoscope of different forces.

1   Engineering Spaces

Engineering invokes ideas of "hard" construction, maintenance, and repair work that goes on from time to time in commuting spaces.[6] Indeed, for commuters, the very word might be enough to cause a shudder, given its association with the threat of a disrupted routine. However, when understood more broadly, engineering can also alert us to the wider set of subtler processes in commuting spaces that can transform experiences for commuters. This part examines how institutions and commuters can "engineer" specific experiences of passage into commuting spaces and also considers the limits of these engineering logics.

Seamless Passage

Mel has the unenviable task of managing one of Sydney's scourges: congestion. In our conversation, she explains her guiding philosophy: "I think there's a weird perception that we start off with in life that that is going to be easy and seamless, right? And that's like our baseline: It's supposed to be like that. Right? And, in actual fact, it's probably not. You know, every time water hits earth, there's a fork in the road; there's a division, there's a point of stress." I'm struck that her illustrations from two rather different spheres suggest that stress occurs when forces act on other forces. This is refreshing when compared with the more common psychological definitions of stress as an affliction of individual human bodies. Her point is profound: Life is full of "points of conflict and points of exchange," as she puts it, where the materiality of the world makes itself felt. This resonates with anthropologist Anna Tsing's claim that frictions are about being in the "grip of worldly encounter."[7] However, when it comes to thinking about journeys, Mel says that we tend to downplay these in our expectations. She grounds this point in an appropriately mundane illustration: "When I leave my backdoor and I have to get to my car, my pedestrian trip, I have to undo the gate. Sometimes the gate sticks a little. Do I get annoyed at that gate? Well, *I* don't, but some people will. That's just my journey being interrupted."

Mel raises an important issue: "One of the concerns for me about congestion and the way we tackle congestion ... is that, every time we make a journey, it will be multimodal. There's not a journey that's not multimodal." Her point is that all commuters, regardless of whether they drive, will experience these "points of conflict and points of exchange," something she later terms *interruption space*. "If I can make people's journey much more seamless, and they accept that the component parts each have their contribution to their journey, then perhaps some of the stress might go." Part of this is about changing expectations. She illustrates her point with an example of a car trip along the Princes Highway south of Sydney. "You know, mathematically, might it be that if I get all greens, it's going to take me ten minutes; if I get three reds, it's going to take me twelve minutes. Now, they're small quantums of time; but that's the bit that's bothering people. So how do we actually say, 'Can you embrace it as part of the journey, not as something that's breaking your journey?'" Her point is that "it's not the actual time factor or the hold-up or whatever else," reminding me that many parts of our day are spent waiting.[8] Travel has a specificity, because "the expectation is that travel should be very quick and efficient, and it's not purposeful in itself."

Much of Mel's job involves thinking about interchanges—a special kind of transit space all about conflict and exchange. "It's this ebb and flow in that interchange space that bothers people," she tells me. To alleviate this, she says that "the very specific environment of the interchange has to be seamless." This logic of the journey is often backgrounded in infrastructure planning that focuses on delivering a particular part of the transport jigsaw.[9] She describes her role at meetings: "I say, 'We have to stop building abutted modes and actually start building interchanges.' And what we do is we build abutted modes. And, you know, I'll say, 'So where are the bus services?' and they'll go, 'Oh, they're there.' 'So what's that journey look like between that bus service and the train service? How efficient is it? What grade's it at? What about the paving and the lighting?'" Mel traces these design imperatives back to our expectations. "Our society today is a distracted society," she says, echoing sociologist Georg Simmel's observations that urban life is characterized by "stimulations, interests, and the taking up of time and attention."[10] "So they want to be able to walk, without thinking, to their next mode," Mel notes. "They don't want it to be convoluted. They want it to be intuitive."

Mobility theorist Gillian Fuller describes how transit spaces are full of signs and symbols, such as the humble arrow.[11] These devices cue movement, often at a subconscious level, so that it can be intuitive, as Mel suggests. Beyond this, Mel says that "efficient seamless interchange" means "continuity." Interestingly, she describes this in relation to her own previous commute, which involved changing trains: "I got off one train and I walked across the platform and got on another train and it went. I didn't care at all: no waiting time. And, even if I had a minute—even if I'd got on to that train and it didn't go straight away but I actually hadn't turned my laptop off, I was still in the middle of my text message, my music was still going, my notebook could have been open and my glasses were still on—it's functionally no change."

Entertaining Passage

In a labyrinthine passage at Martin Place that joins the underground railway station below with the financial district above, something is happening. A wash of close-up green palm fronds adorns the walls, floor, and ceiling. The distinctive sound of cicadas and crickets joins with the clickety-click of high-heeled shoes and the characteristic major key arpeggio of the railway station announcement tone. A faint whiff of coconut scents the air. There is something about this simulated underground rainforest that is mildly disorienting, as though a brief daydream before the passage transitions to the ambience of sugary fried food and eventually bursts into the daytime above. "Live the life exotic," instructs a decal on the floor, next to the logo of a well-known sunglasses company.

Alongside the transport agencies, the task of which is to engineer commuting spaces for seamless passage, this experience at Martin Place reminds us that there are other agencies that shape these spaces according to rather different imperatives. Sociologist Ann Cronin writes that "advertising forms part of what our sight 'stumbles over' in the busy visual clutter of contemporary cities."[12] This is strikingly revealed in commuter spaces. Meg works for the advertising company that conceived this installation. I'm interested in learning what a commercial perspective can tell us about commuting spaces. When I meet her, I tell her about my experience at Martin Place. "'Station domination!' It's incredible!" she exclaims, radiating enthusiasm. She describes how these immersive advertising campaigns are designed for commuters; they are "high-frequency audiences," so the displays are in situ for only one or two weeks to "create that impact." It turns out that commuters are particularly receptive, "especially on their way home, when they're even more relaxed. They're definitely in that mindset to really be absorbing that message," Meg says. I mention another advert that I passed earlier at Town Hall station that day—a huge floor-to-ceiling screen, the pixels of which combine to dazzle even the most insensitive retinas after exiting the ticket barriers. "That's what we call the 'wow wall,'" Meg says with a grin. "You don't even realize that you're saying it—you just go, 'Oh, wow!'" Meg's description illustrates well how contemporary advertising

works through the immediate, sensate registers of bodies, rather than rely-
ing on cognitive thought.[13]

Backgrounded against what others have called the *attention economy*,[14] I
ask Meg about how her agency imagines the relationship between these in
situ adverts and commuters' immersion in their mobile phones. She says,
"Our advertising drives people online to search for more information. So
they might have their phone in their hand, which is great, and they see
our advertising, and then they go down on a train platform and on their
train, and that's when they've got time to search." In other words, it is the
rhythmic interplay of waiting and proceeding that characterizes commuting journeys, or "store and forward," as Gillian Fuller puts it,[15] that makes
commuting spaces particularly attractive to this company. Meg reinforces
this later when she says that her agency owns over sixteen thousand bus
stop panels that aim to capture the "dwell time" of commuters.

We should keep in mind geographer Kurt Iveson's critical discussion of
how these adverts are transforming public spaces. Although historically
such adverts have been critiqued for their visually polluting "crass com-
mercialism," Iveson writes that there is also something undemocratic about
how public spaces privilege commercial media over other media, such as
noncommercial posters or community messages.[16] Meg is, of course, more
upbeat. "Our advertising has definitely improved the rail environment,"
she says. "We've got the numbers to back it up," she adds. "It entertains
commuters. You know, they're looking at it; they're engaging with it. So,
yes, it's really brightened the place up." This concept of entertainment per-
vades much of our conversation about bus stops, too. Meg notes that from
time to time, they remodel a bus stop to create a temporary "immersive"
experience. "A recent one was the Australian Open," she says. "They put
tennis seats in there and just really dressed it up." She reiterates: "Entertain
the commuter and really get that wow factor!"

Like the exoticism of the simulated rainforest at Martin Place, many of
the adverts that I saw in city stations were windows onto worlds beyond
the commute. Gleeful expressions, rich color palettes, and bodies liberated from the rucksacks, umbrellas, and other paraphernalia of commuting were the common features of these worlds. Tantalizing and taunting
in equal measure, a huge floor-to-ceiling advert for a cruise line company
asks, "How's this for a daily commute?" in dingy underground Town Hall

station; in the ad, a youthful bronzed couple pulls a kayak from a perfectly azure sea beneath an endless blue sky.

However, not all advertising campaigns rely on grandiose escapist tropes. Dan devised a campaign for a chocolate company that addressed commuters rather differently. More modestly, he tells me that the message his client wanted to get across was about how their chocolate could add "little moments of joy in consumers' lives." The thirty-second TV ad shows expressionless commuters waiting on a busy platform for their train. Unexpectedly, a purple steam train pulls up to their platform, and dancers, musicians, and people carrying trays handing out chocolate bars exit the train. One of the most powerful aspects of the ad is how it works to capture the expressions of the commuters. "I hope you can feel it when you watch the watch the commercial," Dan says. "It really is capturing the surprise and the delight on people's faces that sets it apart." He assures me that no commuters were primed for the experience. Cameras were hidden all over the station. "We actually didn't think of it as shooting a TV ad at all," he says. "We thought of it as an experience that we wanted people to talk about." Dan acknowledges how the affectivity of levity and humor were key to the success of the campaign. "If you're going to unlock emotion, make people laugh, make people feel something, then it's much more powerful," he adds.

Sociologist Anthony Elliott writes about how new forms of experimentation in service provision are at the heart of today's "experience economy."[17] Contrasting with Meg's desire to smooth frustrating interruptions, discussed earlier in this section, Dan tells me that this campaign was meant to be a small, experimental interruption of a different nature. "It offered the opportunity to really transform a dull environment into something quite different and sort of surprise and delight the consumers in that environment." The choice of a commuting space for the campaign was no accident. Drawing on familiar dystopic tropes of the commute that the exotic holiday adverts also respond to, Dan tells me, "We looked at the areas that were more dreary or negative or laborious, and had a critical mass of people." He also recognized the latent potentials of the past lives of commuting spaces. "There is a kind of old-world majestic nature to train travel a long time ago, and by bringing an older style 1920s train back into a modern commuting environment, there's just a bit of magic that we could unlock with that as well."

Curating Passage

From the perspective of the transport agency and advertising agency, this section has so far discussed how distinctive logics attempt to engineer commuting spaces to provide different sorts of experiences for commuters. However, now we will question the ubiquity of such logics by exploring how commuters themselves curate their spatial experiences in ways that introduce other logics.

Ann commutes by train from the Central Coast to a station in North Sydney. She changes trains at Epping. Her description of this interchange experience is rather different from Mel's ideals of seamless passage. She says: "I have noticed three other people; we have a bit of an exercise regime going in Epping where, I always just walk down the elevator and then do a figure-of-eight around the platform, waiting for the train to come, because when else do I get to exercise? So I do it twice, two loops. And, if I'm feeling extra energetic, I walk up to the elevators again, which means walking up sixty steps, and then down again the other side; and that just keeps the lungs moving." I picture the scene: four people, acquainted only through their looping around still passengers, their eyes perhaps meeting briefly, maybe prompting a weak smile. What I like about this image is how this space is being used in an experimental way. Ann explains her motivations through her desire to exercise. She says, "I've always walked in the mornings and always walked at nights and, because I do that commute, I can't do that. So now I build that into the commuting time and the changing trains' time." However, and perhaps more pertinently, this also illustrates how commuters explore the latent potentials of even the most mundane and seemingly constrained spaces.[18]

The final example comes from an early time in my fieldwork. John lives in the eastern suburbs and performs contract work all over the city, changing his workplace every two to six months. He tells me that his bike provides the flexibility to take on these jobs, because he can ride short distances and put his bike on the train for longer distances. This is how he traveled to his most recent contract job at Olympic Park. However, it is his description of his commute home from Olympic Park that sticks with me. "I did a totally different thing," he says, "and it costs more to do this! But, just for the heck of it, I would ride my bike to the ferry wharf at Olympic Park, put my bike on the ferry to Circular Quay, and then I'd get off at Circular Quay. I had to buy a different public transport ticket that was more expensive." I'm intrigued about the experience. "It's full of international tourists," he says, "and, in the afternoon, these tourists go on bus tours to the Blue Mountains, and they come back and get dropped off at a ferry wharf. And so you're waiting at the ferry wharf with this busload of international tourists, who've all been at the Blue Mountains and they're nattering about their great trip and what they're going to do when they get back to their CBD hotel, and I'm sort of one of the four or five people that actually are local. It was always quite interesting and quite pleasant to get this different view of the city from these people who are seeing it all for the first time. And they're on the ferry, and the Sydney Harbour Bridge comes into view, and the Sydney Opera House comes into view, and they all jump up and start taking photos, and they'd often strike up a conversation with you. It was kind of fun."

John's description of how he "curates" his homebound journey is another reminder that seamless passage is not necessarily the overriding logic at work; after all, his ferry commute takes longer and is more expensive. In an inversion of the tropes implied in the exotic holiday advert wooing commuters in Town Hall Station, where joy is to be found elsewhere—and certainly not in the commute—being caught up in the excitable chatter of tourists having returned from a day at the Blue Mountains is infectious. Although John is fortunate to have this journey choice available to him, it is a scene that belies the dystopian dreariness of commuting spaces that Dan's ad campaign responded to. John's description shows how commuting with tourists not only changes the ambience of the space, but also enhances John's capacities to sense his city. Like Ann's figure-of-eights, John's account provides a further indication of how commuters are experimenting with the potentials of these spaces in ways that transform their experiences.

2 Connecting Spaces

So far, this chapter has focused attention on a range of different commuting spaces, from interchanges to station passageways and from platforms to ferry wharves. However, over the past decade or so, the increasing prevalence of digital technologies—especially location-aware smartphones—has invited us to consider how commuting spaces are changing in other ways. This section explores how digital technologies are changing commuting spaces by giving rise to new senses of connectivity, new forms of accessibility, and new interfaces.

Compressing Space in Real Time

I often used Google Maps to find the quickest way to reach my interviews. As I walked to my nearest bus stop, I would also use an app called *TripView*, which would tell me whether the service was running on time, thereby providing an extra layer of timing information. Today, I was meeting with the designer of TripView to learn about how real-time mobile apps have transformed the experience of commuting. Having paced to this stop in Zetland many times over the past few weeks, I know that I can get there in about six minutes if I run. As I leave the apartment, TripView's simple interface indicates that the next 343 bus to Central Station is running three minutes late (lateness is indicated by a little red square) and is due in fourteen minutes. I hesitate, wondering whether I should head back, but decide instead to take a more leisurely walk to the bus stop, taking the time to enjoy the sweet aromas of the lemon-scented gums that line most of the route to the bus stop.

I meet Nick in a café after taking the train from Central to Chatswood, using his app just before I got off the bus at Central to figure out from which platform the first service would depart. Nick tells me that he developed this app to solve a commuting problem. He says, "I thought there would be some utility to just being able to glance at your phone and see when the next train comes, just so you know whether you need to walk or run to the station. And it was just aimed at regular commuters, because I worked in the city at the time, always got the same train, and just wanted to know whether I'd have to wait." Chiming with literary theorist Harold Schweizer's assertion that waiting is often interpreted as an aberration,[19] Nick designed his app to deal with his commuting problem. He tells me, "I used to catch a private bus, back when I was at uni, and you had no level of confidence that the thing was actually going to turn up. You arrived at the stop around about the time of your service, and you weren't quite sure if it had come early. But, if you do have that real-time information, that's sort of reassuring." Echoing my experience earlier that day, Nick tells me, "I used it at home and I used it when I was walking, to get an idea of how fast I had to walk, and at work or if I was just out and I wanted to make sure I didn't miss the last train." Reflecting on how I got to the interview, I could appreciate how his app did indeed reassure.

As a software developer, Nick tells me that his relationship with commuters is important, not least because their feedback and ideas for new features is vital to the app's ongoing development. "Everything that I've done has been in response to customer feedback," he tells me. "Because the initial app met my own requirements. I didn't really catch buses, didn't really catch ferries, and so the first things that I did were to add buses and ferries—because people asked for them," he says. He tells me that he evaluates changes by monitoring Twitter. "If it's wrong," he says, "they'll have a whinge on Twitter. But there was a huge positive response on Twitter to adding bus real-time data at the time." Learning how his app has created new possibilities for traveling by public transport has been a particularly pleasing aspect of user feedback for Nick. He says, "I've got general feedback from people who I think probably use public transport more than they previously did, because they just didn't have the information available previously. ... It's just knowing that there's a bus route that goes from near you to where you want to go."

Nick is also thrilled that his app has created new commuting experiences for differently mobile bodies. He tells me about an occasion when a visually impaired woman rang him to provide feedback. "She said she'd go to a bus stand—and she obviously couldn't read the timetable; so it was cool to have voice-over to know when the bus was coming," he says, commenting that many phones now have a voice-over option as an accessibility feature. "Another person told me—also sight impaired—that they could go to the station and know what platform the train was coming on, without asking somebody," he adds, suggesting how the app has generated new forms of confidence for some commuters.

Curiously, Nick also talks about the new behind-the-scene relationships between private app developers and the state government. That much of TripView has been customer-driven suggests that the lines between grassroots and mainstream app development are blurred. In contrast to cities in other states, where the transport provider develops its own apps, the New South Wales state government has enthusiastically supported private app developers—for instance, through a recent competition to develop apps that display real-time bus information, which they then advertised through posters. I witnessed this enthusiasm for app development a few weeks later when I spoke with one of the directors of Sydney Trains, who was excited to show me how Nick's app can now display a map showing the precise locations of trains and buses across Sydney, something that I had not seen before, but was mesmerized by: a bird's-eye view previously only accessible to "backstage" transport operations staff.

I walked back to Chatswood Station while reflecting on my conversation with Nick. I was struck by how his mobile app offered a new way for commuters to sense space. This echoes geographer Ash Amin's point that our senses of proximity and distance in cities is becoming crumpled and folded in new ways.[20] Previously, waiting for a bus involved using the lines of sight available, or maybe, with practice, seasoned commuters might listen for the tell-tale grumble of a bus engine in the far distance, but now the real-time location information in Nick's app brings into view the precise locations of buses and trains that would otherwise be out of sight. This is a strange effect of what geographer David Harvey calls *time-space compression*, in which advances in travel and communication technologies can compress the relative distance between places.[21] As geographer Juliet Jain notes, because of this knowledge, we can reduce the time that we spend waiting, making journeys potentially more seamless and enabling small amounts of time to be juggled and utilized.[22] I also recalled geographer Stephen Graham's darker argument that software is a powerful tool whereby the experience of mobility is splintered between people who can afford access to Internet-enabled devices and those who cannot.[23] However, showing that these technologies impact on different bodies in different ways, I also remembered an interview with one train commuter who pointed out that she didn't like using real-time applications as part of her journey. Affirming the value of not knowing, she tells me, "If it's late, what can you do? I'd rather not know than spend more time feeling annoyed."

Space-Sensing Technologies

Mia has only ten percent vision. "I don't see far," she says, early in our interview. "I can see meters. I don't see color." I didn't know this about Mia before we met, and I realize that I've cooed about the view toward the Sydney Harbour Bridge from our café at Circular Quay and feel a little ashamed. This revelation is a reminder that we are all "differentially mobile," as media theorist Kim Sawchuk puts it.[24] Mia's whole life revolves around public transport. "Because I don't drive, I get trains and buses everywhere," she says. She lives north of the harbor and takes the train mostly to her two part-time jobs: one at Circular Quay, and the other near Town Hall. She also attends sports training twice a week in Strathfield, west of the city.

Our conversation begins with a discussion about the significance of luggage in her commute—an ostensibly older technology. This has become a rather tedious conversation point with colleagues: "'You have so much stuff all the time!' 'Where are you going now? What are you doing?'" People are forever saying such things to her. "And I have to say, 'Well, I don't have a car to put my junk in.' I don't have a spare pair of shoes in the back of the car." She describes the tensions she feels between aesthetics and utility. "You want to go to work and you want to look good," she says, "but then you've got to have a comfortable bag for your back at the same time." She sinks her shoulders: "You just feel like a mule the whole day, just carrying stuff between everywhere," she notes, indicating how these mobile prostheses are differently enabling and constraining.[25]

Mia reaches for her tablet. "You have to be organized to work it all out," she says, tapping it into life. "The apps now are the best thing!" she says excitedly. "With TripView, you can plan everything so well." She tells me how difficult it was before this technology. "I had a million timetables in my bag—and it was just useless; and they were the tiniest print that you couldn't read anyway, so I had to get my magnifier to read the timetable," she says, as she mimes holding a magnifier. She bought her tablet a year ago, and I sense that it has changed her relationship with the spaces that she moves through. "Train timetables: I don't bother looking at things; I just look at my TripView now and just confirm the platform with the guy at the gate most of the time."

Sociologist Rob Imrie describes how many urban spaces are designed to unintentionally prioritize able-bodied people, which has the perverse effect of alienating impaired bodies.[26] This point comes to the fore when Mia describes the challenges of commuting by bus. "I can't see bus numbers," she says. "They're really hard to see because they're that sort of white transparency where you have to get on an angle to see. ... So I just have to flag down every bus and be like, 'Are you going to this place?' and they look at you like, 'Well, can't you read the sign?' 'No, I can't read the sign; just tell me where you're going.'" She tells me that she hates catching buses because of the awkward interactions with drivers who often don't know about the free pass that she is entitled to. "They just think, you know, 'Oh, you're blind; you should have a guide dog or a cane.' Well, actually, no; I can see enough; I don't need it." These moments of suspicion are clearly humiliating. "It's just kind of like a slap in the face," she says flatly.

Mia mentions that she has developed a set of visual cues on her familiar routes. "Strathfield: There's a little hut thing on the end of the platforms, like little dog houses on the end. So, when I see them, I'm like, 'All right; I'll get off here.'" On buses, it is often much harder. She recounts a story about commuting to her first day at university: "I prepared my trip and got on a bus. I got off at Raneleigh at the stop, but it was the national park at Ku-ring-gai Chase! And I was just like, 'There's no uni here!'" She sighs. "It took forever to get to uni, and that just makes you feel like crap, because you're starting uni, it's a big thing. I don't want to rely on my—I lived with my parents at that stage and then I just rang mum, and I'm like, 'Mum, you've got to pick me up.'" But her GPS-aware tablet has transformed her sense of space, providing her with a more trustworthy sense of location while on the move. She recounts a recent journey to Mosman: "I needed to get a bus and I didn't know where the stop was, and, again, the bus driver wasn't very helpful. So I had to get my iPad out and I followed the route on my iPad map to the road I needed to get close enough to get off. So now, when I'm really stuck, I just follow where I am on my map.'"

Mia tells me that she recently moved away from her family in the north-west of the city to a place near a station just north of the harbor to give her more independence. However, my encounter with Mia suggests that sense of independence is always a relative concept. Even with her tablet, she says that bus journeys can be difficult. "They're always give and take a little with stops, and they don't always stop at the same spot," so she still asks the bus driver to stop at her stop. In peak hours, she'll ask a passenger to call out to her. "It sucks that you can't just be independent," she says.[27]

Automatic Spaces

Monday mornings in commuting spaces have a distinctive ambience. There is a freshness, a sense of the cache being reset, and with it—for those who work a five-day week—a sense of time telescoping out to an almost imperceptible Friday horizon. For some, there is a sense of being snapped back too quickly into the rhythms of the working week after adjusting to happier, perhaps more indulgent weekend rhythms. Few things have marked this time of the week more strikingly than the Monday morning lineup at railway stations in Sydney, as commuters across the city queue to purchase their weekly travel ticket, a perfunctory, expressionless encounter with a face behind glass. The topic of the Monday queue sprang up repeatedly during interviews with train commuters, who needed to make sure that their Monday routine had a little more slack to accommodate it. Yet almost overnight, this perennial time-stamp vanished, its fate sealed by a product introduced by a new personality unleashed on Sydney's commuting spaces.

"We went for a mix between the explorer and everyday man," says Bea, describing this new personality. "I quite like the sense of humor that they've gone with in the advertising campaign." At this moment, I recall a recent spate of cheeky TV adverts in which a young guy in a black body suit, his head haloed by an oversized black card emblazoned with the word *Opal*, woos the people he encounters. Bea helped develop the brand for the new contactless travel smartcard introduced in Sydney. In our interview, she describes how a carefully constructed brand world has been assembled around this small plastic card, bringing it to life and bestowing it with powers that can move commuters both emotionally and physically. "The customer value proposition was based on being simple, value for money, fast, convenient, safe and secure, and open and honest," she tells me while flipping open her phone cover and prizing out her Opal card with her thumb. The four-toned *O* and azure letters glow against a black background. "They're beautiful," she says with pride, her distinctly unromantic, business-inflected description giving way to quiet adoration.

Sociologist Tim Dant writes that it makes little sense to imagine a mobile body in isolation from all the materials and objects that help it move.[28] In this regard, the Opal card has become an indispensable part of what makes a Sydney commuter. Bea reminds me of this, saying that it is one of only three cards that she carries with her, indicating the intimacy of this relationship. Yet though she stresses that the card is replete with local symbolism (the black opal is the official state gemstone, and the colors of the O represent the four modes of transport that the card can be used on), she also indicates that it has transformed the sensory experience of commuting. She notes that the new card readers at train stations and ferry wharves won a design award. "I'm so proud of them," she adds, indicating how a ferry wharf upgrade provided the inspiration for the readers. "They're beautiful stainless steel."

The Opal card is a powerful example of what sociologists Mimi Sheller and John Urry describe as a convergence between the physical mobilities of bodies and the virtual mobilities of information and software.[29] Bea indicates that this convergence has created a new sense of convenience, saying that when she worked in the city, she would often drive in "because there were days when I hadn't bought my weekly, particularly on a Monday; so I would go, 'I can't be bothered to line up today.'" But the Opal card has removed the Monday queue. "The Opal card is so convenient. I love it, I love it," she says, indicating how this technology has changed routines in subtle but powerful ways.

This sense of ease extends further. I recalled my interview with Nick, the app designer, who recounted his confusion about how getting a bus used to require people to know how many fare stages they would pass through. But Opal changes this: All these calculations are devolved to the system. This deferral chimes with what sociologist Patricia Clough calls a new *techno-logical unconscious*, in which software algorithms increasingly condition our everyday existence without us being aware of it.[30] Nigel Thrift and Shaun French take this argument further, describing how intelligent transport systems have led to the "automatic production of space," in which decisions are made automatically by machines.[31] In the context of Opal, the ease of automation creates new opportunities. Previously, different tickets corresponded to different modes of travel and different transport providers. Opal has removed these confusing local distinctions, a key to unlocking the city, making it more easily accessible by public transport. Although some have warned that openness comes at the cost of increased surveillance, because commuter movements can be tracked,[32] Bea reassures me that it was important that "we had an option for someone to remain completely anonymous, which is why you can purchase one and fill it up at the news agency."

The Opal card has created a new sensory experience for Sydney's commuters. It has given rise to new bodily gestures. Bea tells me that the card's creators were concerned about introducing a new and unfamiliar gesture on buses: the tap off. "I'm okay about tapping on; I don't like tapping off," she says. "Yesterday I held up the bus because it wouldn't work, and that made me stressed." The card has also given rise to a new interface through which your card's balance is displayed. There are new sounds for the card readers, with different beeps to indicate the balance status of the card (e.g., balance getting low or balance too low). Commuters can opt for automatic top-ups when their cards reach ten dollars, creating a different relationship with commuting economics. Perhaps most curiously, the technology has also created new forms of playfulness about saving money. The year the card was introduced, the transport minister declared, "I want people to beat the system. ... I want people to find the savings, because they are there to be had."[33] This "gaming the system," avidly discussed on Internet forums, involves taking unnecessary, short, cheap trips on public transport, often over a lunch break early in the week, to rack up the eight journeys per week that unlocks free travel for the rest of the week for people's more expensive commutes.

3   Sensing Spaces

Commuting spaces can be designed to generate specific experiences. As the interviews indicate, some advertisements in stations attempt to generate entertaining experiences, the design of interchanges attempts to generate seamless experiences, and smartcards attempt to generate new traveling opportunities. However, this final section cautions us about imagining that these techniques work in determinist ways. Although such logics are certainly in play, they might not be as all-pervasive as some analyses would suggest. This section explores how commuting spaces are sensed, revealing how they are much more multiple and therefore much richer than any singular logics would imply.

Ordinary Moving Intensities

We previously encountered Kim in chapter 3, a public service manager who discussed how she deals with the complexity of the timing of her morning routines. Here, we return to that interview, just after she talks about timing complexities. She says that this morning, she and her two children, eleven and thirteen, left home in the car at 7:30 a.m., parked in the back street (only an "ordinary" parking spot today, not the golden "rock star" spot they hope for; the builders are blocking much of the street parking), and walked up the hill to the station. The station platform here is an unexceptional space. Yet hearing her account, I sense that it is a space infused with more moving intensities,[34] for the station is where the three of them part ways each day.

"One catches the train left to Hornsby; two of us catch the train right to Sydney. My daughter gets off at Gordon, and then I keep going," Kim says in a matter-of-fact sort of way. Yet without prompting, she continues by saying, "And, you know, where we stand on the train platform depends on whether I'm in the good books or the bad books." I smile at her delicate predicament. "My son, I'm not allowed to talk to on the train platform; it's not cool." She says that they do have a "goodbye moment," but it happens before the concourse: "That's a, yeah, 'Bye, mum,'—and we can't be seen by any friends." She continues, "And then we walk down onto the train platform and then I'll say goodbye to my daughter, who will actually still recognize me at the moment." She frowns and says, "My daughter still will talk to me, unless she's having a tiff and in a grumpy mood, and then it's 'Go away, mum.' So usually I try and go right down the end of the platform to the last carriage." Kim retells this event with a glibness of tone that works to conceal some of the more melancholic dimensions of this moment. She pauses momentarily, purses her lips, and shrugs ever so slightly. In this pause, I imagine the three of them moving apart at this small station to stand separately. Caught in a play of recognition and avoidance, I imagine other commuters spilling onto the platform to fill the spaces between the three of them, tangling the invisible threads that, until this moment, knotted them tightly together. Now they are just someone's daughter, somebody's son. I wonder whether Kim's eyes ever meet her son's across the platform.

I sensed from Kim that the station is a space where the evolving relationship between her and her children becomes palpably felt. It is a space where complex tensions of growing together as a family, especially as her children are on the cusp of adolescence, play out in ways that are not dramatic, but feel poignant. Among these tensions, we might imagine how the shame of the possibility of being seen with a parent by friends rubs against the alienation of a mother feeling distanced by her children. Of course, this moment might also fizz with the quiet relief for Kim of finally not having responsibility to manage her children—a sentiment that becomes palpable a little later when she says, "When they were little, I mean, they hunt for your attention and they're needy."

Interviewing Kim introduced a cluster of intensities that would not have been open to me had I stood on that platform this morning, preoccupied with the dance of my own attention. However, there are other ways of becoming attuned to different intensities in commuting spaces, as I would later discover at a pedestrian crossing at Wynyard.

Time-Lapse

Commuting is an intensely collective activity. Whether we're driving along a highway or pacing along the sidewalk, we are carried along by the momentum of the people moving alongside us. As Peter Adey points out, this quality of moving together can create a sense of solidarity and connection between people.[35] Moving together shapes the kinds of perceptions and feelings that we have while commuting. What would happen if we suddenly stopped and withdrew from this flow? What kinds of perceptions and feelings might stopping create? How might stopping present an opportunity to sense qualities of commuting that might otherwise be obscured?

Wynyard Square in Sydney's CBD is one of the city's most significant commuting spaces. A bus terminus was established here in the 1880s, and a train station opened in 1932. Today, it is the place where buses and trains that start north of the harbor release most of their passengers. From the far-flung growth center of Castle Hill to the Northern Beaches, many people here who have traveled by bus have journeyed for over an hour to arrive here, enduring yet another round of stop-start traffic along Military Road, the Pacific Highway, and the M2 motorway. Significantly for me, Wynyard was where I got off the bus on my first fieldwork journey for this project. This space marks a transition in the commute from the sealed metal capsules of buses and train carriages to the differently exposed experience of walking through the city—another reminder that commuting is always multimodal. This space is a threshold in the progression of people's journeys to and from work. It is a transition marked by a change of atmosphere, where the intensities of light, shade, sound, and smell become different.

Sydney converges on Wynyard Square—or so it feels at seven in the morning. It is a Tuesday morning in late November, and I am standing on the side of the pavement at the corner of Wynyard Lane and York Street, just past the place where most people are getting off these buses. I am standing opposite a pedestrian crossing, another brief suspension in the *store-forward* protocol of travel, as Gillian Fuller puts it.[36] My camera is set up on a tripod, low to the ground, and I have a remote to operate the shutter. As an experiment, I plan to capture one image every ten minutes, to the second, for two

Figure 4.1
York Street crossing, Wynyard, 7:10 a.m., December 3, 2013. Photo by David Bissell.

hours, starting at 7:10 a.m. I'm mildly delirious from a mixture of adrenaline and curdled sleepiness. Nerves make me feel like stone, and I can barely
turn left and right to look along York Street. I can feel that my face is red. It
is 7:09 and fifty-six seconds. I silently count down the final four seconds on
my phone and slowly depress the shutter button.

During the 1970s, sociologist William H. Whyte was interested in how
people used urban public spaces.[37] He used time-lapse photography as a
way of capturing the mundane details of people's practices, which might
help explain why people do what they do. Because he was interested in
how social life is organized, through his time-lapse photography he was
drawn to the patterns and regularities that he discerned. Yet to use time-
lapse photography to focus on regularities, where repeated events become
interpreted as occurrences of exactly the same thing, can overlook the
differences that are occurring, however small.[38] Indeed, ten minutes on
the milieu at Wynyard has changed. The nerves of ten minutes ago have
already ebbed away a little. I count down the three seconds to the next
time marker.

Figure 4.2
York Street crossing, Wynyard, 7:20 a.m., December 3, 2013. Photo by David Bissell.

Something is happening right now—a now that is so often obscured by projections and retrospections. After printing it out, I sit with this photograph later in the day and allow the scene to inflate. A young man with a rucksack on his back is looking at what I later saw was a missing person flyer. *Lost! Has anyone seen Danny Teneglia?* A woman in black is stepping down to the crossing, her left foot just about to touch down onto the angled paving slab, its shadow about to meet her foot. A man is walking past the crossing, his right trainer heel about to meet the pavement, hand in pocket. A car is speeding in from the right. Three dead leaves. Look, glance, wait, step, hold. A bus is breaking close to me. A breeze from the direction of the harbor catches the Christmas banner hung on the opposite lamp post. A cool blue tone cast by the shadows of the surrounding buildings is offset by the illuminated red light glow. The glass door opposite is reflecting the red glow from this side. The now is created in these encounters, these moments in process never to be stabilized. This photo is a cut through countless ongoing histories.

Rather than identifying similarities, I am interested in the shifts in intensities taking place in this space that might otherwise fly under the radar.

Although we might recognize something of what might be going on in this scene, that is a sign of the way that we so often objectify and refer difference back to that which has already been recognized and experienced. Recognition leaves out the new and virtual qualities of difference.[39] Any new values and senses emerging are overlooked. Therefore, by marking time in this way, I'm becoming differently occupied by the specificities and uniqueness of this space, creating a photographic series in which each image poses its own problems and in which the set performs as a collective.[40] Treating these images as evocative objects for thinking with, rather than reflecting on how they differ from an ideal, carves out a space to keep relations open, rather than closing them down. Fast-forward to the second day at York Street, Wynyard, and I'm much more serene. It is coming up to 7:30, and I press the shutter button once again.

After printing yesterday's photos and spending time with them, my capacities for attending to the scene have changed now being here again. I've become much more sensitive to small differences. Yesterday, I didn't see a white stencil on the pavement next to the crossing: *Now open: pub, kitchen, rooftop bar. Sussex St.* Neither did I notice the yellow line along

Figure 4.3
York Street crossing, Wynyard, 7:30 a.m., December 4, 2013. Photo by David Bissell.

pavement. The suited man with the stroller is definitely here earlier today. The sky is greyer, which makes colors warmer and less blue. The glare from the buildings is less intense. I notice that the pedestrian crossing button has a red advert placed around it for the Bristol Arms Hotel. Was this here yesterday? Danny Teneglia's head has been torn off. The leaves have gone. Particular figures are punctuating the scene in a way that they didn't yesterday. After I take this photo I recognize a woman with auburn hair wearing white trainers that I saw yesterday; upon realizing this, my attention has subconsciously become drawn to the game of seeing who I remember.

Fast-forward to day three: I have now stood still in this somewhat unremarkable commuting space for over six hours. I have witnessed people getting off buses and crossing the road, again, again, again; I am taking photos, again, again, again. However, each repeated iteration becomes entangled with something new each time. It builds on the last and is oriented to the next. Although each iteration is similar to the last, new acquisitions are introduced each time, however imperceptibly.[41] I count down the final few seconds to 7:30 again: three ... two ... one ... *click*.

Figure 4.4
York Street crossing, Wynyard, 7:30 a.m., December 5, 2013. Photo by David Bissell.

Different people, different postures, different weather: It is drizzling, and the air is cool. The space has changed. Rather than matte gray, the pavement and road now glisten silver. Tightly folded umbrellas punctuate the scene. I get a funny smile from a lady that I recognize. Then, very unexpectedly, a man in a blue shirt approaches me. He asks what I'm taking photos of each day. Caught off-guard, I say I'm working on a project on commuting rhythms. "Are you here all day?" he asks. "Why did you choose this crossing?" My heart is racing as I attempt to answer. A few minutes later, a woman walks past me, hesitates momentarily, and turns back to me. "Are you doing a jaywalking thing? I saw you yesterday, and then I saw the police down there." A short while later, another man approaches and says, "Now, I've seen you here for three days." A provocation rather than a question! "I'm looking at changing rhythms over the week." "So it's a qualitative study?" he asks. "Yes, that's right." "Ok." He walks swiftly to the crossing.

What is significant here is that these questions and provocations are happening *today*, not during the first two days. This shows that, however subtly, the distribution of desires in this space have changed. My presence has been retained by the attention of the commuters that move through this space every day. I have become part of the memory of this space. After four days in this space, my own fieldwork arc here has come to an end. The excitement of Monday's location-finding morning; the nerves and apprehension of the first day of photography on Tuesday; and the sense of being a suspicious part of the scene today have telescoped into a mild sense of sadness that I'll be leaving. Yet I'm also aware that I'll never really leave. Being here means that in small ways, my capacities to attend and sense have changed. In small ways, this experiment has changed the commuters who have passed me, cuing questions, intrigue, humor, and incomprehension. In small ways, this experiment has changed this space, becoming part of its memory: a memory that continues to have capacities for affecting, as I am reminded every time I pass this spot.

Multiple Durations

In the commute, it is tempting to imagine that people are moving and space is still. This understanding holds some weight. As mobilities theorist Kevin Hannam and colleagues explain, mobile people and objects require a complex array of relatively immobile infrastructures to make movement happen.[42] Yet as the time-lapse experiment indicates, this more static understanding of space as a container for action overlooks the way that spaces might be much more transitional. The Wynyard commuting space does not have a permanent "essence," because it is always in transition. The photographs themselves draw attention to and continue to evoke a series of unique intensities that created space at that time. Doreen Massey makes one of the most convincing arguments for thinking about space more dynamically. Her argument is that space is not only the product of interrelations and interactions, but also the "sphere in which distinct trajectories co-exist."[43]

Here, I turn to an interview encounter with Alice, who commutes between her Central Coast home and the eastern suburbs of Sydney. Her commute is just under six hours, which involves a walk, then a bus, a train, then another train, then a bus, then a walk. She has been doing this for around ten years.[44] Striking in our conversation is her attention to the past lives of commuting spaces. She tells me, "In the early days in particular, I found myself in total awe of the wonderful work done by the engineers who constructed the line. And you think, 'Some poor bugger went through here with a tape and compass and worked out where to put these train tracks.' And it wasn't a thoughtless choice; they've actually gone for the best views. It's not just about the gradient." What feels significant here is how Alice's reminiscences attend to the multiple pasts that continue to inflect her experience. This not only disrupts a linear sense of temporality but also is a reminder of the multiplicity of space.[45]

Alice says: "You know, living leaves detritus; there are markers all around." Becoming sensitive to the presence of these markers is important for Alice, because they help intensify her sense of place. She worries that missing such markers is troubling, because it means that some people are potentially "losing their sense of place. They are not attached to a place." Yet as Doreen Massey suggests, developing a progressive sense of place is not about being aware of all the durations, as though some totality could exist, because that would place us in a position of deficit from which we were always falling short. Instead, it is about retaining "at least some sense of contemporaneous multiple becomings."[46]

Alice bemoans that many commuters do not seem to notice these inheritances, saying, "I have numerous times been waiting at the train station and have said to people, 'The architect that built this place has a funny sense of humor.' Like, you can go, 'Look at the detail in there that is referencing that over there.' And they go, 'Oh, yeah; isn't that funny?' You know, people get it. But they need to have things pointed out to them because they can be standing somewhere but they do not see. They need somebody to show them what to look for." Her frustration about people not being so receptive echoes Marc Augé's contention that commuters on the Paris Metro, far from being affected by the specific histories of stations, are instead "occupied by the urgency of their everyday life and spotting on the map they are consulting or the stations that go by nothing more than the more or less rapid flow of their individual duration, estimated only in terms of being ahead or behind schedule."[47] This *goal-oriented* attention that Augé describes creates a tunnel effect through which commuters are effectively "missing" the city.[48]

However, the multiple durations of spaces can affect us in ways that are not necessarily so conscious. Philosopher Bernard Stiegler says that the technical environments that exceed the lifetimes of individuals have their own strange agency that cues our experiences in subtle ways.[49] He points out that our very experience of being human is constituted by a form of memory that is exterior to the body, regardless of whether or not we are alert to it. He is interested in how experiences are "archived" and the idea that these archives are not inert materials, awaiting our conscious attention for them to do their work. Instead, they have their own agency that transforms our experience in less conscious ways. In the context of commuting practices, these might include archives such as the Sydney Powerhouse Museum and its transport-related artifacts, but they would also include the memory of how commuting practices are grooved into spaces and how these grooves then work on us. As I stood at the pedestrian crossing at Wynyard, I noticed that the repeated passing of vehicle tires over the surface of the road had made two more pronounced tracks into the road. I imagined how the experience of negotiating the wheel ruts on York Street would ever so slightly pull a vehicle into these ruts, thereby adding to this "impersonal" memory. It is through the bodily unconscious that these *tertiary retentions*, to use Stiegler's phrase, make a difference. The technologies of the road and tires have, in a small way, shaped the parameters of this commuting space, where the traces of previous practices provide the bedrock for future experiences.

Conclusion

Our bodily experiences of mobility are intimately connected with infra-structures. Architectural forms can enable and constrain not just the movements of different bodies, but also different bodily sensations and emotions, indicating how power can be engineered into space in subtle ways. For example, Peter Adey describes how airport architects employ what he calls *affective techniques* in different spaces of the airport to provoke certain unconscious behaviors and emotional responses according to the logics of, for instance, security or commerce.[50] What he highlights are the material capacities of space to affect: that surfaces, lighting, and positioning can cue behaviors and augment certain feelings while dampening others.

Yet commuting spaces are different than airports. They prompt us to consider the power of these spaces differently. As Mel pointed out, all commutes are multimodal, and therefore all commutes bead together a series of diverse spaces, which might include sidewalks, street crossings, bus stops, car interiors, and platforms. Whereas airports are "total" environments, the design parameters of which can be prescribed to a large degree by architects and designers, the urban spaces that make up the commute are more complex by virtue of their multiplicity. Some commuting spaces might be subject to a high degree of engineering—for instance, Nigel Thrift describes how unconscious cues are engineered into the design of cars to make their use more pleasurable[51]—but other, less privatized commuting spaces are not necessarily so "engineerable," owing to the range of institutions and individuals that might stake a claim to that space.

Commuting spaces are also being transformed by new technologies that can induce new senses of connectivity. This unsettles our understanding of power in these spaces even further, because these new "code spaces" are often automatic, with lines of code bypassing any human intermediary.[52] Furthermore, access to real-time and location-aware technologies such as smartphones and tablets raises questions about who is excluded from these benefits. We could speculate on what the dominant powers are in commuting spaces, and indeed, the intensification of advertisements in these spaces might make commercialization a ripe contender. However, as this chapter has illustrated, the range of forces at play in commuting spaces cannot be reduced to the workings of a supposedly dominant power. This is a point that Ann Cronin makes when she invites us to question whether ads *really* operate in the ways that agencies imagine. She says that if we think about how ads are being encountered, on the go, in spaces of mobility, then "commercial messages may be reduced to snatches of text and glimpses of color and images that are detached from the semiotic coherence of the original advertisement."[53]

This chapter has emphasized that encounters in commuting spaces matter. As Doreen Massey points out, space is not something that is pregiven and therefore determined by designers and architects, but is better imagined as an emergent effect of the multiplicity of different trajectories and processes happening simultaneously.[54] Commuting spaces are therefore always transforming, however subtly, because of the interplay of these different trajectories and processes. There are many other intensities that these spaces generate that cannot be reduced to imperatives of engineering "from above."[55] These intensities might involve the memory of a certain space and how its past use cues certain feelings in some commuters. These intensities might also involve the folds of commuters' own biographical memories that become threaded through these spaces, adding richness and density to routine journeys. Commuting spaces, then, are formed as much by the eddies and flows of commuters themselves as by the agencies and authorities that manage and have a certain jurisdiction over them. Rather than an inert and passive backdrop to the activity of commuting, commuting spaces are a dynamic force, fizzing with potential to make commuters feel differently about their journeys.

5 Impassioned Voices: Moving Tones and Murky Speech

"All talk and no action" is a familiar gibe often uttered by opposition party politicians and commuters alike about the state of investment in urban transport infrastructure. This has become something of a common refrain in Sydney. For all the talk about transport in the form of master plans, scoping studies, and promises of new roads and railways, concrete infrastructure investment is often slow to materialize, as chapter 6 will explain. Because investments in large infrastructure projects are frequently postponed—the short-termism of a political system that does not reward investments for which benefits are only realized over much longer timescales—the political worth of speaking about urban transport becomes somewhat suspicious.

However, though talk is so often equated with inaction, this chapter explains how speaking and writing about commuting is anything but passive. From the cheery conversations of waiting in lineups with friends[1] to the tenser encounters with strangers on a bus,[2] and from annoying mobile phone conversations on trains[3] to the informative loudspeaker announcements in transport hubs,[4] different forms of speaking have different capacities for action. As geographer Katherine Brickell has suggested, speaking is "a practice that provokes meanings in, and of, different spaces."[5] Speaking is not just the words that we say about things; in the actual saying of words, things change. Speaking or writing about commuting can crystallize a mood, it can provide relief, it can instruct, it can console, it can berate, it can organize, it can bring something inchoate into sharper focus. Voicing commuting can change it.

This chapter explores how different methods of voicing the commute can change the experience in powerful but often overlooked ways. Practices of voicing through speaking and writing are not just passive, representational reflections of a supposedly objective reality "out there." If we appreciate that speech has performative dimensions,[6] then practices of voicing are active players that change how commuting takes place and how it is experienced. What this means is that voicing the commute through speaking and writing produces particular kinds of spaces and particular kinds of bodily experience.

This chapter unfolds in three sections. First, section 1 explores how commuting is reported on. Through descriptions of interviews with reporters, we see how different forms of journalism can change how commuting is experienced. We first take to the air and meet an eye-in-the-sky traffic reporter, whose role is helping commuters negotiate their way to and from work. Back down to earth, we then meet a transport journalist from a leading daily newspaper, whose job is to keep commuters up to speed with the latest transport developments in the city while at the same time creating an entertaining read. We then catch up with a citizen journalist, whose blog about the city's transport has become an important source of information for academics and policymakers alike.

Section 2 moves from the voices of expert reporters to the sorts of everyday reporting that commuters themselves perform. From the letters that commuters send to newspapers to their postings on social media, and from the everyday rants and raves that commuters engage in at home and work to the sorts of mental chatter that takes place during commutes, this part explores how the way that we talk about commuting can change the experience, for good and for ill.

Section 3 brings experts and commuters together by turning to drive-time radio, an iconic part of the commuting landscape in many cities, to explore how this medium creates different forms of intimacy for people during their commutes.

1   Traffic Reporting

Over to the Eye-in-the-Sky

Hovering high above the M5 motorway, Vic Lorusso is making his afternoon pilgrimage into the humid skies of Western Sydney.[7] Miked up and head clamped between a pair of industrial headphones, he turns to the TV camera and speaks with a lexicon only comprehensible to the Sydney motorist: "A truck overturned on the M5, causing delays around the Liverpool overpass; slow westward on the M4 tonight, with queues going back to Ashfield." Haiku-like in its perfunctory lyricism, these words become dramatized by the piercing whirr of the helicopter blades. TV and radio traffic reports have been a central part of the commuting landscape of Sydney for a long time now.[8] Indeed, as I journeyed across the city over many months conducting interviews, I became acutely aware of the sound of chopper blades during these evening peak hours, layering a familiar sonic drone over the weary late afternoon atmosphere.

Cultural theorist Caren Kaplan writes about how elevation above a landscape can produce a privileged kind of knowledge about and authority over that landscape.[9] On this basis, I was keen to learn what sorts of knowledge the eyes in the sky have developed and the kinds of authority that they have over commuting in Sydney.[10] Intrigued by this curious combination of aeromobility and reportage, I journeyed to Bankstown airport, a small airport in Sydney's southwest to meet Vic at his workplace. I was excited about meeting Vic. The delivery of traffic information from a helicopter beamed to the living room television seemed, at first blush, like an anachronism: a format of an earlier era, considering that information on traffic conditions is now an integral part of mobile phone map apps in our digital age. Yet, as I was to learn, Vic's organization provides a valued combination of empathy, consolation, and information to thousands of commuters who travel by car across Sydney each day.

"We have a lot of people who actually rely on us," Vic tells me unequivocally as we begin our chat in his office. Vic is passionate about traffic, and his enthusiasm for his job is clear. He joined the organization straight out of school twelve years ago and has been a household name in Sydney ever since. His face is beamed from his "flying newsroom," as he puts it, to televisions across the city every morning and evening. Anticipating my question about why people in their living rooms need to see the traffic, he says, "People like to know what's happening now. And, if their husband's stuck in the traffic coming home, they can tell: 'He's on the M4; oh, he's going to be home late.'"

Geographer Paul Simpson reminds us that the symbolic content of sound—the part that we might register as information—is only a part of how sound affects us.[11] Before I met Vic, as I sat on a very low sofa at the end of the vestibule area, I was reminded of this point. Every few minutes, the silence was momentarily broken by a short traffic report, read from one of the adjoining rooms with a characteristic delivery, the sound of which could only be that of a traffic report. Listening here, what I found so striking were not the actual descriptions of road conditions but the rises and drops in tone, or the "prosodic 'tune'" of the commentary, as linguist Judy Delin puts it.[12]

Rising from this tune, I recognize the name of a street being mentioned and am surprised that the report is about the road conditions in Canberra, momentarily reminding me that everyday life in my home city continues. I discovered that this unassuming airport outbuilding is something of a national traffic *nerve center*, a hub for collecting and disseminating information to every radio and TV station in Australia. As Vic later tells me: "We've got all our data channels flowing to our reporters at the moment. We've got a traffic reporter position in the Transport Management Centre at Eveleigh and they're looking at all the cameras. And so we've got all the social media feeds that we have that we work on: our listeners, scanners, our informal, our formal Internet-gathering system that's scooping all the traffic data nationally. So we've got abreast of everything that's going on. We are the number one incident reporting mechanism in the country by far, so we have a feel of what's happening now."

In the phrase "what's happening now," Vic hints at the present-tenseness of how his organization operates. I ask whether he can anticipate what each day will be like. He points to the window and says, "Today's going to be horrible because of the weather, so the Channel 7 chopper will go up shortly, and then I'll go up before five o'clock for the afternoon. So we pretty much have an idea of what we're doing before we go up." However, the contingency of traffic is unpredictable. Emphasizing the drama of his job, Vic says, "Things change, traffic changes; so, if something goes off 'bang,' we're up there early and we do it. So you really don't know where you're going; I will never make the call until I'm sitting in the machine." Just like commuters' keen sense of timeliness described in chapter 3, making seconds matter, Vic emphasizes how a similar sense of timely discipline characterizes his reporting. He tells me, "It's all live, and every segment of every piece is timed to precision, although some of the radio and TV crosses are prerecorded a few minutes before they go to air."

I'm particularly struck by the compassion with which Vic speaks of Sydney's commuters. Early in our conversation, he tells me, "The commuters are number one. They get stuck in awful traffic every day, and we just try and be there as part of their anchor." This sense of companionship seems to go beyond the hard-nosed task of information provision. He tells me, "We try and be there for them as that familiar voice, for consistency, to allow them to have someone in the commute with them." Echoing sociological writing by Arlie Hochschild, who devised the term *emotional labor*[13] to highlight jobs that increasingly involve creating particular feel-good emotions, Vic refers to this sense of emotional companionship later by saying: "Our main focus is helping the listener out and trying to get them home quicker, if we possibly can, or detour them away; have some entertainment and involve them in the reports—that's our whole goal."[14] He says that this empathy is intensified during the car journeys he makes in the city. He discusses a recent journey, telling me, "I had to drive through peak hour traffic and it was the most stressful, terrible— I never drive through peak hour, because I'm working peak hour, so it was horrible. And I was thinking— 'Wow, people do this every day.' So you have an appreciation of the roads. I was sitting on the roads I talk about!" His expression turns more somber. "To actually feel and experience it; it's horrible to sit in; it's not fun. You know, these guys are sitting in it every day. So we have a level of compassion of what people are experiencing."

Having watched several of his eye-in-the-sky reports recently, I can't help but feel a little starstruck in Vic's company. He exudes the same energy that I recognize from his traffic reports. His enthusiasm is clearly enjoyed by others. He says, "Friends call and ask, 'I'm stuck on the M5; what do I do?' And I'm at home and I go, 'I'm at home, but I'll check.' So we've built up a major show around town that all of our reporters are known to a lot of people; we're the traffic guys!" The intimacy that his presence creates with commuters is palpable when he tells me of an encounter a few days ago. He was stopped by someone in the supermarket, who said, "'Oh—you flew over me; I was in that accident; do you remember that accident on Pennant?'—'Mm, I think I do.' But I don't remember," he says, honestly. "You know: 'Oh, I was in the red car and you flew over me and I waved.' So, we're there—people see us as we're there in the sky and we're assisting."

Vic tells me that he has been doing this job for seventeen years, and I'm keen to hear about the sorts of expertise that he has developed. Has Sydney's traffic changed from his perspective? "Have people's driving habits changed?" Vic muses. "I think they have," he answers. Early in our conversation, his evaluation becomes clear. He says, "We've just seen Sydney get worse and get worse and get worse and get worse every single year." The repetition of this phrase seems to intensify the sentiment. He qualifies this by referring to differences that he perceives in the morning traffic. "When I first started … we used to fly down to the M5 every morning at about six and you'd see the traffic start to build up at about Liverpool. Now, at six, you see the traffic build up right about two k's out of Campbelltown," a point he attributes to the expansion of the southwestern suburbs of the city. "We were there fifteen years ago, when traffic was bad; now it's horrible," he remarks grimly, reinforcing how important traffic reports continue to be. This has a temporal effect too. Vic reminds me that "peak hours now start from 5:00 a.m. instead of seven before and then six." Arcing back to his earlier point on the issue of timeliness, he says, "People now are so time poor and time conscious." I'm intrigued to learn that although the traffic patterns have remained broadly similar, the delays around well-known corridors have become more intense. "The significance of the delays have just extended in—from the southwest and the greater west, the biggest corridors," he says, a point that he connects with the issue of rocketing house prices in the city.

Making Commuting Interesting

Newspapers played a dual role in this project. On one hand, they were key to my fieldwork: I placed a small advert calling for "stressed commuters" in the city's largest daily broadsheet, in the hope that it would attract the attention of such people reading it on their way to and from work. On the other hand, news media was also my ongoing source of information about transport news in the city. Significantly, it was the means through which I learned about the city's commuter discontent in the first place, as well as about the ongoing developments that took place over my three years of fieldwork, such as the rollout of the Opal smartcard ticket. I met with one of the broadsheet's transport reporters to learn about the role of newspapers in shaping commuting life in the city.

Stephen and I arrange to meet at the shiny foyer of the newspaper's harborside offices, amid the buzz of lanyards and security passes. Over coffee, he tells me that he's had the transport portfolio for over four years now, which he says is fairly long in journalism terms. He says that there are advantages to this: "You know what is significant and you know what's new" in terms of the issues, the people, and the contexts in which they are embedded. He suggests that the expertise that he has developed over four years has given him the confidence to be able to search out new stories, rather than rely on government media releases. What I am really struck by is the tension that Stephen articulates around the repetitious nature of stories involving commuter pain—something that I had become very aware of—and the threshold of newsworthiness required to write interesting stories. This tension seems to pervade his professional subjectivity.

As cultural theorist Sianne Ngai writes, there is an important performative dimension to judging something as being "interesting," because it is the first step toward truly making that thing interesting.[15] The word *interesting* formed a persistent refrain throughout our conversation, indicating Stephen's mode of evaluation when choosing which commuting-related stories to raise to prominence. Early in our conversation, he admits that "there's a lot of meat-and-potatoes reporting that you have to do," acknowledging that "a lot of people still rely on newspapers or newspaper websites to give them basic facts about things," such as information about fare changes and bus breakdowns, information similar to that provided by Vic's eye-in-the-sky reporting. Stephen's social responsibility for this aspect of his practice is explicit. "You're a media figure," he says, "so you just have to get that information. Even if it's not going to win you a prize." Rolling his eyes, he smiles and says, "I've written too many stories about the Opal card! Like, I just can't deal with it, you know!" Whereas traffic reporting and social media provide almost real-time commentary on unfolding events, Stephen indicates that news media reporting is commuter commentary of a different nature, taking place over a more extended time frame.

The endemic nature of commuting frustrations in the city is both the lifeblood of Stephen's job and one of his occupational hazards. He notes with breezy conviction, "People always bitch about transport in Sydney, as they should—like, you know, it's one of the frustrating things," reinforcing a point that I had come to learn. However, this doesn't constitute newsworthiness in and of itself. This is reminiscent of media theorist Daya Thussu, who writes that the pressures that journalists face to capture audiences in new ways have given rise to a new genre, which he calls *infotainment*.[16] Stephen describes how he inhabits this tension later in terms of thresholds of interest. He says, "It's when that bitching becomes interesting enough or is bad news—an issue that's interesting enough to kind of want to write about." Emphasizing this tension, he says, "You can't write about every bus that's late, even though we should be writing about late buses, but we can't," empathizing with those caught up within these endemic frustrations.

What makes a commuting story interesting enough to write about, I ask? The four years in this particular role have clearly sharpened his barometer. He confidently admits, "If I'm interested in it, I'm going to want to write about it, because then I imagine other people might be interested in it." He provides an example related to urban planning issues, such as a proposed second harbor rail crossing. A key aspect of Stephen's barometer involves anticipating the reach of geographical interest in a story. I learn that he is a regular point of contact for many transport community groups across the city that want to draw media visibility to their campaigns. However, though he recognizes the importance of local interests, he admits that "because you're writing for a broader audience, you're wary of doing something that's too local. ... The standard is, if their issue is going to be interesting to people who are not just in that immediate area, or if there's some issue of principle or precedent, or if it's particularly outrageous!"

While on the topic of "interest," Stephen moves our discussion forward to remind me how much the media landscape has changed during his eight-year journalist career. Indicating the challenges currently faced by news media, he points out that a sister tabloid paper has reduced its staff to a third or a quarter of the size it was when he started. In short: "You're producing more content with fewer people, and so you've got less time to do it," he says. Echoing scholars such as Jonathan Crary who have diagnosed the current appetite for nonstop, round-the-clock news,[17] Stephen describes how this push to write timelier online content is especially designed for commuters heading home. Describing the interplay between different online and offline versions of his stories, he says, "You might just get the first take of it up by 11:00 a.m. and then, often with the stories that I do, there's a push to have just people read them on their mobile phones when they're commuting. You'd have a different take on it for 5:00 p.m., and that'll be the story that will be in the paper the next day."

Cultivating an allegiance with commuters is clearly a significant part of Stephen's practice. The commercial imperatives that partly drive this relationship is expressed most clearly in our discussion of the reader comments sections that appear below some stories in the online paper, encouraging readers to leave their (often impassioned) opinions. This section is a "funny beast," Stephen jokes, admitting that reading some of the comments can be quite a chastening experience. He says, "They like us to do it with more stories than not because it increases the amount of time that people stay on a story," which, he goes on to point out, increases advertising revenues. Yet the comments section is also where Stephen finds "real people" to interview for his stories. As if suddenly remembering the value of this, he admits, "I probably should just have a comments section on all my stories!"

What I find fascinating is that, while referring to this crowded mediascape, Stephen describes how different sorts of commentary have an interdependency. For instance, though he describes his reluctance to use social media such as Twitter himself, he describes how it provides him with a useful barometer for diagnosing sentiment. "Social media, in terms of getting a real-time feed of what's happening, is really important," he says, "so I use it for that, and you can use it to disseminate your stories as well and just to get a sense of what people are saying about an issue." In the other direction, he acknowledges that bloggers have become an important constituency in reporting on the city's transport. These commentators, however, rely on *his* information: "What I'm contributing is trying to find out new information and then bloggers can 'blog it up,' if they want to."

Citizen Commuter Journalism

The volume of commentary on commuting has grown significantly through online publishing. Where print media was once the key source of information on city transport, the Internet has given rise to new sorts of "citizen journalists," whose voices have expanded the nature of commentary.[18] Bambul has been one of the city's most prolific transport bloggers of the last four years. I found his blog while researching for the project and was impressed with his capacity to explicate the policies concerning the city's commuting challenges in such an erudite manner—so impressed that I began to check the site on a weekly basis for updates, folding it into my research habits.

I met him at his suburban workplace overlooking the Tasman Sea on a sultry summer afternoon to learn about his practice. Bambul is a Sydneysider with knowledge of many different parts of the city, having lived in both far-flung and inner-city locations over the course of his life. It is often difficult to pinpoint how our passions about a topic develop, yet I'm instantly struck by how lucidly Bambul recounts how his interest in urban transport has emerged. "I've generally been interested in the movement of things," he tells me. "Mass migration of people or the transfer of electricity from power plant to where people use it." His interest in movement, in a more abstract sense, resonates with my own. For Bambul, watching a TED talk given by Melbourne's chief urban planner in 2010 was a tipping point. "It often doesn't happen much in life," he tells me, "but I actually will say that that's a video that changed my life; that's the one that really sparked me into it!" From this moment, "I just started reading a lot of government reports and I decided to start the blog as a way to write something," he says, a technique recommended to him by a journalist friend.

Following my conversation with the broadsheet journalist, I was interested to learn of Bambul's relationship to other media. He tells me that he perceived a gap between "all of those really dense information-heavy government reports" and "three hundred–word articles in the newspaper, which cover it all and don't go into a huge amount of detail." Although he still gets much of his information from the press, he laments that their sensationalist tone means that they "sometimes gloss over certain things." He says, "I wanted something that went into more detail, that was accessible to the average person but that wasn't so over the top that you needed to have a degree in transport planning to understand it." As a way of making complex transport information more digestible to generalist audiences, Bambul describes himself as a "citizen journalist" who tries to avoid the dogmatism that he says is often characteristic of print media, which pushes agendas instead of providing more balanced perspectives—suggesting a rebuttal of the infotainment tendencies of news media.

I'm impressed that Bambul has been blogging for four years now. Just as Vic the traffic reporter's expertise has developed over time, I prompt Bambul to reflect on how his practice might have changed. He laughs and says, "I sometimes go back and have a look at some of my earlier posts and I find myself doing what I just criticized others for doing!" I ask him what he means by this. "I've found myself sort of shifting around with my views a bit to be a bit more nuanced," he says. "I've also moved to be more evenhanded; that's a more recent thing." I'm particularly struck that part of this development involves anticipating people's responses. "I do find myself before I publish, sort of rereading and going, 'How are people going to respond to this?" he says. "Are they going to savagely attack me? Are there any holes in what I'm saying?" This involves subtle changes in vocabulary, being more moderate, being "a little bit more honest."

I'm struck that one of the targets of Bambul's moderation is the popular discourse about the city's poor transport that has become such a common refrain. "The standard joke," he says, "is 'make fun of the transport system in the city.' You can't go wrong with that, wherever you go. You go somewhere like New York or London, where everyone goes, 'Oh, there's fantastic transport in this city,' and even the locals will say, 'Oh, the tube and the subway are rubbish.'" He suggests that people's dispositions toward different city transport systems are, in his experience, shaped by comparisons that are wildly different in context. For instance, while visiting a city on vacation, we might be staying in the inner city and using the transport system outside of peak hours, which might sharply contrast with the more routine travel practices in our home cities.

Sociologist David Beer contends that new media such as blogging is characterized by a "politics of circulation," which means that these voices can take on a life of their own beyond what an author had possibly intended.[19] Bambul remarks that part of his newfound nuance and moderation has emerged as his blog has attracted a community of regular commenters, which was somewhat unexpected. "After a while," he notes, with a tone of surprise, "once you get a few people, they start replying to each other. And that's where you get some real communication going, because it's not just them responding to me." What's interesting here is how this has presented Bambul with a real dilemma. "Do you try and stay above it all? Do you try and put your opinion out there? Do you try and sway people's views? Or do you try and give them all the information so they can make up their own mind?" he asks. "I'm still not sure what I want to do." Yet despite his professed uncertainty over his own motivation, his readership is impressive. "My blog—I know that it's read by the shadow transport minister, the transport correspondent for the Herald, the head of transport for the Sydney City Council, and people from other councils. An academic at UNSW [University of New South Wales] apparently puts my blog up as recommended reading at the start of his lectures on urban planning." This roll call prompts Bambul to reflect on the power of his practice. "I may not necessarily have a lot of readers," he says. "I have a few—but, if you can get people listening to you who make the decisions, I think that's the real element of power where you can actually influence people." This represents a curious evolution of Bambul's blog, from a personal site borne of a passionate interest in wrestling with complex transport ideas to a community of writers whose voices are becoming listened to by decision makers.

Bambul's blog has taken on a pedagogical role in the city's commuting debates. Toward the end of our conversation, he suggests that some people's frustration is from a lack of understanding of how complex systems operate, judging decisions as a personal affront. "People will see things from their little perspective," he says, "their individual perspective, from the ground up; they rarely see the big picture. And that I think often leads to frustration where you don't understand: 'Why is this happening? Why are you doing this to me?'" Yet folded through this citizen journalism is a clear enthusiasm for knowing the infrastructural fabric of his city better. No illustration is more appropriate than his reflections on completing the "all stations challenge" of visiting every station on Sydney's suburban network in one day, a challenge that requires an intimate knowledge of "how the network operates, how a delay can affect you and how changing at different stations can be fast or slow." With a mixture of deadpan seriousness and intense wonder, he recounts the knowledge he gained by performing this challenge, discovering secret platforms and hidden crossings.

2   Rants and Raves

Ranting

I have lost count of the number of times that telling someone I'm researching how commuting affects city life has unleashed a flared retort that few other opening gambits seem to match. Throughout my interviews with commuters, at times I feel like I've become something of a "commuting counselor," providing a kindly ear to soothe agitations in need of attention. "I'm so glad that you're doing this project," one woman confides on finishing our interview. "I haven't been able to talk about this with anyone else," she says, as though having disclosed a painful secret.

Yet, as I discovered, talk of commuting bubbles up in all kinds of unexpected places. I learned that two standing items of dinner party conversation in Sydney are house prices and commuting. Commuting talk also saturates written forums. As well as letters to the editor and the public comments below transport stories on online newspapers, the city's free newspaper given out at stations to commuters has a daily double page in which commuters can vent their spleens in a section bearing the same name. This section is packed with tightly bundled commuting rants, often judging the conduct of other commuters ("Standing gripe: I wish people who stay on the train for the longest get first pick of the seats. I dislike having to stand for forty mins while others who have seats get off after five minutes").[20]

During interviews with some commuters, I learned that commenting on commuting experiences has become a part of the way that they deal with the strains of traveling. During my interview with Alan, the bike commuter from chapter 1, he told me that he often rants to colleagues when he arrives at work about incidents that happened on the way. "My colleagues," he says, "you know, I'll get to work and there'll be an occasional incident which I've found unpleasant and a little bit, you know, nerve wracking where you've locked up brakes or someone hasn't seen you—and I come to work and I rant, and my colleagues just sort of: 'Yep, okay.' You know, if I've been shouting on the road and I come to work and I 'raah!'—and then I'll feel fine about it, actually." Unlike the more informative commentary of traffic and news reporting earlier in this chapter, this way of voicing the commute is more about dealing with the mental churn of commuting events that linger long after they have happened. In fact, Alan is explicit about the cathartic quality of ranting. He tells me, "I do rant when I get home occasionally as well and I just—yeah, that's sort of released; it's gone then."

Literary theorist Dina Al-Kassim writes that ranters are not necessarily in control of their own speech. She says that the rant is a "haphazard and murky speech" that "loses the subject in the stream of words that overwhelm his speaking."[21] Although this sense of being possessed by the intensity of injurious events might be an apt description for Alan, for others these stories are a little gentler. During my chat with Francesca, who commutes mainly by car between her home in the Inner West and Parramatta, she says, "A lot of my colleagues do seem to live around here [where she lives] and do more or less the same commute." Because of this shared route to work, a different sort of voicing the commute happens. "Some are a bit later than me," she says. "And it's this whole sort of, you know, 'Oh'—you know—'what about that accident this morning?' and it's almost like you've got to offload to each other how bad the commute was, when you first arrive. You have about a three- to five-minute whinge and then it's just,

'Oh, right; well'— you know—'get on with the day.'" Through this ritual anecdote sharing, there is something much more habitual about Francesca's commentary than Alan's.

As sociologist Mike Michael writes, the telling of an anecdote creates a relationship with context.[22] Telling an anecdote therefore creates something new. For Francesca, it might be intensifying a connection with her colleagues. However, the telling of anecdotes, especially ones that become cliché, can have other effects. Where Alan's rants have positive, cathartic effects, and Francesca's are more ritualistic, I was struck by my conversation with Lauren, a bus commuter who travels between her home in outer northwest Sydney to her workplace just north of the CBD. Her commentaries seem to have a very different effect. Here, she flips the point of view by giving us a sense of someone who has to listen to these anecdotes. On the topic of her husband's arrival at home, she says, "'Don't talk to me; I don't want to know! Just let me—just let me get ...'" She continues by describing how she has changed her commute to avoid listening to these anecdotes, which clearly have a depleting effect on her: "That's why, as I said, I get the bus now to home instead of him coming and picking me up, because that conversation used to start when he picked me up. It's like, 'I don't want that.' So I actually prefer to sit on the bus through all the back streets, getting jerked around the place and having that little bit of a walk, and then, when I get in the door, he's at least busy cooking dinner. It's so reverse, it's—oh, it's sort of funny. And he's like, 'Don't talk about it; I don't want to know!'" Philosopher Judith Butler acknowledges the precarious nature of repetitious performances when she reminds us that they "always run the risk of becoming deadening clichés."[23]

Voicing to No One

The spectrum of voices commentating on commuting frustrations have multiplied in recent years through social media platforms. Some have even suggested that the use of social media effectively democratizes commentary, freeing it from the preserve of "expert voices," such as the reporters and journalists discussed in section 1.[24] However, as sociologist Monika Büscher and colleagues suggest, the way that social media is being used to know and sense events in new ways is creating more "agile publics,"[25] which respond to incidents as they happen, providing traffic reporters like Vic with immediate feedback from events. This indicates that there are intricate relationships between different sorts of commentary. Although there are several official transport feeds that commuters can subscribe to, through the use of hashtags such as #sydneytraffic and #cityrail, commentary is increasingly being voiced by commuters caught in incidents.

Social media provides real-time commentary that unfolds in parallel with the events commented upon. One participant, Clara, who commutes daily by train between the Blue Mountains and Sydney, reflects that she "got straight onto Twitter" in response to a disruptive event not uncommon in the heat of the Australian summer. "One little incident—a few weeks ago," she recounts. "It was a super-hot day; it was, like, forty-something degrees [Celsius]. Central Station was bedlam because none of the trains could cope, because all of the tracks buckled. And I know they have to put safety as the priority, but I just—the entire network came to a standstill because of the hot day. I just don't get it. I mean, I got straight onto Twitter and said something about it. There's a lot of people tweeting about CityRail stuff."

There is clearly a symbolic dimension to Clara's commentary, in that she is sharing what is going on with other people, but it seems secondary to the performative dimension, in the sense of needing to externalize her feelings of frustration at being delayed. Although social media has been lampooned by some for being narcissistic and egotistic,[26] a more sympathetic evaluation might be that these commentaries get their force from the heat of the moment, rather than the indulgence of the commuter-commentator. Unlike commentaries directed at specific individuals, these commentaries are directed toward no one in particular. However, there are similarities with Lauren's account presented earlier, in that tweeting has, for some, become a habitual response to disruptive events. Getting "straight onto Twitter" certainly suggests such unreflexive immediacy.

Specific hashtags have emerged on social media for people to vent about disruptions to commuting by train in Sydney. Interestingly, though operator CityRail changed its name to Sydney Trains several years ago,[27] #cityfail continues to be the hashtag of choice to commentate on railway grievances. The content of tweets using #cityfail often display particular stylistic conventions, such as acerbic humor, as a Twitter user showed in a recent tweet: "Sydney train air conditioning appears to have 3 settings. Fridge, Freezer or today's setting Liquid Nitrogen #cityfail."

Autoventriloquy

I am seated on a sweaty, non-air-conditioned train heading to Central Station to meet someone for an interview in five minutes' time. Mine is the next stop, but the train has come to a halt in the tunnel. The carriage is silent. There are no announcements, no onboard commentaries—yet this moment is brimming over with my own silent commentary that is gurgling away. "Oh this is so predictable, why does this always seem to happen? Oh for goodness sake, can we just get going sometime ...?" Trying to present what is going on here is not straightforward, as a linear account risks betraying not only the irrepressible relentlessness of this voice, which I sort of identify as being mine, but also the jumbled and graceless nexus of words that form across me in this heated moment. Among the split-ended strands of commentary pertaining to the mildly panicky event of being late are muffled shards of conversations I've had with people over the past day or so, a few bars of songs on seemingly endless repeat, words I see on adverts in the carriage that then might repeat a few times, and a piano ostinato that melds into a familiar but irritating song that has been on my brain for a few hours.

Voice-over commentary has been used extensively in television and film, often for its capacity to reveal contradictory or voyeuristic dimensions of experience that might otherwise be repressed by everyday conventions of speech.[28] In the 1970s British sitcom *The Fall and Rise of Reginald Perrin*, the protagonist, Reggie, uses this audible voice-over technique extensively. The voice-overs during his morning commute on a packed but characteristically silent British Rail carriage reveal Reggie's wry and often critical observations of his fellow passengers. Akin to daydreams, in some episodes these observations morph into fantasy conversations with work colleagues. Indicated visually through frowning, eyebrow raising, subtle mouth movement, and grinning, these voice-overs apparently reveal Reggie's inner thoughts, sculpted as they are by the utter routineness of his everyday life and his dissatisfaction about his job. Some of these inner thoughts occasionally become voiced out loud to comic effect, indicating Reggie's increasingly unhinged disposition, doubtlessly induced by the ennui of his bland suburban life.

This commentary contrasts markedly from the clipped care of traffic reports and the blustery but more or less coherent narratives of anecdotes discussed previously. Similar to Twitter outbursts, these voices are not directed at anyone in particular. Instances of road rage might provide examples in which an inner voice suddenly becomes spoken out loud.[29] Similarly, car drivers might talk to themselves in the process of navigating traffic.[30] However, this vocalized speech represents only a thin slice of inner speech, reinforcing the idea that this is what someone is *really* thinking, unconstrained by the normative conventions of speech that often characterize talk between people.[31]

Literary theorist Denise Riley describes the chaotic untidiness of this inner speech beautifully. She says, "My swollen (because word-suffused) psyche can ... assume the most unbecoming shapes. Some graceless prose of the world has got me in its grip, and my word-susceptible faculty is seized and filled up by it. It's a neurolinguistic circus, this wild leaping to my tongue of banally correct responses, bad puns, retold jokes ... and many other kinds of stock formulas."[32] This description seems to get at what I was experiencing, not only on the way to the interview, but through so many of my fieldwork experiences. Riley says that this "inner language is not composed of graceful musing, but of disgracefully indiscriminate repetition, running on automatic pilot."[33]

But is it really *our* own voices that are muttering away during commuting journeys? Riley's description of inner speech as *autoventriloquy* suggests that these are voices that might be coming from elsewhere. She ventures to define this autoventriloquy: "my repetition to myself of whatever authoritative positioning I've caught from the world."[34] What is so interesting about this description is that it suggests that something much more contagious is going on here. Rather than a private, Goffmanesque "backstage" realm in which the demands for self-presentation subside and we're saying to ourselves what we're *really* thinking, the commentary of an inner voice is much more contagious. It is whatever preoccupies our attention at the time.

Some of my interviewees gave a sense of the things that were preoccupying their inner voices during their journeys. For some, this was a time filled with inner speech related to work; a time when office conversations were replayed and the events and encounters of the day were cogitated over. Just like the afterlife of forms of malignant speech that linger long after they have been spoken, sustained by their own momentum,[35] for some the evening commute was a necessary opportunity for this commentary to take place. Recall, for instance, Liz in chapter 3, who described how her homebound train journey enables her to process the day. This was commentary that would otherwise consume time at home; thereby, in a small way her commute freed the home space from the preoccupations of work.

Just like the rant and debrief, the commentary of the inner voice can have different effects for commuters. Sometimes, it might be helpful, while at other times it might be more depleting. If this inner voice is so inescapable, as Riley suggests, how might we moderate its effects? Although we might not be the authors of our own inner speech, there are certain powers of editorship that Riley calls *linguistic will*. She explains this by describing how "an expression flashes over me and it will have its way, but only if I don't throw it out."[36] *Throwing it out* might involve techniques that help modulate the force of inner speech. Empathetic to my susceptibility to being strangled by knots of self-commentary, a friend's recommendation to read Eckhart Tolle's *The Power of Now* became a salve during difficult times.[37]

As some commuters indicated, somatic techniques such as mindfulness meditation can provide a way of becoming less ensnared by this silent speech and more accepting of its anonymous, indifferent nature. As Riley suggests, "We can still elect to suffer our subjugation moodily and darkly, or we can treat it much more lightly and indifferently, as a by-product of the disinterested machinations of language."[38] Accepting the impersonal contingency of being accidentally spoken might go some way toward providing light relief from the sometimes oppressive burden of having to entertain the dance of these commentaries. Yet at the same time, unlike the speed and closure of the clichéd anecdote, this mode of commentary—its obsessive lingering, persistent refrains, eddies, and feedback loops—has its own strange durations that do not coincide with the temporal unfolding of the commute.

3   Drive Time

Drive Time on the 370

It's late afternoon in late February, and a late summer sun sears the group of people waiting for a late bus from Chippendale. The smell from the braided urine streaks on the pavement mixes with purple vehicle fumes, depending on the direction of the wind. Yet my mildly heat-stressed irritation is being tempered by a debate currently unfolding about the medicinal use of cannabis for cancer patients. Through my earbuds, I'm listening to Justin Smith's drive-time radio show on call-in station 2UE while traveling home, as has been my habit for the past few weeks. The current caller is describing her painful cancer ordeal. Justin is clearly moved by her story. As he interjects, I notice the bright white illuminated numbers "370" lurch around the corner. Previous annoyances are forgotten and perhaps even forgiven. I step onto the bus and absentmindedly swipe my Opal card through the reader, my attention latched onto an earlier interview snippet being replayed of a caller upset by the prospect of legalized cannabis. After I sit down, Justin cuts to traffic and public transport updates. Reports of traffic jams following a truck accident on the Great Western Highway immediately seem to bring the traffic surrounding the bus into full view.

Unpolished, unedited, and unabashed—there is something about the rawness of call-in (or talkback) radio that I've always rather enjoyed. Although social media means that many people can broadcast themselves to the whole world whenever they please, there is something venerable— stately, even—about both radio as a medium and call-in as a format. Legalized in Australia in 1967, and growing in popularity soon after, "talkback programs on the AM band lead the ratings surveys in most Australian metropolitan markets at prime time," as cultural theorist Graeme Turner notes.[39] What struck me most about my journeys home while tuned to 2UE was the heady mixture of topics Justin placed side by side. Today, the traffic news segues to an interview with the member of parliament for Reid, who is talking about children being held in detention. That segues to an advert break for the *Second Best Exotic Marigold Hotel* movie. That segues to an interview with a sixteen-year-old boy, who saved a blind woman who fell onto a railway track in Melbourne. That segues to traffic again—an almost word-for-word repetition of the previous report. Like a slide carousel stocked with slides randomly picked from very different collections, there is a seamlessness to the show that belies the almost outlandish differences of topic. I was hooked.

Intimate Tipping Points

The following day, I had the privilege of talking to Justin by phone about his show. I was interested to learn how Justin reflects on his role in people's commuting lives in the city. Nerves steadied by Justin's instantly personable phone manner, I tell him how much I enjoyed being taken beyond the traffic on my previous afternoon's commute. "Great! Look, I really hope so; I really hope that people get taken out of themselves a bit because being stuck in traffic for a long period of time is obviously pretty awful," he confides. Justin shares a story with me. "As somebody once told me, ask yourself this question: 'Have you made the drive home shorter?' and I think it's a terrific question to ask and I've never forgotten it." I smile, remembering how just yesterday his show dissipated my frustrations with the late bus. He continues: "You sort of think to yourself, look, it would be great if you presented something so engaging that, while they were stuck in that traffic, not only would they get the information but, when they pulled up at the doorstep to get out of the car, they had to stay in a few more minutes to hear you finish your interview." Justin's comments echo geographer Ben Anderson's point that what we are listening to can change our perception of time by speeding it up or slowing it down, thereby altering our orientation to what we are doing.[40]

For Justin, this experience of listening is about creating a collective. "You want people to break up that drive by being a part of it," he tells me, an idea that would thread through our whole conversation. "The thing about radio, which is nice, is that it's a bit of a collective drive home together," he says, echoing eye-in-the-sky Vic's point earlier. However, Justin tells me, the difference in his show is that people can share their first-hand experiences with others in real time. He says, "We put these callers to air sometimes because they say, 'Oh, Justin, something happened on the M5 at around about this exit; can you tell me what it is?' We'll say, 'Oh, we don't know; let's put the call out.' The next thing you know is that a caller rings in and says, 'Yeah, I'm stuck on it right now'—you know—'It's a real pain in the arse.' So that immediate back and forward is what is terrific about radio." It is the sense of care for other commuters that Justin notes with astute bluntness when he says, "It is that nice feeling where people would like other people to avoid the crap, so: 'I'm in the crap; I want to keep you out of the crap.'" Sociologist Richard Sennett has bemoaned that cities are becoming disconnected spaces in part because many people spend so much of their time driving alone,[41] but these commuters seem much more connected than Sennett implies.

I want to hear how Justin curates his slide carousel of topics. He provides an idea of his daily routine, which involves scouring the newspapers in the morning, followed by a meeting with his producers at lunchtime to decide on topics. "There are only two stories that you can do on air," Justin tells me. "One of those is something that people are already interested in. ... And the other one is ones we *want* them to be interested in. The medicinal cannabis campaign that we've been on over the last year, I'd say, is probably one of those ones," he says, reminding me of Stephen the broadsheet journalist's criteria of interest for his stories. "And then you make sure that there's a mix of important stories and a bit of fun," he says. "When we put the show together, we look at how we're going to balance that: 'Okay, we've got an interview here about children in detention. Why don't we—after the break, when that's finished, why don't we do something that'—'oh, that thing was a bit of fun; let's have a chat about that.'" Turner suggests that "many talkback hosts are entertainers rather than journalists, and all are charged with keeping the program moving and upbeat."[42] Unlike the distanced reporting that Bambul described earlier, here "the investment [is] in selling opinion rather than impartiality."[43] Yet I'm struck by how Justin points out that this juxtaposition creates an intimacy. "It's like friends having a conversation," he tells me. "You know, you'll talk about something that's a little serious and the next thing you'll be telling a rude joke. I mean, that's friendship, and I think radio's the best medium of all to be able to be, like a real relationship with people."

Like a virtual backyard fence, this intimacy is marked when Justin talks about his "regulars." "It's like some people feel really connected with the station," he says fondly. "I think they've just got in the habit of calling. And there's a large chunk of people—they're in the habit of calling because it's sort of what they do; it's like staying in contact with your family. They feel that staying in contact is part of what they are, part of what they do, you know. It is beautiful, really." Casting my mind back to the interview that I heard Justin perform with the MP during yesterday's show, I am struck by how this sense of intimacy seems to extend to his "expert" interviewees as well as regular callers. Justin describes how radio permits a more intimate relationship than TV, partly because of the time restrictions of the latter. "In a normal conversation when you talk to somebody," he says, "you warm up, you have a little bit of chit-chat, you get sort of to know the person, the feeling of the conversation, and then it just starts to drop down into that little deeper area."

This intimacy can create unexpected tipping points that, for Justin, make for good radio. As he puts it, "The person starts to feel more relaxed, and then you can slide them down into it, and then you can hit them with something that they weren't really expecting to say on radio." I'm struck by how he strives to create a similar sort of tipping point for listeners, too. "I like to be able to tell a story so that people go, 'Gees, hang on; that guy's never going to be the same again after today. That's an incredible thing that's happened to this person; it's really changed their life.' And I hope that I can be a bit of a conduit for those stories." Justin is clearly skilled at drawing out these tipping points, as I cast my mind back to yesterday's interview with the pained cancer patient that moved me while I was stilled by the traffic of King Street. "Sometimes we forget what those moments are, you know, or we don't quite recognize them straight away," he says humbly. "When people have been through those moments of: 'Gee, nothing's ever going to be the same again'—I don't know if *enjoyment* is always the right word, but they're the stories that get to me, you know, to creep inside of that person."

My conversation with Justin helped crystallize some of what I experienced while listening to his show commuting home: a sense of companionship and a sense of being liberated from the relentless mental churn described earlier. That being part of this dispersed, mobile community of listeners could give rise to profoundly moving encounters made it a part of the day that I would look forward to. Yet Justin was acutely aware that his community of listeners is a commuting community. Toward the end of our conversation, he says unequivocally, "Congestion is always top of mind for people driving in Sydney. ... So we thought, 'Oh, well, let's do the entire show from a car. We'll take callers, we'll do interviews, we'll cover the news that we would normally cover but, with it, we will also talk about where we'll go.'" I'm excited about what this forthcoming show promises and I count the days to the following Wednesday.

Drive Time Live from the Streets

"We need these streets. But we seem to curse them these days!" says Justin, as the intro music for today's show, "She Drives Me Crazy" by Fine Young Cannibals, fades out. In a twist of roles, Justin is mobile, with this afternoon's show being presented from a studio 4x4, and I am sedentary, having decided to listen from my apartment so that I can take notes on what unfolds. It is only a few weeks until the state election, and Justin has invited the roads minister, Duncan Gay, to join him in the mobile studio to talk about the city's traffic problems as they encounter them firsthand, starting from Parliament House in the city center.

"We'll get the latest from Bali first," Justin says, these words unexpectedly zooming listeners from the traffic concerns of the CBD to the plight of two Australians who have been imprisoned in Bali for almost ten years on drug-trafficking offenses. The story has been the subject of intense media interest in recent weeks, as the pair have become unwitting pawns in a fraught political tussle between Indonesia and Australia. Cut to a newsroom segment: "They have just been dispatched to an island for execution." Cut to the mobile studio: "Do you believe that pink undermines authority?" Justin asks Duncan, referring to a news story about changing the rugby league referees' strip from pink to blue.

After a few wrong turns, the mobile studio is approaching Anzac Bridge. I know this because on the radio station's website, a map is tracing the movements of the mobile studio, giving the show an added authenticity. Cut to first caller: "Look, I drive a truck all day. We've got major infrastructure problems going on. You've got all these crap roads between the city and Waterfall. You've got to do something, because we've got nothing." The minister responds: "We will have a southern exit to WestConnex, we're looking at routes for the A1. The money we've spent on the Princes Highway is incredible, Berry and Kiama. It just goes on and on." Cut to second caller: "I've just received a statement from the E-way toll on the M2. I'm a courier by day and I have to travel thirty-seven kilometers home. It costs $967 in tolls a year. That's a week and a half's wages!" The minister responds: "It is a whack, it is a cost, but it is as low as possibly can. Sitting idle is worse than paying a toll." Cut to news—a three year-old child has possibly been murdered—and to adverts—no one can beat the Lounge Suite Warehouse.

"The traffic doesn't look too bad now," says Justin, sounding disappointed. It reminded me of my first week of fieldwork in Castle Hill, when I was trying to sniff out transport blackspots. The minister is delighted. "Some of the pinch-point updates must be working!" Soon enough, the mobile studio hits traffic. "Welcome to my nightmare! It's my life!" says the next caller. The majority of callers in the first two hours have called to talk about the infrastructure problems that they experience in the city. They speak with expert authority about specific intersections, grade separations, flyovers, and merging lanes through a vocabulary that only people with an intimate familiarity with that patch of the city would likely appreciate. Many callers offer suggestions for improvements to the minister. "Why can't we have a flyover going over Milperra Road?" questions one. "The only impediment is the cost," replies the minister. "Selling off poles and wires would help," he adds, slickly cementing infrastructure shortcomings with his party's controversial public-asset selling plans. "The biggest problem with the M5 is city-bound merging from King George Road onto the freeway, merging with Bexley Road on the right-hand side. They have to go across both lanes," insists another caller, demonstrating intimate knowledge of what works and what does not.

Three hours later, the mobile studio is heading back to the radio station headquarters north of the harbor. "The fact is, the roads are a mess. There are a lot of cars." Justin's weary but triumphant final sign-off at the end of the show sympathizes with his commuter audience. I sense his exhaustion in the unambiguous nature of his statement. Reflecting on my experience of listening to the on-the-road drive-time show, the different sorts of suffering being experienced by people was stark. Commuters were calling, and they were frustrated about the traffic. Commuters were calling, and they were frustrated about the death penalty in Indonesia. These two sorts of suffering seemed to be held side by side in tension together, without diminishing each other.

Rolling with It

The following morning, I speak with Justin about his experience with the mobile show. "It was really good," he says. I agree. "It does put a different perspective on your talking about the traffic while you're in it. Particularly with Parramatta Road and a couple of spots like that, you're just sitting still; I had something to keep my mind occupied, by being on air at the time. But I could imagine if I was just sitting there, tapping the steering wheel, I'd be feeling a bit cheated." He says that his biggest surprises were the lack of carpooling and that so few people seemed to want to talk about public transport. More poignantly, he speaks at some length about being affected by the faces of commuters stuck in traffic. "I got looking at the faces of the people though, when they were driving, and they were sort of stuck in the heaviest bits, there seemed to be this calm resignation that, you know, this was what it was," he says. "No one was sort of arms out the window, you know, beeping horns and pushing people to go through there," he says. "Everyone was sort of sitting there, just waiting for it to clear and waiting to move and waiting to roll in to the evening."

I comment on the combination of discussions of the death penalty and traffic frustration and ask whether it felt strange shifting between the two. "It's very interesting that you say that," he says. "I hadn't thought about it like that before." There is a momentary silence, and I fear that my representation has troubled him. "When you do a radio show like that, you can't really think along those lines because, otherwise, say you have terrorism attacks in Martin Place and things like that; well, everything could seem trivial to that." Echoing his comments to me a week earlier about how friendships are formed of these sorts of topic switches, he continues: "So I guess I've just conditioned my brain that you switch between different things. One minute you're having a laugh about something and the next minute, you're, 'Oh, how was the siege in Martin Place?' So I guess you just learn to roll with it a little bit more."

Geographer Doreen Massey argues that our ways of imagining places have often tended to tame them, to overly order what is going on. This is problematic, she says, because it overwrites the existence of multiplicity, or the "ever-shifting constellation of trajectories" that make up places.[44] Her word *throwntogetherness* seems apt in describing the multiple worlds that rub side by side on Justin's show. Indeed, it is through this throwntogetherness that Justin describes his ethos toward his listeners. "The other thing is that I don't ever want to trivialize anything that someone would call in about," he says sharply. "If they call in because somebody put milk up by twenty cents, for their family, for that person, who might be on a pension, it's really important. And, if I were to say to them, 'I don't give a shit about the price of milk'—you know—'Don't you know we had a siege in Martin Place?' I think, if you do that, you can really trivialize the things that they've got to grapple with every day." His comment strikes at the heart of the issue of commuting pressures that the project has been grappling with. It reminds me that my task as a researcher has been to cultivate a sensitivity toward my participants in order to appreciate the significance of commuting in their lives.

Conclusion

Geographer Yi-Fu Tuan makes the curious point that some things we do are so instinctively routine that they surely don't require speech at all.[45] Although there might be an instinctive familiarity to commuting, such that it can "go without saying," to use sociologist Pierre Bourdieu's words,[46] this chapter has shown that commuting is brimming with all kinds of speech and is anything but silent. They might not be classically beautiful or even breezily poetic, but there is an ordinariness to the sorts of voicing that this chapter has described. This ordinariness might make them seem insignificant or even inconsequential. After all, what could be more banal than hearing another traffic report? What could be more mundane than talking about something that happened on the way to work again? What could be more commonplace than skimming another newspaper article about bus fare hikes? Yet these *are* the expressions that course through commuting lives, giving definition to everyday journeys.

There are so many ways of voicing the commute, and there is a specificity to each medium that generates significance. Each mode of voicing unfolds according to different durations. From the knee-jerk responsiveness of Twitter to the almost near-real-time updates of traffic reports, and from the more delayed simmering debriefs at home to the much more refined reflections of journalists, these voices have distinctly different capacities to affect and be affecting. They have different spheres of influence; the workplace rant is much more local than the city-wide newspaper article. They evidence different degrees of authorial control; the mental chatter of auto-ventriloquy perhaps is more difficult to tame than a blog post. They create different sorts of intimacy; the drive-time community is perhaps more dispersed than a group of work colleagues. Yet these different modes of voicing are intimately connected, forming an ecology of sorts that takes us well beyond the confines of the journey. As the rants and debriefs indicate, the effects of commuting can spill over into workplaces and homes. They can also become entangled, as the Twitter feeds on social media might make their way to traffic reporters, the voices of blogs might make their way to newspaper journalists, and the everyday rants and raves of commuters might make their way to the comment sections of newspapers.

What these different voices have in common is their capacity to change commuting. Sydney's transportation problems have become a conspicuous point of concern of late, in part owing to the way that these voices give definition to the otherwise more vague and ambient forces that make up commuting: the sinking feeling of sighting a traffic jam ahead, the resentment of another fare rise, the shock of being cut off by another car unexpectedly. Certainly, interviews with commuters indicate that the experience of traveling to and from work has a uniqueness shaped by a person's own biographical commuting history of moving around the city. However, these experiences are folded through the experiences of others—through the commentaries that circulate on call-in radio shows, Twitter feeds, work conversation, and dinner parties—each of which helps create a more extensive apprehension of the city's transport problems that extends beyond the horizon of individual experience. Voicing is powerful because it contributes to a collective understanding of the forces that make up the experience of traveling through cities.

The performativity of these voices make them a subtle but powerful agent of change in the city. For instance, hearing accounts that we might recognize might be incredibly consoling, providing a collective apprehension of a problem. Speaking out loud might rid us of things that we are chewing over. These voices can also change the experience of duration. For instance, drive-time radio might make time stuck in traffic speed up. On the other hand, our automatic commentaries might make time slow down to a crawl. The point here is that the changes that voicing creates are complex and are by no means determinate. Traffic reporting can dampen the forces generated by traffic incidents, but it can also give rise to suspicion and mistrust. Telling anecdotes about commuting can be cathartic, but it can also become a tedious habit, intensifying stresses and thereby extending their durations. The commentary of inner speech can orient us from moment to moment, but it can also carry us away and become debilitating.

6 Stranded Expectations: Still Waiting for Infrastructures

Validating one of the central frustrations commuters talked about with me, a recent report raises serious concerns about the adequacy of infrastructure provision in the state of New South Wales, stating that "this is especially true for transport infrastructure where, by international standards, Sydney's service levels and costs are poor."[1] Geographers Steven Graham and Simon Marvin provide historical evidence that might explain this situation. They argue that postindustrialized cities have been experiencing an infrastructure crisis since the 1960s; population growth and the associated demand for mobility has outstripped expenditure on transport infrastructures, putting cities under severe strain.[2] In response, this chapter explores the ways that "hard" infrastructure changes only come about through the delicate interplay of practices enacted by different institutions and organizations. Although it might often seem that nothing is happening to improve transport infrastructures on the ground, focusing on the backstage techniques, materials, and performances employed by different institutions and organizations helps us better appreciate the forces actively at work to change commuting experiences.

Taking Steven Graham and Colin McFarlane's cue that infrastructures are always in formation rather than rigid constants,[3] this chapter highlights that these practices and processes of advocacy are a vital part of how infrastructures change. Furthermore, focusing on these practices and processes helps us expand what we mean by infrastructure. Geographer Derek McCormack points out that by focusing on processes, the infrastructures of mobility are made up of a "generative interplay between bodies, movement and materials."[4] This means that infrastructures "are always bound up in webs of meaning and affect excessive of, but not entirely opposed to, their physical engineering and construction."[5] This chapter takes up this point to show that advocacy practices are not separate from infrastructure, but are instead part of the medium through which transport infrastructures take shape.

To take on this task, we visit different sites in western Sydney to learn how infrastructure change materializes. Through encounters with commuters, politicians, and media statements, section 1 explores how waiting for infrastructures can create particular dispositions in communities where transport infrastructure investment is not keeping pace with rapid population growth. Focusing on the formal governance of state and federal politicians committed to improving commuting experiences in the city, this section draws attention to three challenges to infrastructural change: the short time frame of election cycles, a perceived lack of transparency, and the persistence of ideologies.

Section 2 illustrates that these intangible dispositions have powerful effects. We learn this through examining an information center for a new transport infrastructure project, where advocacy strategies are needed to respond to these dispositions through specific demonstration techniques.

Because one of the key challenges of changing infrastructures is the sheer length of time it takes for changes to materialize, section 3 turns to a different sort of advocacy group in western Sydney. This grassroots group uses a different set of tactics to show how smaller, more incremental changes can change commuters' lives in profound ways. This chapter concludes by evaluating how these political forces must be considered in tandem with each of the other sites of transformation that have been explored in this book. As will be clear by this point, rather than a silver bullet to solve the commuting crisis, hard infrastructural interventions are ultimately only one dimension of the solution.

1   Still Waiting for Transport Infrastructures

It is ten past seven on a late summer Monday morning. I have returned to the Castle Hill transport interchange, two years after my very first fieldwork encounter. Things have changed since I was here two years ago. In a practical change, I no longer need to buy a MyMulti paper ticket to catch the bus here, because the Opal smartcard is now accepted on these services. From a more bodily perspective, I have been changed by the encounters that I have experienced with commuters across the city. As I approach a group of people waiting for the bus, I realize that there are different queues, as there were two years ago. I approach a woman whose gaze is fixed on the war memorial opposite. "Are you waiting for the CBD bus?" I ask, a little shyly, the volume of my voice constrained by the silence of the scene. She looks at me. "Yep," she says. "Great, thanks!" I reply. "Still waiting," she adds flatly, drawing out the vowel sound and dulling the *t* of the second syllable of *waiting*. I find a spare patch of pavement. In my morning dazedness, I realize that her words are still echoing, and I find myself repeating the phrase in my head a few times. As I look at my watch, it occurs to me that she might be waiting for a bus that is overdue. *Still* waiting. A minute or two later, a red Metrobus draws up.

Still waiting. This innocuous phrase kept returning to me over the course of that day. As it did, it seemed to open out, expanding its reach to suggest different things. The tone initially suggested frustration due to a delayed bus. Then again, *still waiting* seemed to speak of something a little deeper: something more profound about her situation, finding herself at the bus stop again and again. This double sense of waiting reminded me of anthropologist Peter Dwyer's[6] useful shorthand distinction between what he terms *situational waiting* and *existential waiting*. For Dwyer, situational waiting is waiting *for* something. Existential waiting, on the other hand, is much more a condition of our existence.[7] This duality is reminiscent of the distinction that Henri Bergson makes between time as thought and time as lived.[8] Thought time is a mathematical, abstracted time that comes from our habit of dividing time into measurable blocks that can be used. *Still waiting.* Lived time is the flow of duration that is embodied and endured. *Still waiting.*

Drawing on this distinction, literary theorist Harold Schweizer writes that in waiting we become conscious of time as something other than that which can be measured or thought. He says, "The time that is felt and consciously endured seems slow, thick, opaque, unlike the transparent, inconspicuous time in which we accomplish our tasks and meet our appointments."[9] Yet Schweizer points out that too much emphasis on situational, task-oriented understanding of waiting obscures the potential that lurks in existential waiting. He says, "The instrumental nature of ordinary waiting—where we usually wait for something that is supposed to be better than waiting—conceals this intimate, existential aspect of waiting."[10] I wonder whether the woman at the bus stop would agree?

Intensifying Waiting

As the residents of this part of northwestern Sydney know, waiting has political dimensions. Anthropologist Ghassan Hage reminds us, "There is a politics around who is to wait. There is a politics around what waiting entails. And there is a politics around how to wait and how to organize waiting into a social system."[11] Politics often revolves around the question of who moves and who stays stay put,[12] but what Hage's observations add to this question is an important but often overlooked temporal dimension to such politics. He points out that waiting can reveal "certain features of a social process that might have been foreshadowed by others or entirely hidden."[13] Over the course of my fieldwork, this politics of waiting kept returning in different guises at different sites. One of the sites where I sensed it most intensely was during interviews with state and federal politicians whose portfolios included urban transport issues.[14] One of these interviews is with a New South Wales state MP. Although our interview covers many different issues, what particularly strikes me over the course of our conversation is that the concept of waiting for the construction of public transport infrastructures keeps returning.

Toward the start of the interview, it becomes quickly apparent that the MP is frustrated with the lack of action taken by the current New South Wales state government to solve commuting problems in the city. Referring to the relatively short election cycles in Australia, she says with some emphasis: "It's a *very dire picture* here, unfortunately, and, it is that thing about ... slowly governments have become, you know, very short term, four-year to four-year, and not thinking beyond that." She describes how the federal government's current obsession with roadbuilding is contrary to what city commuters need, especially in the west. She puts these short election timescales in the context of the timelines required for the benefits of public transport infrastructures to materialize. She says: "When you look at ... the shorter term, then roads become cheaper in that sense. It's public transport and other environmental social benefits that have a longer time span for a payback." Referring back to these longer time spans later on during the interview, the MP says that the biggest challenge that Sydney has to face is "real gridlock in the city." With an unequivocally steely tone, she says, "I mean, I'm seeing a disaster looming here, really." After the interview, as I walk across Macquarie Street next to the New South Wales

Parliament, her words continue to resonate in my head and give the queues of traffic an added sense of foreboding. *Still waiting.*

The following week, I find myself in Canberra, sitting opposite an Australian politician who has devoted much energy to campaigning for public transport infrastructures as a way to improve urban livability. Similar to my interview with the state politician, it was the unhelpful temporalities of party politics that dominated our conversation. We talk about the changes the politician has seen since he has been in office. With a concerned look, he says: "I think we've gone very sharply backwards. So I came in 2007, which was the turnover year in which the Howard government lost office and the Rudd government was elected for its first term, and, for a period of a couple of years, there was actually quite a bit of energy about. ... But obviously, most recently, in the last eighteen months, we have seen the trends really go into reverse.[15] We've got an election of a government that actually appears to be completely opposed to public transport, such that all of the funding has been withdrawn. ... There's a massive push on road building, particularly urban freeway building. And so in a way it feels like—I think the tide's turning and popular feeling is still pretty strong, but institutionally we're actually amidst, I think, quite a profound and really unfortunate reversal."

His frustration becomes even more conspicuous when he says: "The underinvestment and opportunism like we're getting are just really advanced case studies in political opportunism here, now. And in Sydney, sometimes they're multi-billion-dollar commitments; they take a heap of planning and they are disruptive when you're putting them into the ground. And, if you're got people who want to play games, you can wreck them and you can smash them up pretty badly." I'm struck here by how he describes transport infrastructure projects as at the mercy of party politicking. He goes on to say, "I think that just denotes a degree of political immaturity that we've got to get over, because we're going to strand a lot of people. I think people are going to be pretty pissed off." Echoing the sentiment of the state politician I previously interviewed, and referring to suburbs like Castle Hill, he says: "You will see a lot of very angry middle-ring and outer-metro populations pretty pissed off at the underdone state of infrastructure, and they're going to want to know what's going to be done about it."

Stuckness

With the politicians' words still resonating, I cast my mind back to my recent encounter at the Castle Hill interchange. "We're going to strand a lot of people." The phrase *still waiting* now seemed to gain another sense: a sense of how people living here might be feeling stranded, just waiting for something to be done about the current state of transport infrastructure. Indeed, the direct link between transport infrastructure and social inclusion has been described extensively by researchers who have shown that inadequate public transport infrastructure provision can intensify a sense of being stranded.[16] Tim Cresswell calls this *stuckness*.[17] As I learned from speaking with commuters, stuckness can be a one-off event, such as an infrastructural breakdown caused by a broken-down train,[18] but stuckness can also be a much more everyday experience. For example, cultural theorist Phillip Vannini's detailed ethnographic portraits of island life in British Columbia, Canada, reveals that stuckness is a normal part of being at the mercy of the (ferry) transport system.[19] It is this more everyday rather than exceptional sense of stuckness that feels most fitting to the situation in northwest Sydney in places like Castle Hill.

Stuckness has tended to imply being passively held at the mercy of a stronger force. However, Ghassan Hage reminds us that though stuckness has tended to imply a lack of agency, *enduring* an experience of stuckness could actually be taken to be much more active, because it is a demonstration of *not* giving in to circumstances. He says that our current social and historical conditions are arguably those of "permanent crisis," and not only has this "led to a proliferation and intensification of this sense of stuckness,"[20] but this stuckness has become normalized as a test of endurance, in which our capacity to "wait it out" becomes celebrated. Consider here how the idea of the "battling" commuter has become such a pervasive media discourse. As Hage points out, this stuckness "involves both a subjection to the elements or to certain social conditions and at the same time a braving of these conditions."[21] It is a form of waiting in which "one is not waiting for something but waiting for something undesirable that has come ... to end."[22] Hage's definition of stuckness as *waiting it out* for something undesirable to go away certainly resonates with encounters I had with some of the longer-distance commuters, in which their subjectivities emerged through experiences of endurance. These commuters told me that they were only going to have their current commutes for a few years, a refrain indicating that setting time limits could establish a weak sense of authority over an otherwise stuck situation.

Hage's argument is that what we have in waiting it out is a new form of governmentality that "invites and indeed valorises self-control in times of crisis."[23] Although he is especially interested in how waiting it out is an experience socially differentiated by class and race, this everyday notion of waiting it out as endurance seemed to echo the kinds of "strandedness" evoked in my interview encounter with the politician. I cast my mind back to the interview. The statement that "I think people are going to be pretty pissed off" suggests that endurances are being pushed to their limits, especially in northwest Sydney.

Stuckness in Northwest Sydney

Castle Hill is a place that I kept returning to during my years of fieldwork because it is a part of the city that has been embroiled in ongoing transport infrastructure controversies. This is an area where the city's population growth over the past two decades has been particularly concentrated. To illustrate, from 2013 to 2014, the population of the Parklea-Kellyville Ridge statistical area, part of the Hills District, grew by 9.4 percent,[24] the second-highest area of growth in the whole of greater Sydney. This growth has been underpinned by urban development strategies in the 1980s and 1990s that facilitated the growth of business services in the area, in hubs such as the Norwest Business Park.[25]

However, the provision of public transport infrastructures in this part of the city has not kept pace with the high population growth. In 1998, the state government acknowledged the detrimental economic, public health, and well-being impacts of congestion in the city. The northwestern growth corridor of the city was singled out as an area particularly poorly served by transport. Geographer Peter Thomas offers an incisive summary of events between 1998 and 2014.[26] In short, the 1998 transport plan proposed the construction of eight new urban railway lines by 2010, one of which was the North West Rail Link (NWRL), to serve the Hills District. Yet over this twelve-year period, only one of these lines was constructed and a second begun. The NWRL was not constructed. As Thomas points out, in successive reports during this period, "Transport problems were identified, continuous road-building was rejected as a solution, and progressive commitments to deliver a more sustainable transport solution through public transport were advocated."[27] Clearly, there has been a mismatch between promises made and delivery.

The NWRL, in different guises and configurations, has been announced, canceled, and reannounced several times. The railway was originally proposed in 1998 to Castle Hill. In 2000, doubts about the project's economic viability came from delays from the state government to release a report on the proposal. In 2001, the project was deferred indefinitely. In 2002, the state government announced a feasibility study and began public consultation, with the majority of respondents being in favor of the project. In 2005, the state government published its Metropolitan Railway Expansion Plan, which included the NWRL, which would be constructed by 2015. In 2008, the state government changed tack by making the NWRL a "metro-style" railway, rather than a traditional, "heavy" railway. However, the government's focus was on constructing a metro in the CBD. Later in 2008, the entire NWRL was cut due to budgetary pressures. In 2010, the state government devised the Metropolitan Transport Plan, canceling the CBD metro (which cost A$93.5 million in compensation for canceled contracts and tenders), but reannouncing the NWRL. Yet by 2013, during my fieldwork, no railway had yet materialized. Set against this story of oscillations, a line from the politician's interview takes on renewed significance: "If you've got people who want to play games, you can wreck them and you can smash them up pretty badly."

Thomas's account of these oscillations cites tensions between and within the jurisdictions of federal, state, and local governments as the main reason for these oscillations. He also suggests that these oscillations are underpinned by a more fundamental tension about how the longer durations involved in railway construction are not compatible with the shorter-term benefits that four-year election cycles demand—a point that was made in the first interview with the state politician. That is, the "historical relationship between railway construction, cost overruns and the inability of such forms of transport to repay their direct capital costs can lead to unease for those charged with making the financial decision for the go-ahead. The longer-term social, environmental, and economic benefits brought about by railway infrastructures cannot be easily accounted for."[28]

Thomas spotlights some of the possible triggers for these political oscillations, but how did these oscillations themselves change the public mood in northwest Sydney over time? As described in chapter 4, collective bodily responses to events or places can be engineered below the threshold of people's consciousness[29]—for example, through the judicious design of environments such that bodily capacities are primed to affect and be affected in particular ways.[30] However, the oscillations here are less derived from the effective management capacities of the "sovereign" power of the state government, and much more an effect of the state's *incapacity* to provide for the transport infrastructure needs of the population of northwest Sydney. Such a situation resonates with geographer Mitch Rose's idea of *negative governance*. In reflecting on Michel Foucault's focus on the technologies and capacities of the state, Rose says, "We become over attentive to what power does and blind to that which power fails to do—not only power's various losses, but its various non-attempts."[31]

The oscillations of announcements, postponements, and cancellations by the state government over the fifteen-year period starting in 1998 changed different capacities to affect and be affected across different arenas. As Thomas notes, these arenas range from investor confidence to commuter well-being. Media accounts from the *Sydney Morning Herald* after policy "backflips" in 2007 provide a sense of the simmering frustrations that were accruing. Reporter Bellinda Kontominas wrote:

Public transport and roads are by far the biggest issue for this commuter-belt electorate. Residents say they are still waiting for the long-talked-about North West Rail Link. "I think I'll be dead before it goes in," says Bob Caldwell, who lives on the border of the electorate at Castle Hill. "It should have been in 20 years ago." Mr Caldwell has lived in the area for 35 years. In that time it has undergone plenty of change, but planning has been poor and government perception that people in the area are well off has affected policy, he says. "West Sydney and South Sydney get rebates on their tolls and we don't.[32] If we do a trip to the airport it will cost $25 for a return trip unless you go the back way, which will add another 30 to 40 minutes." The Lane Cove Tunnel will be another toll to budget for, he says. Mr Caldwell and his wife are moving to Queensland in the next few months. "Our state used to be the premier state 15 years ago... [but] we are joining the exodus."[33]

Later in the same year, reporter Sunanda Creagh reported on the news that the state treasury might put a stop to the NWRL: "'I am quite outraged,' said Tamer Galil, of Kellyville. 'We moved out here even though it's a bit of a hike because the infrastructure was going in. We all knew about the rail link; the promise was made and if they have broken the promise, the Government should give commuters an explanation.'"[34]

Through his account of the NWRL's troubled history, Thomas points out that these repeated failures of the state generate their own responses. For instance, he singles out the way that technologies such as route diagrams, maps, and new visualizations of the city create *imminent mobilities*, a sense of a future transport link that can have material consequences, such as property speculation. When these plans are abruptly withdrawn, we are reminded that "ruptures and disruptions are equally a part of the imminent mobilities of future urban transport plans."[35]

Significant here is that the affectivity of infrastructure announcements, their capacities to change, is contingent on the situated and singular memory of place. As the media commentary presented earlier indicates, "New plans and announcements do not occur in a temporal vacuum but slice through an urban landscape that is already overflowing with the affective charge of previous plans and announcements."[36] In section 2, we visit another site in northwest Sydney to probe how the NWRL is responding to this charged atmosphere.

2   Managing Waiting

Sensing Disbelief

One afternoon during my first fieldwork week at Castle Hill, I noticed a sign reading "North West Rail Link Information Center," adorning an otherwise forgettable white building right next to the bus interchange. Cognizant of the troubled history of the project, I ventured inside. A promotional video played on a large flat-screen TV, flashing the keywords *growth* and *future* in time to a rousing, anthemic soundtrack. CGI renderings of new stations adorned the walls. The woman at the desk told me that the information center opened in 2011. She told me that she commuted into the center of Sydney for fifteen years from Kellyville, even further out than Castle Hill. She was desperate to find a new job closer to home. "I couldn't do it anymore," she says. "This is my dream location!" I understand why she speaks passionately about this infrastructure project, but the history of failed action over the past decade and a half hangs in my mind. Before visiting the center, I had been talking with a barista in the café on the opposite side of the transport interchange. I pointed to the information center and asked if he'd been inside. He shook his head. "Nah, it's not happening," he says, bluntly. "We've been here before."

Interested in learning about how the state government sensed and managed these dispositions that experiences of *still waiting* have created, I arranged to talk with a representative associated with the North West Rail Link project. After moving a folding glass panel partition to create a pop-up meeting space within the information center, Kate tells me that her role has changed considerably as the project has evolved. "Initially it was about the engagement and consultation around the planning process," she says. "So we needed to bring community and stakeholders along with us and get their input, and that resulted in some changes to the project." Next came a planning phase. "This is where we needed to say to people, 'This is *actually* happening.'" Kate pauses, and then says, "Which was a challenge in itself." I ask her why this might be the case. "This project was on again, off again, on again, off again," Kate admits, waving her hand from side to side, intensifying a sense of oscillation. "So, when we arrived, it had been on again and off again for over ten years, so—this iteration of it, so initially people didn't want to engage with it." The timbre of her voice here suggests empathy. She says, "I think they were so disheartened that they didn't want to invest anything into the project. ... When we first started, people's main concern was: 'This will never happen.'" She describes how they would talk to people, saying, "'Well, we letterbox dropped you some information about this,' and they said, 'Yeah; well, I looked at it, but I threw it in the bin, because I just don't believe this is going to happen."

The community information center was set up as a response to this lack of confidence, "to do what we call *reality messaging*," as Kate puts it. "'So here it is; it *is* going to happen.'" Kate stops herself and says more slowly, "It's more likely it's going to happen this time," as though, despite her role, the force of the oscillations has planted a seed of doubt. I nod. "The cynicism was extraordinarily high ... in that initial phase, and there was great cynicism, making it hard to get through to people," Kate says with weary irritation. "People just can't imagine, with these huge infrastructure projects, a government ever getting on with it. I think that's a legacy of previous governments' performance. So there's still every time you say, 'We're planning something'—'Yes, that's fine, but it'll never happen!'" I cast my mind back to the aborted Sydney Metro scheme and add, "I suppose they can be forgiven in that respect." Kate smiles. "Oh, absolutely. I think government needs to deliver on a lot more things like the North West Rail Link. You know, they need to see them through to the end, for people to start actually believing that they will do what they say they're going to do."

Generating Belief

Emphasizing the importance of appreciating the ongoing adjustments that infrastructures undergo, urban theorist AbdouMaliq Simone writes, "Infrastructure exerts a force—not simply in the materials and energies it avails, but also the way it attracts people, draws them in, coalesces and expends their capacities."[37] Highlighting the way that infrastructures are both social and material, he says, "The distinction between infrastructure and sociality is fluid and pragmatic rather than definitive. People work on things to work on each other, as these things work on them."[38] Simone writes that part of the task of maintaining sociomaterial infrastructures involves the "calibration of expectations."[39] This sense of calibrating expectations is particularly helpful when considering Kate's role in attuning the community to the project. Reflecting Simone's idea of infrastructure as both material and social, with infrastructural engineering tending to foreground brute material dimensions, Kate describes her role as about engineering something much less tangible, yet no less significant: belief. Persuading people to believe in something that doesn't actually exist on the ground yet is her main challenge. This is difficult because "you won't be able to prove that this is the best product, until it's actually up and operating," she admits, a point consistently exploited by the local media, from which commentary on the project has tended to be negative. She says that three strategies in particular have been instrumental in creating belief in the project.

The first strategy centers on the strategic vision of the state government. She says, "What really helps us explain this is having a strategic vision for Sydney's rail future, and we can explain where [this project] fits into that—that it's not just some little spur line that will never go anywhere—and people really respond well to that bigger strategic picture." This echoes architect Ilze Paklone's point that planning messages need to be simple to digest, given their wide audience.[40] The second strategy is the repetition of key messages. "We just keep saying the same things over and over again to the media," she says. "We just try and use as much as we can ... to explain actually what this product is, why it's different, and what the benefits of that are." She says that this strategy has been particularly important when talking to people about their concerns about privatization: "So we have to say again and again that the control of the fares will be retained by the government and they'll be the same as the rest of the network. And people are quite relieved when they hear that." The third strategy uses the power of social media, especially Facebook. She expresses surprise at how self-moderating this strategy has been. "When people have expressed their concern on the Facebook page, you have that self-moderation of the community. So someone'll say, 'Oh'—you know—'these single-deck trains: They're dreadful and there are going to be no seats,' and then someone will come on and go, 'These are all around the world; this is what Sydney needs.' So that's much more powerful than if we're saying it."

About evaluating the efficacy of these strategies, Kate tells me that community surveys have been an important way of diagnosing changing beliefs toward this future infrastructure over time. "[Survey respondents] would say their main concern is that it will never happen," she says, "and that's disappeared now. So that's how we track it." Anecdotal evidence is important, too. "So just when we go out and engage with people, what are they telling us?" she says. "Now people come up and are really excited and want to know where the station is and how often the trains come." She says, "So now we have really strong support out in this area for the project, and, even across the rest of Sydney, we know that they believe that this project will be good for northwest Sydney."

Demonstration

Geographer Sam Kinsley writes that future-oriented "simulations" are not just passive depictions of things to come. Their very presence has powerful performative effects. With reference to "vision videos" of the sort that technological companies create, Kinsley writes that these materials "produce futurity" by 'establishing the presence of what has not happened.[41] This dynamic is at play in the information center, as Kate explains that demonstration is a key technique for creating belief in the project. The materials that make up this information center work to do just that. On every wall are striking renderings that provide viewers with a window onto the future of this suburb, complete with its new train line. "We have a really defined product now," she says. "So initially all we had were some plans and we could show people what we thought it was going to be. As we get closer and closer, we can make it more tangible. 'This is really what your trains will look like; here's what your stations will look like,' and people are really excited about that." These visualizations have transitioned from speculative design to procured product. As sociologist Monica Degen and colleagues remind us, such digital images are not just glossy representations but a new way in which cities are becoming visualized.[42]

A second form of demonstration is provided by the scale models of new stations and trains. Kate says that these have been "hugely successful" in helping people visualize the project. These models are themselves mobile, having traveled extensively around the community. "They don't have a railway out here, and the railway that they've probably experienced in other areas of Sydney is very different," she says. "So it brings the project to life." An older couple are looking at one of the station models, walking around it, viewing it from different angles and pointing. "You see," says Kate, "you have people poring over those models, going, 'Oh, that's my street' or 'my neighbour's street; oh, right, I can see where that's going.'" The scale model of one of the trains has a side cut out so that you can see inside. Kate says that this has been helpful for assuaging people's concerns about the lack of seating on these metro-style trains. She says that a man visited the center recently, looked at the model, saw the tiny orange grab handles coming from the ceiling, and admitted that he was "relieved and persuaded."

A third form of demonstration is provided by the more immersive, hands-on experiences at the information center. A virtual reality headset offers a six-minute tour of the tunnel-boring machines. This experience provided a sense of depth and peripheral vision that I had never experienced with any other form of media. I'm struck by the technical dimensions of the tunneling, but also the magnitude of the operation, which feels sublime. I wanted to reach out and touch what was in front of me and found myself leaning forward to do so. The video heightens my perception of the immense forces required to create this transport infrastructure. At one point, we zoom into the steel-cutting blades, which the voice-over informs me are tungsten-tipped and need to be replaced every few weeks. The toughness of the rock seems to intensify the magnitude of the project. My desire to reach out and touch is satiated when Kate shows me to a table containing rock cores from the test drills of different rocks at various points along the route. I picked up one of the smaller cores with one hand and was startled by its weight.

Like Kinsley's analysis of vision videos, these materials in the information center are designed to encourage a familiarization and an embodied disposition toward this proposed future transport infrastructure.[43] This was important because, as Kate indicated, a pervasive sense of cynicism existed in this part of northwest Sydney, caused by fifteen years of political oscillations that delayed construction of this rail link. What is particularly striking is how the information center has been designed to cut through this cynicism through the creation of particular bodily experiences.

As philosopher Brian Massumi has argued, contemporary power can no longer operate through appeals to reason alone, but instead has to operate through affective channels, through the creation of particular experiences.[44] In the context of waiting for infrastructures to be constructed in this transport-poor part of the city, Kate described how the information center aims to produce experiences that intensify enthusiasm and excitement, and thus form an affinity with the project. Key to the operation of the information center is the aesthetic potential of demonstration. The materials at play, such as scale models, core samples, and VR headset tours, are designed to work haptically, at the level of immediate sense, rather than reflective discourse. These materials are designed to facilitate encounters that create affinities with the project, rather than just transmit information about the project. This echoes Nigel Thrift's point that "the practices of worlding demand the use of a much greater sensory palette in order to produce ambience as well as message."[45]

Of course, this is not the only site at which these kinds of disposition shifts are taking place. Through our everyday lives, we are constantly having encounters that subtly shift our capacities to affect and be affected.[46] These include encounters that might involve the force of materials in the information center, the force of political announcements, and the force of media presentations. These encounters are folded through countless ongoing encounters that make up people's everyday commuting lives in this part of the city, such as *still waiting* for a bus.

3   Taking the Next Step

After three years of fieldwork, I was becoming all too aware that "solving" the commuting problems people in cities face is a challenge of almost overwhelming proportions. Although investment in new public transport infrastructures is a part of the response, storying the undulations of just one infrastructure scheme, the North West Rail Link, indicates just how long and drawn out the processes of planning and constructing new transport infrastructures can be. It can often feel like waiting for infrastructures is an endemic condition of living in cities such as Sydney.

Urban transport can feel stubbornly recalcitrant when it comes to change, but at the same time, I was aware of how easy it can be to submit to a "paranoid critical stance," to hold our hands up and claim that transformation is an unlikely, if not hopeless, project. Such a position can be dangerously paralyzing. As Brian Massumi notes, constantly looking to the future for our salvation, for some utopian dream of a better life, neglects all kinds of potentials that exist here and now in our present. He writes: "In every situation there are any number of levels of organization and tendencies in play, in cooperation with each other or at cross-purposes. The way all the elements interrelate is so complex that it isn't necessarily comprehensible in one go."[47] Such a diagnosis certainly feels apt for describing the giddying complexities of urban transport. His point is that even in the most constrained and seemingly intractable situation, there is always some wiggle room for maneuvering, owing to the complex tendencies in play. However, rather than figuring out what needs to be done in terms of large-scale grand plans, as is often the aim of urban planning, Massumi's point is that it might be as important simply to figure out what the next step is. He writes, "The question of which next step to take is a lot less intimidating than how to reach a far-off goal in a distant future where all our problems will finally be solved."[48]

Rather than waiting around for a time when urban transport will finally be sorted out, Massumi alerts us to our responsibility to experiment with what is going on here and now.[49] For changing transport infrastructures, this might on the face of it seem more difficult than engaging in some of the other modes of experimentation that the other chapters in this book explore, especially considering the costs that are often involved in developing infrastructures. However, in this section, we visit a different site in western Sydney to explore how one advocacy organization is taking on this challenge of championing smaller-scale infrastructure interventions that have potentially life-changing implications for commuters in the city.

Assembly

"Who do we sing for?" calls a lone voice facing the assembled crowd. The audience responds: "We sing for western Sydney!" A little awkwardly and hesitantly at first, this call and response builds and builds, each iteration a little more confident than the last, until the whole hall becomes caught up in the infectious rhythm of this syncopated refrain. Nervous smiles turn into wide grins as the simple song weaves its spell. There are over four hundred people assembled here in the main theater of Parramatta Hall on this spring evening, many of them members of unions, religious groups, and care organizations, as indicated by the banners some are holding. This is a local meeting of the Sydney Alliance, a nonparty political organization that brings together different community organizations, unions, and religious organizations to advance common good issues. One of their three main advocacy issues is city transport.

A little south of Castle Hill, the area around Parramatta is a part of the city where the strains of commuting are also being acutely felt. Parramatta itself was one of the first colonial settlements in Australia, once a small village at the country end of the sluggish Parramatta River, reachable only by river or dirt track in the early days of colonial settlement. It is now the geographical center of Sydney and is a city in its own right. Outside, a forest of sleek glassy towers dwarfs the grand Victorian building we are in, and an assortment of slender cranes promises more. At least half of the population of western Sydney works outside this region of the city, necessitating lengthy journeys to and from work. Underinvestment in public transport in this region forces many commuters into cars, resulting in the chronic congestion that is familiar to this part of the city.

The mood in the hall is an odd torsion of light-hearted camaraderie mixed with serious ambition. It is a demonstration of a different kind from that represented by the NWRL information center, explored in section 2. This is more akin to riding a wave of collective energy than quiet contemplation. After the roll call of organizations, Kurt, the assembly's transport spokesperson, is the first to address the warmed-up crowd. "Improving transport in this part of the city is not just about grand infrastructure projects," says Kurt, echoing Massumi's point about taking the next step. "It's about making the best of what we've got right now." As he says these words, people holding placards above their heads emblazoned with railway station names parade down the center aisle through the assembled crowd. They make their way up the steep wooden stairs onto the stage. Appropriately, the placards bear the names of the nineteen stations across Sydney's rail network that are yet to have step-free access, impeding access for many commuters. The sign-bearers are followed by a few people dragging heavy suitcases and one woman with a baby carriage. They ascend the wooden stairs to the stage with decidedly less grace than the sign-bearers; the power of this simulation is revealed to the assembled organizations and local MPs through their authentically pained grimaces.

Alliance

What made the Sydney Alliance choose step-free access as a transport issue to champion? To learn about this, I met with the man addressing the assembly to discern how the group advocates for commuters. Kurt tells me that, first, transport was identified as an issue that crossed the many diverse organizations that make up the assembly. The next step was about figuring out what transport goal they wanted to achieve, through discussions with each organization and with experts in the field. "We didn't want to just be one of those organizations who are just saying, 'Transport's rubbish; do something,'" Kurt tells me. "So we came up with this little formula, four hundred to fifteen to one." This formula highlights important aspects of accessibility: four hundred stands for public transport within four hundred meters of where people are and where they want to go. Fifteen is for the frequency in minutes of public transport. One is for one ticket, even if your journey contains multiple parts. As Kurt says, this was "a neat way of trying to encapsulate what it was that we thought was at least a vision for what we should be aiming for with policy improvements." When they road-tested this formula with members, other issues were raised, especially safety, so SCA^2 was added to the formula, standing for *safe, clean, accessible,* and *affordable.*

The next step was about identifying "measures that we can actually start trying to pin the government into making a commitment to acting upon, rather than just a vague idea." Kurt tells me that one of the first alliance campaigns was about staffing at interchange stations, because a previous government had closed ticket offices and removed staff. "That was a good campaign to get a lot of people fired up," he says. "We did all sorts of little actions where we had all of our people in different districts going and doing nighttime safety audits at different train stations." Although he admits that it was harder to get the state government to act on the staffing issue, he tells me that they made some good progress in related areas. "For example, at Redfern, lighting came up and we went to the City of Sydney and got some improvements in lighting there. Similarly, in some of the western suburb stations around Blacktown, we got the council doing stuff."

"It's about making use of the stuff that we've got," Kurt says. Rather than announcing another "big vanity project," he says, they asked: "'What could we be doing now? What are the baby steps that would actually make a difference? What about just doubling the frequency of the buses in between the train lines that we've got? What about fixing the train stations?' That isn't ten-year, *Alice in Wonderland* stuff, you know. You could take the fee off the train station to the airport with a stroke of a pen tomorrow," he says, referring to the station entry surcharge for commuters and travelers using the airport railway station. "There are a few thousand people whose lives would be very different if they could catch the train to work," rather than alighting at the previous station and walking to the airport to avoid the tax.[50] "Just seeing the difference that makes to people's lives, when you actually get that infrastructure in, is really, hopefully, a positive thing to be campaigning around," Kurt says.

Part of the alliance's tactics are about bringing issues to the attention of the state government. Their tactics are different from those of other organizations. "We don't do submissions and we don't do consultation," Kurt tells me. "We're actually about organization." He gives me an example of a recent meeting that members of the alliance had with the state transport minister. "We were trying to get them to commit to a timetable of improvements across the network for the next ten years," he says. Drawing attention to the spatial politics of infrastructure investments across the city, he says that the group wanted a transparent sense of how resources were being allocated and how priorities were being determined. "What we were starting to get into was a discussion about priorities and about process. ... Is it just who shouts the loudest?"

J. K. Gibson-Graham's writings on what they call *post-capitalist* economy are instructive for helping evaluate the politics of the alliance. Their argument is that to invoke large and unwieldy entities such as capitalism, as traditional economic analysis often does, blinds us from appreciating the countless diverse practices and relations that make up the full spectrum of economic activity, most of which are not formally recognized in more traditional analysis, which focuses on waged labor. Translating this point to the realm of urban transport, focusing just on the success or failure of large, grand-plan infrastructure overlooks the countless potentials that all kinds of diverse, smaller-scale, incremental infrastructural changes might provide. As they point out, "We are being called to read the potentially positive futures barely visible in the present order of things, and to imagine how to strengthen and move them along."[51] Thus, though step-free access or removing the airport station access fee might be a relatively small issue that becomes lost in the sweep of policy debates that tend to focus on large-scale "vanity projects," as Kurt put it, such small steps could be potentially life-changing for many commuters in the city.[52]

Storying

As Kurt suggests, like most advocacy groups, one of the key challenges that the alliance faces as an organization is to how to have its message heard by local and state governments. This is important because these are the institutions that provide capital for the interventions proposed. Now, we turn to a member organization of the alliance to learn about the tactics that it uses in campaigning.

Ruth is a transport representative for a community forum based in Parramatta that advocates for western Sydney. "I think transport has a tendency to be about large numbers," she says. "But we're interested in representing those issues that may be left out of the major planning." These issues are about challenges that many people face, especially in this region of the city that has received disproportionately low investment in public transport. "Transport, it's unevenly distributed," she says, "and so, while you're trying to provide something that is a mass thing for a whole group of people, not everybody benefits." She gives an example of this geographical unevenness: "If you live on a certain line, you might get lots of express trains and fast trains; whereas, if you live, for instance, in Liverpool, it actually is still quite comparable in the peak to drive in on the congested M5 as it is to come in on the train, because there are a lot of stops on the Liverpool line, which means the trains go a lot slower." Ruth emphasizes that "people highly value their right to move around; and the minute that changes, you know, people are up in arms." Ruth's point here mirrors Mimi Sheller's term, *mobility justice*, which turns the spotlight firmly onto these uneven distributions of mobility.[53] Sheller argues that this uneven distribution is deeply political given that people's differential capacities to move impacts on their opportunities. She alerts us to how different axes of identity, such as gender, age, class, and race, intersect these distributions of mobility.

Ruth has a privileged perspective, having worked for both state government transport and for local community organizations, making her well-placed to reflect on their relationships. "I can actually take that knowledge and use it in a very different way to actually be an advocate for transport," she tells me. However, knowing the transport-planning terrain, she is aware of the challenges of sorting out the city's transport problems. "It's very hard to get a train line put in," she admits, "or get this put in or get a road decongested or sort out the parking; I mean, it's very complex." In a slightly world-weary tone, and reflecting the tenor of conversations I had with commuters I interviewed, she concedes that "many of us can't actually do anything about transport; that's something that's just given to us, and everybody has their own personal, individual transport challenges." Ruth's challenge, then, is to figure out who their message is for and who will listen to it. "Quite a lot of advocacy goes on," she says, "so it is actually about having to know how to get in through the doors."

Out of this knowledge and acknowledging these challenges, a project has emerged. The Transit Makes Such a Change project generated a diverse set of stories from people who live in western Sydney to emphasize the central role of transport to their lives. As a tool for guiding policy decisions, the booklet that the project produced is "trying to bring that human element into the transport conversation," Ruth says. The ethos of this project is the positive capacities that transport creates. "They're not just complaints," Ruth says. She tells me that focusing on these benefits is important, because so much talk about the city's transport problems tends to be negative. "I've been on the inside! I can see what it's like when a whole bunch of people turn up and 'this isn't right' and 'that isn't right' and they don't really know what to do about it." Warning of the dangers of negative feedback, she says, "If you get too much negative input, [the government] will just pull the shutters down." Because of the way that transport has become politicized in the city, Ruth tells me that "complaints tend to be managed, rather than used as a qualitative input." Instead, Transit Makes Such a Change "tries to showcase best practice and suggest, in that way, the government could possibly invest more."

Ruth gives me a sense of what was involved. First, she had to develop skills to become a "story activist." Then, once ten community organizations were committed to the project, these organizations were provided with a skills-development workshop and asked to bring back four stories each. "We've got stories from the refugee—the migrant stories, the aging stories, the story from Michael about vision impairments," she says, giving me a sense of the diversity of issues.[54]

"Collecting stories is one thing, but what are you going to do with them?" Ruth asks, rhetorically. Joking cynically about how such issues can often be dismissed in mainstream transport planning, she says, "You sit in a meeting and you talk about enablement, and it's like, 'Oh, excuse me while I vomit!'" I smile, having witnessed similarly dismissive responses. "I heard a lot about how the community are reflected upon in government," she says bluntly, "and it's not very kind. What I've done then with that and coming back out to the community is to try and find something which brings those two a little bit closer together." Through stories and accompanying images, Ruth says that this project is "trying to deliver to the bureaucratic system something which is a little bit more personalized." She situates this within the changing role of advocacy organizations, which she says "are a little bit passé now, in the way that governments operate. They're 'We're there for the people,' supposedly." So stories give, in her words, "a tad more validity. When I can show somebody a video of Michael, that's Michael saying those things, it's not me saying those things on behalf of Michael."

Validating this approach and evoking the enthusiasm she has witnessed, Ruth says that every bureaucrat she has talked with has been excited about this project. "You show this picture, and then suddenly people are going, 'Okay, I get it.' When you see a picture, you can kind of start relating it to yourself and your own humanity." Part of this efficacy is down to the way that the project has responded to the new landscape of social media. "The stories project is building a bunch of resources that will actually appeal in this new way that we share information and communicate," she says. "We've got six main stories that we will design up into an electronic postcard and then that postcard will be sent to politicians and to people—so this is also a strategy for the upcoming election."

"It is about trying to change the conversation that we have with people about transport and to be talking about the benefits and to try and turn on some lights for people," Ruth says, such as showing how investing in flexible transport options can open up multiple benefits for people. Especially palpable in our conversation is the joy that Ruth has witnessed from the storytellers themselves. "When I've been with people and encouraging them to get someone and to get a story and to try it out, there is their absolute joy in being able to enter into this space and realizing, 'Wow, I can do this'—you know—and who knows?"

Conclusion

In Sydney, like many other cities, debates addressing commuting problems have often revolved around formal national, state, and city government responses to these problems. The construction of new transport infrastructures has often been viewed as the silver bullet that will solve commuting problems once and for all. Accordingly, the question of *which* transport infrastructures should be constructed is therefore a charged political consideration. As this chapter has illustrated, there is a complex politics behind transport infrastructure projects. One transport project gets the go ahead and another is shelved not necessarily due to the outcome of supposedly impartial, democratic, or even rational evaluation processes, such as the use of cost–benefit analyses. Geographer Bent Flyvbjerg alerts us to the complex workings of power in relation to large infrastructural "megaprojects."[55] Through his detailed ethnographic account of a transport interchange in the Danish city of Aalborg, he exposes and untangles the hidden webs of influence at play to reveal how such projects are saturated with different powerful interests that call into question the idea of rational government. Such an analysis certainly shares parallels with the troubled history of the North West Rail Link that was the subject of this chapter.

In policy debates, it is commuting's "macropolitical" dimensions that receive the most attention.[56] The assumption is that political action, properly understood, takes place through the maneuverings of national-, state-, and city-level institutions that have the financial and institutional jurisdiction to build infrastructure and manage transport operations. It is important to trace the workings of these powerful interests. As urban theorist Ole B. Jensen points out, policymakers can intensify social inequalities by perpetuating certain interests "from above."[57] As the politicians interviewed in this chapter intimate, policies that facilitate road building over public transport investment or seductive megaprojects over less alluring incremental upgrades not only are often ideologically driven, but also result in unevenly distributed benefits. It might be tempting to try to definitively locate where commuting politics is *really* determined in the hands of the decision makers in the state government.[58] As this chapter has shown, such people certainly do play an important part. However, focusing on the power relations of decision makers and the success or failure of their ambitions is only one way to understand power in relation to transport infrastructure projects. The problem with this focus, though, is that it neglects the spectrum of other forces at play.

Much of this book has explored the significance of micropolitical, moment-to-moment transitions in capacities that are at play in any commuting event or encounter. These micropolitical transitions can enlarge or restrict people's capacities to do and sense things. For example, chapter 2 explored how the unfolding of a skirmish in a train carriage changed the capacities of the people in situ. What this means is that power is never predetermined prior to an event or situation. It is the relationship of different forces at play in events themselves that alter capacities, changing the course of events. With this in mind, this chapter has attended to some of the micropolitical dimensions of these macropolitical practices and processes. Storying my engagement with different sites of infrastructural advocacy draws attention to how, even when there is no concrete action being undertaken—such as the building of a road or the installation of a lift at a railway station—there are all kinds of micropolitical fluctuations going on, involving different combinations of forces.

Seen from this perspective, transport infrastructure changes are composed of events and encounters with the different forces of media stories, political statements, and demonstration materials, each of which have different capacities for affecting what people can do and feel. Just like any experience, these events and encounters are linked together in an ongoing manner. As section 1 demonstrates, a brief encounter with a commuter at a bus stop became looped into media headlines, which became looped into a politician's statements. Each of these encounters changed my capacities to sense what is going on. Each of these encounters built up to sensitize me to the concept of waiting as one way of thinking about this situation. Performing the story in this way shows that it is never possible to stand back and have an objective and complete bird's-eye view of a situation. Such a view is impossible because we are all immersed in worlds of experience that affect us. Retrospective analysis could attempt to identify threshold moments or trigger points with the aim of producing a cold, disembodied analysis, but such an approach would not be faithful to the worlds of experience that we are a part of.

Although it is often tempting to diagnose how events might be the product of dominant powers, Peter Adey warns that there is "a danger that we see mobility strangled, sorted and denied, or overdetermined as an outcome of some other practice, regulation or policy."[59] From this top-down perspective, events such as the demonstration in Parramatta Town Hall can only ever be understood as small openings of resistance that chip away at a dominant power, but only after that power has had its way.[60] Therefore, rather than understanding power in terms of forces that have been decided on in advance, we can think of power as being much more situational or immanent. In other words, it is the actual range of forces at play in the event itself that matters.

This immanent understanding of politics is beautifully expressed through Kathleen Stewart's description of an emergent system. She notes: "Its elements are thrown together not through the conspiracy of a state power, or a pre-existing common ground or ideal, but through events of articulation, histories of use, unintended consequences, and experiments that register. Its lines of force propel forward, spread laterally, and diverge into distinct trajectories."[61] What is so exciting about this is that what comes next can never be predetermined. For example, the instabilities of belief and disbelief continue to resonate at this site in northwest Sydney, discernible in key moments such as in the interview when Kate is momentarily hesitant about the prospect of the railway being built, as the force of years of government backflips on the project continue to make their presence felt. In a different context, as Ruth says while reflecting on her community project, who knows what is next?

This fizzing sense of indeterminacy needs to be appreciated through the fieldwork events and encounters themselves, but it also needs to be extended to the very logic of new infrastructures. Macropolitical decision-making is ultimately concerned with changing capacities. As Brian Massumi reminds us, "It would be naïve to think that [micropolitics] is separate from that kind of macro-activity. Anything that augments powers of existence creates conditions for micropolitical flourishings."[62] Investment in new public transport infrastructures is important. However, Massumi notes,

"Success at the macropolitical level is at best partial without a complementary micropolitical flourishing."[63] In other words, though new transport infrastructures can be built, doing so doesn't guarantee that the commuting challenges described in this book are solved, because different situational enablements and constraints will emerge. Macropolitical decision-making is always complicated by virtue of there being a much greater range of forces at play.[64]

This is why infrastructural change needs to be situated within each of the other sites of change that have been explored in this book. Rather than stabilizing power in a nested hierarchy of interests in which the beleaguered commuter languishes passively at the bottom, always at the mercy of a dominant government or private enterprise, power is always much more distributed and much more situational. This is exciting because it opens our eyes to the transformative potentials of each of the sites of change beaded through the experience of commuting. This is a much more "differentiated landscape of force, constraint, energy, and freedom."[65] To revisit Ruth's final words, affirmatively: What will happen next? Who knows?

Epilogue: Commuting Interventions

"Overslept. So tired. If late. Get fired. Why bother? Why the pain? Just go home. Do it again." In 2011, this poem on the New York subway received an edit by two students who papered over some of the characters in the original with different characters to create a new sentiment: "Overexcited. Energized. All smiles. Time flies. Come, brother. Much to gain. Just be proud. Do it again!" In a media interview at the time, the students claimed that the original version of the poem was simply too depressing and that it didn't capture the more uplifting aspects of transit life. The Metropolitan Transit Authority, however, wasn't in favor of this optimistic poetic adjustment; four days later, the original, more sobering poem was restored.

Indeterminacies

The tension of depletion and uplift that hovers over this soft subversion highlights an ambivalence that strikes to the heart of this book. To claim that commuting is either a negative or positive activity belies its fundamentally indeterminate nature. The indeterminacy that characterizes the oscillation between the depleting and uplifting versions of the poem in the New York subway are captured by philosopher Jacques Derrida's discussion of the ancient Greek word *pharmakon*.[1] This word refers to the capacity of something to be both poison *and* cure, rather than only one or the other. As the events and encounters in this book suggest, commuting has "pharmacological" characteristics. Commuting can tire, deplete, and cost—but commuting can enliven, excite, and energize. Commuting is differently enabling and constraining—both poison and cure.

For good or for ill, commuting is one of the most significant collective daily movements in the city. It contributes to the distinctive rhythms of urban life. Through rich and singular descriptions of events happening in commuting spaces and encounters with commuters and others who are implicated in the activity of commuting, this book has drawn out the significance of the myriad practices of moving between home and work. Far from a zone of "dead time," as has often been the assumption, the commute is a time when people work on their sense of self and engage in all manner of activities. Putting these events and encounters at the fore provides us with a richer apprehension of some of the complex experiential textures of everyday transit life in the city. In doing so, it gathers different sites in the city and beyond that together contribute to the distinctiveness of this mobile practice. From train carriages to traffic helicopters and from living rooms to board rooms, the practices that take place in the sites explored in this book each shape transit life in specific ways.

The significance of commuting is only likely to increase as processes of urbanization intensify around the world. The urgency of understanding how commuting impacts city life is heightened by the multiple infrastructure, public health, and environmental crises that presently haunt our cities. However, the indeterminacy that characterizes the artistic intervention noted earlier needs to be kept front and center when we evaluate what commuting is doing to city life. Although commuting is a shared event, snapping us into collective daily rhythms, we each bring our own habits, tendencies, and sensibilities into the picture, which makes any event or encounter fizz with instability. Brian Massumi's concept of *differential attunement* emphasizes that collective events, such as the mass daily movements of commuters, are *differently* lived.[2] This concept provides a reminder of the dangers of making grand pronouncements about what commuting is *really* doing to life in our cities. Generalized diagnoses of depletion or uplift ride roughshod over a much more intricately patterned ground.

Evaluations

Since completing the fieldwork for this book, shifts have taken place in the transport landscape of Sydney—a reminder that cities are continually evolving.[3] The North West Rail Link that was the subject of chapter 6 is almost complete, and several light rail schemes in the inner city are in the early stages of development.[4] Construction has begun on a controversial toll motorway project that proposes to alleviate congestion in some of Sydney's busiest commuting corridors. A new airport is being planned for the far west of the city. Looking even further ahead, these infrastructural transformations are folded through excited debates about how driverless vehicles might revolutionize future mobility practices in the city.[5]

New transport infrastructures will undoubtedly alter the conditions and experiences of urban mobility, and new technologies will likely have disruptive effects. However, it is vital that we are not dazzled into believing that such infrastructural and technological changes are a silver bullet for addressing the challenges of commuting. If anything, the issues in this book are likely to become even more pronounced, as commuters will continue to learn new ways of moving, experience different sorts of encounters in transit, navigate altered forms of time squeezing, affect and be affected by different transit spaces, experiment with new sorts of voicing, and engage in different forms of advocacy.

The tendency to evaluate technological changes in isolation from wider questions about our indeterminate capacities is something that troubled philosopher Félix Guattari. His writings encourage us to reflect more expansively on the nature of interventions in cities that respond to significant social problems. Writing on urban transformations, Guattari argues that "without transforming mentalities and collective habits, there will only be 'remedial' measures taken concerning the material environment."[6] Much discussion in this book and elsewhere has revolved around how to make the practice of commuting more bearable.[7] On the face of it, to suggest otherwise—that commuting shouldn't be made more bearable—might seem bizarre. However, Guattari's point is that the material environments of our cities, such as transport infrastructures, are only one dimension of a much more expansive ecology. His point challenges us to ask: What good are new transport infrastructures, or driverless vehicles for that matter, if wider questions about what we are commuting for, what we value, and the material impacts of our transit lives go ignored?

Guattari prompts us to consider how any social problem manifests across multiple zones of life, which he calls *ecologies*.[8] His point is that enduring changes need to take place across environmental, mental, and social ecologies for them to be effective. He is particularly concerned with the tendency of capitalism to homogenize and narrow what we value in terms of accumulation and lifestyle. Being effective, from his perspective, means to create new forms of value that develop and extend our potentials as creative beings, rather than have our potentials folded back into the narrow values of capitalist production that merely encourage economic competition, often with very destructive consequences.[9] In this regard, developing new transport infrastructures or driverless vehicles could be interpreted as a "remedial measure" that provides only a partial remedy to commuting problems, because it does not necessarily address some of the more stubborn social challenges and existential dilemmas of the sort that bubble up through the pages of this book.

Guattari is encouraging us to reflect on how new forms of living can emerge according to logics other than those tightly bound up with work. For him, the creation of new values involves tangled pathways across our milieus, our minds, and our social relations. What the multitude of events and encounters in this book demonstrate is how the commute itself comes to question people in ways that can shift their values; in ways that can make people rethink just what it is that matters to them; in ways that allow people to reevaluate what their work, their relationships, and their communities might mean to them. In addition to focusing on the "reek and jiggle" of the commuting journeys themselves, to use Sikivu Hutchinson's wonderfully evocative phrase,[10] the events and encounters narrated in this book gather together many different sites that tangle together milieus, minds, and social relations. It is through these knotty entanglements that it is possible to make out tipping points of different magnitudes, points at which something must give. This means that the politics of enablement and constraint in transit life are far from clear-cut. For instance, it might only be when we are at our most constrained or at our lowest ebb that a new way of going on in life might present itself.[11]

Transformations

Commuting is an activity riven with knotty relations of power. Longer-duration social formations, such as classed and gendered inequalities, can become reproduced through commuting practices. However, these forms of inequality become subtly reconfigured through the actual events and encounters that take place during commutes. These below-the-radar changes to our indeterminate capacities escape capture in rigid transport statistics, which tend to focus on our more rigid identities. Therefore, rather than imagining that commuting journeys are repetitions of the same, tending to standardization, each of the events and encounters reenacted in this book shows how events and encounters make a difference. Through a focus on the experiential dimensions of transit life, what the events and encounters narrated in this book bring out is how commuting can alter our capacities for acting, sensing, and feeling. Each of the sites highlights complex tensions of enablement and constraint that are ongoing and transitional.

Geographer Paul Harrison reminds us that "in the everyday enactment of the world there is always immanent potential for new possibilities of life."[12] This is not to naïvely downplay the significance of some of the most intransigent inequalities that exist in contemporary urban life. Instead, we can take Harrison's point to mean that we need to appreciate how some of the most obdurate forms of social inequality come about precisely through our repeated experiences of enablement and constraint. A one-off confrontation in transit might rattle and agitate, but repeated exposures to a threatening environment might change our constitution much more markedly. One long journey to work now and again might be bearable enough, but doing it repeatedly over years might reconfigure our drives and desires such that we might be drawn to participate in a project such as this. Furthermore, institutions working to change urban mobility that have social justice at the fore get their momentum in part from people whose capacities have been affected by repeated experiences in transit, especially in transport-poor areas of the city.

In short, a focus on regularities and similarities can leave us with the impression that the social life of the commute is merely the playing out of a set of rigid social scripts, in which social life is neat but disarmed. However, focusing in on singular moments in commuting lives, as this book has done, makes social life live again. Rather than prescribing lofty diagnoses of why commuters might be engaging in certain practices and then leaning on relatively bounded meanings that such explanation might provide, the way that the fieldwork has been presented in this book has tried to remain faithful to at least some of the indeterminacies of aspiration and sorrow, confusion and revelation that fizz through these encounters. The storying of transit life in interviews adds further richness by opening a site to heighten all kinds of backward-tracing realizations for commuters, subtly changing capacities still further. Even the event of engaging with these accounts as a reader might prompt small but significant transformations in us, in the way that the accounts might cause us to question ourselves anew.

We might be tempted to imagine that it is only supposedly "dominant" powers that have the capacity to intervene in commuting problems. In the sphere of urban transport, these dominant powers might be different domains of government, urban planners, architects, and policy makers. There are certainly good reasons why we should look to these institutions and actors to help solve some of the most critical transport problems currently faced by many cities. However, when we look only to these supposedly dominant powers for intervention, this obscures the myriad transformations taking place in transit life that are not reducible to these institutions and actors; it overdetermines transit life as the outcome of a limited set of agencies; and it relegates commuters themselves to a passive situation where they are always at the mercy of powers that have been decided in advance. In response, this book challenges us to become more attentive to the more complex, emergent distribution of forces that play out in unpredictable ways in transit life. As we have witnessed, interventions happen across a range of different sites and at different durations: from the moment-to-moment shifts in capacities through events experienced during the commute, to the shifts in capacities that made up the interview encounters presented here. It is precisely this richness and complexity that is transit life.

Notes

Introduction

1. The installation commissioned in 1991 was originally intended to be displayed for a year but has been left in situ ever since.

2. Bill Bryson, *The Lost Continent: Travels in Small Town America* (London: Secker and Warburg, 1991), 49.

3. As Daniel Gilbert notes, "Driving in traffic is a different kind of hell every day." In Tom Vanderbilt, *Traffic: Why We Drive the Way We Do (and What It Says about Us)* (London: Penguin 2009), 141.

4. Tim Edensor, "Commuter," in *Geographies of Mobilities: Practices, Spaces, Subjects*, ed. Tim Cresswell and Peter Merriman (Aldershot: Ashgate, 2011).

5. Douglas Kahneman et al., "A Survey Method for Characterizing Daily Life Experience: The Day Reconstruction Method," *Science* 306, no. 5702 (2004).

6. Elwyn Brooks White, *Here Is New York* (New York: Little Book Room, 2011), 26.

7. Get Living London, "British workers will spend 1 year 35 days commuting 191,760 miles in their lifetime," Get Living London (n.d.), accessed July 6, 2016, http://www.getlivinglondon.com/pressmedia/british-workers-will-spend-1-year-35 -days-commuting-191-760-miles-in-their-lifetime.aspx.

8. Glenn Lyons and Kiron Chatterjee, "A Human Perspective on the Daily Commute: Costs, Benefits and Trade-Offs," *Transport Reviews* 28, no. 2 (2008).

9. Ibid.

10. "British workers will spend 1 year 35 days commuting," Get Living London.

11. John Urry, *Mobilities* (Cambridge: Polity, 2007), 4.

12. Colin Pooley and Jean Turnbull, "Modal Choice and Modal Change: The Journey to Work in Britain since 1890," *Journal of Transport Geography* 8, no. 1 (2000): 14.

13. David Harvey terms this phenomenon *time space compression*. See David Harvey, *The Condition of Postmodernity: An Enquiry into the Origins of Social Change* (Oxford: Blackwell, 1989), 260–307.

14. Pooley and Turnbull, "Modal Choice and Modal Change."

15. Rachel Aldred, "The Commute," in *The Routledge Handbook of Mobilities*, ed. Peter Adey et al. (London: Routledge, 2014), 453.

16. Urry, *Mobilities*, 4.

17. Jennie Middleton, "'I'm on Autopilot, I Just Follow the Route': Exploring the Habits, Routines, and Decision-Making Practices of Everyday Urban Mobilities," *Environment and Planning A* 43, no. 12 (2011).

18. Peter Hall and Ulrich Pfeiffer, *Urban Future 21: A Global Agenda for Twenty-First Century Cities* (London: Routledge, 2013).

19. Lara Tan, "Metro Manila Has 'Worst Traffic on Earth,' Longest Commute," CNN Philippines, accessed October 31, 2015, http://cnnphilippines.com/metro/2015/10/01/Metro-Manila-Philippines-worst-traffic-longest-commute-Waze-survey.html.

20. Visarut Sankam, "Research Reveals Ugly Side to Bangkok Life," *The Nation*, accessed October 31, 2015, http://www.nationmultimedia.com/national/Research-reveals-ugly-side-to-Bangkok-life-30271979.html.

21. John Pucher et al., "Urban Transport Crisis in India," *Transport Policy* 12, no. 3 (2005).

22. Julien Bouissou, "Mumbai's Rail Commuters Pay a High Human Price for Public Transport," *The Guardian*, October 29, 2013, https://www.theguardian.com/world/2013/oct/29/india-mumbai-population-rail-accidents.

23. John Calfee and Clifford Winston, "The Value of Automobile Travel Time: Implications for Congestion Policy," *Journal of Public Economics* 69, no. 1 (1998).

24. Cebr, *The Future Economic and Environmental Costs of Gridlock in 2030* (London: Cebr, 2014).

25. David Metz, *The Limits to Travel: How Far Will You Go?* (London: Routledge, 2012).

26. Howard Frumkin, "Urban Sprawl and Public Health," *Public Health Reports* 117, no. 3 (2002): 201.

27. See, for instance, Peter Baccini, "A City's Metabolism: Towards the Sustainable Development of Urban Systems," *Journal of Urban Technology* 4, no. 2 (2007).

28. See David Bannister, *Transport Planning: In the UK, USA and Europe* (London: Spon Press, 2004).

29. Jared Walker, *Human Transit: How Clearer Thinking about Public Transit Can Enrich Our Communities and Our Lives* (Washington, DC: Island Press, 2012).

30. Vanderbilt, *Traffic*, 142.

31. Jon Shaw and Iain Doherty, *The Great Transport Debate* (Bristol, UK: Policy Press, 2014). See also Robin Law, "Beyond 'Women and Transport': Towards New Geographies of Gender and Daily Mobility," *Progress in Human Geography* 23, no. 4 (1999).

32. Bureau of Infrastructure, Transport and Regional Economics, *Population Growth, Jobs Growth and Commuting Flows in Sydney: Report 132* (Canberra: Australian Government Department of Infrastructure and Regional Development, 2012), 202.

33. Office of National Statistics, *Commuting and Personal Well-being, 2014* (London: Office of National Statistics, 2014), 1. This report states: "Holding all else equal, commuters have lower life satisfaction, a lower sense that their daily activities are worthwhile, lower levels of happiness and higher anxiety on average than non-commuters."

34. Erin Manning, *Relationscapes: Movement, Art, Philosophy* (Cambridge, MA: MIT Press, 2009).

35. Chloe Chard, *Pleasure and Guilt on the Grand Tour: Travel Writing and Imaginative Geography, 1600–1830* (Manchester: Manchester University Press, 1999).

36. See, for instance, Chaim Noy, "Performing Identity: Touristic Narratives of Self-Change," *Text and Performance Quarterly* 24, no. 2 (2004); Avril Maddrell, "Moving and Being Moved: More-than-Walking and Talking on Pilgrimage Walks in the Manx Landscape," *Culture and Religion* 14, no. 1 (2013).

37. Francisco Sionil José, *Tree* (Manila: Solidaridad Publishing House, 1981), 1.

38. Levi Bryant, "The Ethics of the Event: Deleuze and Ethics without Αρχή," in *Deleuze and Ethics*, ed. Nathan Jun and Daniel Smith (Edinburgh: Edinburgh University Press, 2011), 25.

39. Pauline McGuirk and Phillip O'Neill, "Planning a Prosperous Sydney: The Challenges of Planning Urban Development in the New Urban Context," *Australian Geographer* 33, no. 3 (2002).

40. Robert Freestone, "Planning Sydney: Historical Trajectories and Contemporary Debates," in *Sydney: The Emergence of a World City*, ed. John Connell (Melbourne: Oxford University Press, 2000).

41. McGuirk and O'Neill, "Planning a Prosperous Sydney."

42. Bureau of Infrastructure, Transport and Regional Economics, *Australia's Commuting Distance: Cities and Regions: Information Sheet 73* (Canberra: Australian Government Department of Infrastructure and Regional Development, 2015).

43. Delia Falconer, *Sydney* (Sydney: NewSouth Publishing, 2010), 21.

44. Tom Baker and Kristian Ruming, "Making 'Global Sydney': Spatial Imaginaries, Worlding and Strategic Plans," *International Journal of Urban and Regional Research* 39, no. 1 (2015): 71.

45. John Hawkins et al., *IBM Australia Commuter Pain Study* (Sydney: IBM, 2011), https://www-03.ibm.com/press/au/en/presskit/33518.wss.

46. Scott Lennon, *Sydney: Australia's Global City* (Sydney: PricewaterhouseCoopers and NSW Business Chamber, 2010), 11.

47. Edensor, "Commuter."

48. Mimi Sheller and John Urry, "The New Mobilities Paradigm," *Environment and Planning A* 38, no. 2 (2006).

49. John Urry, *Sociology beyond Societies: Mobilities for the Twenty-First Century* (London: Routledge, 2000).

50. Elizabeth Shove, Mika Pantzar, and Matt Watson, *The Dynamics of Social Practice: Everyday Life and How It Changes* (London: Sage, 2012).

51. In this book, pseudonyms are used for the names of all participants to preserve anonymity, with the exceptions of Rob in chapter 2; Nick in chapter 4; Vic, Bambul, and Justin in chapter 5; and Kurt in chapter 6 who were happy to be named.

52. Monika Büscher, John Urry, and Katian Witchger, eds., *Mobile Methods* (London: Routledge, 2010).

53. Within human geography, performative thinking has been developed most extensively through nonrepresentational theories. For an overview, see J-D Dewsbury et al., "Enacting Geographies," *Geoforum* 33, no. 4 (2002).

54. Ben Anderson and Paul Harrison, eds., *Taking-Place: Non-representational Theories and Geography* (Aldershot, UK: Ashgate, 2010).

55. Mitch Rose, "Negative Governance: Vulnerability, Biopolitics and the Origins of Government," *Transactions of the Institute of British Geographers* 39, no. 2 (2014).

56. Mike Savage and Roger Burrows, "Some Further Reflections on the Coming Crisis of Empirical Sociology," *Sociology* 43, no. 4 (2009).

57. Kathleen Stewart, "Regionality," *Geographical Review* 103, no. 2 (2013): 284.

58. Raymond Williams, *Marxism and Literature* (Oxford: Oxford University Press, 1977), 129–130.

59. Lauren Berlant, "Humorless. Serious. Critical" (paper presented at the Moods of Criticism: Theatrical, Humorless, Prurient, Susceptible, Alacritous panel of the MLA conference, Philadelphia, Pennsylvania, January 7, 2017).

60. Monika Büscher and John Urry, "Mobile Methods and the Empirical," *European Journal of Social Theory* 12, no. 1 (2009): 103–104.

1   Impression Zones

1. On the prevalence of car travel as the most likely mode of transport despite initiatives to transform commuting, see John Urry, "The 'System' of Automobility," *Theory, Culture and Society* 21, no. 4–5 (2004).

2. By evaluating practices such as commuting in this way, "the understanding breaks it up into successive and distinct states, supposed to be invariable." Henri Bergson, *The Creative Mind*, trans. Mabelle Andison (New York: Philosophical Library, 1946), 15.

3. Henri Bergson, *Creative Evolution*, trans. Arthur Mitchell (New York: Modern Library, 1944), 102.

4. Graeme Davison, "Australia: First Suburban Nation?," *Journal of Urban History* 22, no. 1 (1995).

5. Wolfgang Schivelbusch, *The Railway Journey: The Industrialization of Time and Space in the Nineteenth Century* (Berkeley: University of California Press, 1986).

6. Marc Augé, *In the Metro* (Minneapolis: University of Minnesota Press, 2002), 6.

7. Ibid., 7.

8. Ibid., 8.

9. David Seamon, *A Geography of the Lifeworld: Movement, Rest and Encounter* (London: Croom Helm, 1979). Seamon is interested in understanding how the habitual "body ballets" of individuals give rise to regular "time-space routines." Here, it is the collective aspects of habit that become important, because these time-space routines coalesce to form "place ballets."

10. The M2 is the highway between Sydney's northwest and the CBD.

11. A study in Cambridge, England, found that contrary to the idea that people weigh how they prefer to travel, then relocate, then travel in their expected way (known as the *self-selection hypothesis*), people's experiences of their new commute are much more changeable and ad hoc as they adjust to new routines. See Caroline Jones and David Ogilvie, "Motivations for Active Commuting: A Qualitative Investigation of the Period of Home or Work Relocation," *International Journal of Behavioral Nutrition and Physical Activity* 9, no. 109 (2012).

12. Tim Cresswell, *On the Move: Mobility in the Modern Western World* (London: Routledge, 2006), 85–95.

13. Anthony Giddens, *The Constitution of Society: Outline of the Theory of Structuration* (Cambridge: Polity, 1984), xxxii.

14. Tacit knowledge is the "mundane frame of reference within which ordinary persons routinely apperceive our phenomenal world." Rod Watson, "Tacit Knowledge," *Theory, Culture and Society* 23, no. 2–3 (2006): 208.

15. Ian Walker, Gregory Thomas, and Bas Verplanken, "Old Habits Die Hard: Travel Habit Formation and Decay during an Office Relocation," *Environment and Behavior* 47, no. 10 (2015).

16. On the significance of differential mobilities over the lifecourse, see Elaine Stratford, *Geographies, Mobilities, and Rhythms Over the Life-Course: Adventures in the Interval* (London: Routledge, 2015).

17. Elizabeth Shove, Mika Pantzar, and Matt Watson, *The Dynamics of Social Practice: Everyday Life and How It Changes* (London: Sage, 2012).

18. Cecily Maller and Yolande Strengers, "The Global Migration of Everyday Life: Investigating the Practice Memories of Australian Migrants," *Geoforum* 44, no. 1 (2013).

19. Kim Kullman, "Pedagogical Assemblages: Rearranging Children's Traffic Education," *Social and Cultural Geography* 16, no. 3 (2015): 257.

20. Ibid.

21. Peter Merriman, *Driving Spaces: A Cultural-Historical Geography of England's M1 Motorway* (Oxford: Blackwell, 2007), 152–160.

22. Kullman, "Pedagogical Assemblages," 257.

23. Horton's research shows that cycling is often perceived as frightening in a car-based environment. David Horton, "Fear of Cycling," in *Cycling and Society*, ed. David Horton, Paul Rosen, and Peter Cox (Aldershot, UK: Ashgate, 2007), 133–152.

24. Félix Ravaisson, *Of Habit*, trans. Clare Carlisle and Mark Sinclair (London: Continuum, 2008).

25. "It is not action that gives birth to or strengthens the continuity or repetition of locomotion; it is a more obscure and unreflective tendency, which goes further down into the organism, increasingly concentrating itself there." Ravaisson, *Of Habit*, 53.

26. Pragmatist philosopher John Dewey describes this as the "stability essential to living." John Dewey, *Human Nature and Conduct* (London: Dover, 2002), 19.

27. Tim Ingold, *The Perception of the Environment: Essays in Livelihood, Dwelling and Skill* (London: Routledge, 2000), 291.

28. On the sensate dimensions of cycling in the city, see Justin Spinney, "Cycling the City: Movement, Meaning and Method," *Geography Compass* 3, no. 2 (2009).

29. As Kullman points out, the focus on traffic education and danger in the literature on mobile learning means that "it is easy to forget that traffic can also be a pleasurable setting, where one learns to collaborate with different road users and acquires new bodily skills." Kullman, "Pedagogical Assemblages," 261.

30. Maurice Merleau-Ponty, *Phenomenology of Perception* (London: Routledge, 2002), 166.

31. Elizabeth Grosz writes that habit enables bodies to "accommodate real forces and effects through the minimization of the energy and conscious awareness that concerted action involves." See Elizabeth Grosz, "Habit Today: Ravaisson, Bergson, Deleuze and Us," *Body and Society* 19, no. 2–3 (2013): 218.

32. David Lapoujade, "The Normal and the Pathological in Bergson," *MLN* 120, no. 5 (2006): 1152.

33. J-D Dewsbury and Paul Cloke, "Spiritual Landscapes: Existence, Performance and Immanence," *Social and Cultural Geography* 10, no. 6 (2009): 697.

34. Ibid.

35. Hubert Dreyfus, "Intelligence without Representation: Merleau-Ponty's Critique of Mental Representation," *Phenomenology and the Cognitive Sciences* 1, no. 4 (2002).

36. Rachel Aldred writes that cyclists undertake identity management to negotiate between appearing too competent and not competent enough. See Rachel Aldred, "Incompetent or Too Competent? Negotiating Everyday Cycling Identities in a Motor Dominated Society," *Mobilities* 8, no. 2 (2013).

37. Graham and Thrift argue that practices of repair and maintenance are the "invisible work" undertaken on an everyday basis to keep cities moving. Stephen Graham and Nigel Thrift, "Out of Order: Understanding Repair and Maintenance," *Theory, Culture and Society* 24, no. 3 (2007).

38. The maximum legal speed on this freeway is 110 km/h.

39. William James writes that the efficacy of habit requires a suppression in consciousness. He says that "we pitch or catch, we shoot or chop the better the less tactile and muscular (the less resident), and the more exclusively optical (the more remote) our consciousness is." William James, *The Principles of Psychology* (Cambridge, MA: Harvard University Press, 1983), 1128.

40. Maxine Sheets-Johnstone, *The Primacy of Movement* (Philadelphia: John Benjamins Publishing, 2011).

41. David Seamon, "Body-Subject, Time-Space Routines, and Place-Ballets," in *The Human Experience of Space and Place*, ed. Anne Buttimer and David Seamon (London: Croom Helm, 1980).

42. This experience of exhaustion mirrors Rabinbach's account of fatigue as a bodily depletion of energy. Anson Rabinbach, *The Human Motor: Energy, Fatigue, and the Origins of Modernity* (Chicago: University of Chicago Press, 1992).

43. See Friederike Ziegler and Tim Schwanen, "'I Like to Go Out to Be Energised by Different People': An Exploratory Analysis of Mobility and Wellbeing in Later Life," *Aging and Society* 31, no. 5 (2011).

44. Joe Moran, *Reading the Everyday* (London: Routledge, 2005), 163.

45. Yi-Fu Tuan, *Space and Place: The Perspective of Experience* (London: Pion, 1977), 182.

46. Michel Foucault, *The Use of Pleasure*, vol. 2 of *The History of Sexuality*, trans. Robert Hurley (Harmondsworth, UK: Penguin, 1984), 10–11.

2   Fizzing Intensities

1. Arlie Walsh, "Sardine Express: Welcome to the Peak Hour Commute on Sydney Trains," *Channel 9 News*, November 11, 2014, http://www.9news.com.au/national/2014/11/11/20/17/sardine-express-for-sydney-trains.

2. Transport for New South Wales, *Train Statistics 2014* (Sydney: Bureau of Transport Statistics, 2014).

3. Nigel Thrift, *Spatial Formations* (London: Sage, 1996), 266.

4. Alfred Hitchcock's 1951 psychological crime thriller *Stranger on a Train* and Agatha Christie's 1975 *Murder on the Orient Express* are two classic cinematic expressions of the dangers of "capsular" travel.

5. Paul Theroux, *Last Train to Zona Verde* (London: Penguin, 2013).

6. Jenny Diski, *Stranger on a Train: Daydreaming and Smoking Around America* (London: Virago, 2002).

7. Tim Edensor, "Mundane Mobilities, Performances and Spaces of Tourism," *Social and Cultural Geography* 8, no. 2 (2007).

8. Nigel Thrift, "But Malice Aforethought: Cities and the Natural History of Hatred," *Transactions of the Institute of British Geographers* 30, no. 2 (2005): 140.

9. Helen Wilson, "Passing Propinquities in the Multicultural City: The Everyday Encounters of Bus Passengering," *Environment and Planning A* 43, no. 3 (2011); Greg Noble, "Pedagogies of Civic Belonging: Finding One's Way through Social Space," in

Cultural Pedagogies and Human Conduct, ed. Megan Watkins, Greg Noble and Catherine Driscoll (London: Routledge, 2015).

10. Doreen Massey, *For Space* (Sage: London, 2005), 9.

11. Eric Laurier and Chris Philo, "Cold Shoulders and Napkins Handed: Gestures of Responsibility," *Transactions of the Institute of British Geographers* 31, no. 2 (2006).

12. Harold Garfinkel, *Studies in Ethnomethodology* (Cambridge: Polity, 1991). See also Erving Goffman, *Behavior in Public Places: Notes on the Social Organization of Gatherings* (New York: Free Press, 1963).

13. David Bissell, "Travelling Vulnerabilities: Mobile Timespaces of Quiescence," *Cultural Geographies* 16, no. 4 (2009).

14. Ben Anderson and James Ash, "Atmospheric Methods," in *Non-representational Methodologies: Re-envisioning Research*, ed. Phillip Vannini (London: Routledge, 2015), 35.

15. Gernot Böhme, "Atmosphere as the Fundamental Concept of a New Aesthetics," *Thesis Eleven* 36, no. 1 (1993): 114.

16. Anderson and Ash, "Atmospheric Methods," 35.

17. Ibid., 45.

18. Allan Pred, *Lost Words and Lost Worlds: Modernity and the Language of Everyday Life in Late Nineteenth-Century Stockholm* (Cambridge: Cambridge University Press, 1990).

19. Ben Anderson, "Affective Atmospheres," *Emotion, Space and Society* 2, no. 2 (2009): 79.

20. Goffman, *Behavior in Public Places*, 39.

21. Michael Bull, *Sound Moves: iPod Culture and Urban Experience* (London: Routledge, 2007).

22. On the changeability of familiar commuting routes, see Tim Edensor, "Defamiliarizing the Mundane Roadscape," *Space and Culture* 6, no. 2 (2003).

23. Peter Adey, *Mobility* (London: Routledge, 2010).

24. Tim Richardson and Ole B. Jensen, "How Mobility Systems Produce Inequality: Making Mobile Subject Types on the Bangkok Sky Train," *Built Environment* 34, no. 2 (2008).

25. Rob Imrie, "Disability and Discourses of Mobility and Movement," *Environment and Planning A* 32, no. 9 (2000).

26. Around 2.3 percent of the whole of Sydney's workforce is now from Wollongong, making that city a large dormitory suburb. See Bureau of Infrastructure, Transport and Regional Economics, *Population Growth, Jobs Growth and Commuting Flows in Sydney: Research Report 132* (Canberra: Australian Government Department of Infrastructure and Transport, 2012).

27. This is well in excess of the average one-way commuting time in Sydney of just under thirty-five minutes.

28. Sound has a specific role within this event. As Simpson clarifies, sound both signifies and affects. For example, there is a symbolic dimension to the boy's line "a dirty mullet"—a reference to his own haircut. However, this is entwined with a complex affective dimension created by the sound itself, involving the boy's timbre of voice, volume, and repetition within the carriage at this time, such that "a dirty mullet" becomes a complex mixture of taunt, irony, disparagement, and humor. See Paul Simpson, "Falling on Deaf Ears: A Post-phenomenology of Sonorous Presence," *Environment and Planning A* 41, no. 11 (2009).

29. Gilles Deleuze, *Expressionism in Philosophy: Spinoza*, trans. Martin Joughin (New York: Zone Books, 1990).

30. Brian Massumi, *The Power at the End of the Economy* (Durham, NC: Duke University Press, 2014), 108.

31. Philip Fisher, *The Vehement Passions* (Princeton, NJ: Princeton University Press, 2002), 15.

32. Sara Ahmed, *The Cultural Politics of Emotion* (London: Routledge, 2004), 103.

33. Thrift, "But Malice Aforethought," 134.

34. Gilles Deleuze and Claire Parnet, *Dialogues II*, trans. Hugh Tomlinson and Barbara Habberjam (London: Continuum, 2002), 126.

35. Ibid.

36. Gilles Deleuze, *Logic of Sense*, trans. Mark Lester and Charles Stivale (London: Continuum, 2004), 176.

37. Billy Ehn and Orvar Löfgren, "Routines—Made and Unmade," in *Time, Consumption, and Everyday Life: Practice, Materiality and Culture*, ed. Elizabeth Shove, Frank Trentmann, and Richard Wilk (Oxford: Berg, 2009).

38. Colin Symes, "Coaching and Training: An Ethnography of Student Commuting on Sydney's Suburban Trains," *Mobilities* 2, no. 3 (2008).

39. Ainsley Hughes, Kathleen Mee, and Adam Tyndall, "'Super Simple Stuff?': Crafting Quiet in Trains Between Newcastle and Sydney," *Mobilities* 12, no. 5 (2017).

40. Colin Symes, "Entr'acte: Mobile Choreography and Sydney Rail Commuters," *Mobilities* 8, no. 4 (2013).

41. Symes, "Coaching and Training," 452.

42. Tim Cresswell, *On the Move: Mobility in the Modern Western World* (London: Routledge, 2006).

43. Maria Hynes, "Reconceptualizing Resistance: Sociology and the Affective Dimension of Resistance," *The British Journal of Sociology* 64, no. 4 (2013): 571.

44. David Conradson and Alan Latham, "The Affective Possibilities of London: Antipodean Transnationals and the Overseas Experience," *Mobilities* 2, no. 2 (2007), 235.

45. Wilson, "Passing Propinquities," 645.

46. Jack Simmons, ed., *Railway Travelers' Handy Book: Hints, Suggestions and Advice, before the Journey, on the Journey and After the Journey* (London: Old House Books, 1862).

47. Steve Woolgar and Daniel Neyland, *Mundane Governance: Ontology and Accountability* (Oxford: Oxford University Press, 2013).

48. Thrift, "But Malice Aforethought."

3 Squeezed Transitions

1. Jane-Frances Kelly and Paul Donegan, *City Limits: Why Australia's Cities Are Broken and How We Can Fix Them* (Melbourne: Melbourne University Press, 2015).

2. Nolan Feeney, "See How Bad Your Commute Is Compared to Other Cities," *TIME*, March 18, 2015, http://time.com/3748746/commute-times/.

3. Alois Stutzer and Bruno Frey, "Stress that Doesn't Pay: The Commuting Paradox," *Scandinavian Journal of Economics* 110, no. 2 (2008).

4. Don DeLillo, *Point Omega: A Novel* (New York: Simon and Schuster, 2010), 44–45.

5. Hartmut Rosa, *Social Acceleration: A New Theory of Modernity* (New York: Columbia University Press, 2013).

6. Thomas Hylland Eriksen, *Tyranny of the Moment: Fast and Slow Time in the Information Age* (London: Pluto Press, 2001); Ben Agger, *Speeding Up Fast Capitalism* (Boulder, CO: Paradigm Publishers, 2004).

7. Judy Wajcman, "Life in the Fast Lane? Towards a Sociology of Technology and Time," *British Journal of Sociology* 59, no. 1 (2008).

8. This contrasts with Rosa's suggestion that social acceleration is characterized by the reduced amount of time taken for "goal-oriented" and "intentional" processes, such as "transport, communication and production." Hartmut Rosa, "Social Acceleration: Ethical and Political Consequences of a Desynchronized High-Speed Society," *Constellations* 10, no. 1 (2003): 6.

9. For a distinction between extensive and intensive, see Scott Lash, *Intensive Culture: Social Theory, Religion and Contemporary Capitalism* (London: Sage, 2010).

10. Eviatar Zerubavel, *Hidden Rhythms: Schedules and Calendars in Social Life* (Berkeley: University of California Press, 1985).

11. On the coexistence of the past in the present, see Henri Bergson, *Matter and Memory*, trans. Nancy M. Paul and W. Scott Palmer (New York: Zone Books, 1988).

12. Helen Jarvis, Andy Pratt, and Peter Wu, *The Secret Lives of Cities: Social Reproduction of Everyday Life* (Harlow: Prentice Hall, 2001).

13. Paul Harrison, "Making Sense: Embodiment and the Sensibilities of the Everyday," *Environment and Planning D: Society and Space* 18, no. 4 (2000).

14. James W. Carey, *Communication as Culture: Essays on Media and Society* (Boston: Unwin Hyman, 1989). Timetables are also a key technique of the social organization of time; see Eviatar Zerubavel, "Timetables and Scheduling: On the Social Organization of Time," *Sociological Inquiry* 46, no. 2 (1976).

15. On how mothers organize their children's schedules, see Dale Southerton, "Analysing the Temporal Organization of Daily Life: Social Constraints, Practices and their Allocation," *Sociology* 40, no. 3 (2006).

16. On how cars permit complex daily routines to take place, see Robyn Dowling, "Cultures of Mothering and Car Use in Suburban Sydney: A Preliminary Investigation," *Geoforum* 31, no. 3 (2000). On how cars are a significant site of parenting, see Gordon Waitt and Theresa Harada, "Parenting, Care and the Family Car," *Social and Cultural Geography* 18, no. 8 (2016).

17. For a critical reflection, see Glenn Lyons and John Urry, "Travel Time Use in the Information Age," *Transportation Research Part A: Policy and Practice* 39, no. 2–3 (2005).

18. Nicola Green, "On the Move: Technology, Mobility, and the Mediation of Social Time and Space," *Information Society* 18, no. 4 (2002).

19. Tim Ingold, *The Perception of the Environment: Essays in Livelihood, Dwelling and Skill* (London: Routledge, 2000), 189–208.

20. New technological developments include apps such as Periscope, which allows users to transmit live video from their phone, thus making it possible for users to

broadcast their commutes to the world in real time. This show and tell nature of the journey to work is becoming surprisingly familiar, although the narrative is a little less well-curated (typically, "Tell me what you guys are up to?" "Well, what do you want to know?").

21. Ben Anderson, "Time Stilled, Space Slowed: How Boredom Matters," *Geoforum* 35, no. 6 (2004).

22. On the differentiation of travel time, see Weiqiang Lin, "Wasting Time? The Differentiation of Travel Time in Urban Transport," *Environment and Planning A* 44, no. 10 (2012).

23. Henri Lefebvre, *Everyday Life in the Modern World,* trans. Sacha Rabinovitch (London: Transaction Publishers, 1984).

24. Melissa Gregg, *Work's Intimacy* (Cambridge: Polity, 2011).

25. On how mobile workers learn to perform intricate tasks while on the move, see Eric Laurier, "Doing Office Work on the Motorway," *Theory, Culture and Society* 21, no. 4–5 (2004).

26. James J. Gibson, *The Ecological Approach to Perception* (London: Houghton Mifflin, 1979).

27. Christena Nippert-Eng, "Calendars and Keys: The Classification of 'Home' and 'Work,'" *Sociological Forum* 11, no. 3 (1996).

28. Michel de Certeau, *The Practice of Everyday Life*, trans. Steven Rendall (Berkeley: University of California Press, 1984), 111.

29. Glenn Lyons, "Transport and Society," *Transport Reviews* 24, no. 4 (2004).

30. John Urry, *Mobilities* (Cambridge: Polity, 2007), 4.

31. However, average figures indicate that the amount of travel time remains relatively constant at around one hour per day. Ibid.

32. Between 2006 and 2011, the number of long-distance commuters in Australia rose by 37 percent to around 213,773, or about 2 percent of the Australian workforce. Hema de Silva, Leanne Johnson, and Karen Wade, "Long Distance Commuters in Australia: A Socio-Economic and Demographic Profile" (paper presented at the Australasian Transport Research Forum, Adelaide, Australia, September 28–30, 2011).

33. Organisation for Economic Co-operation and Development, "How Persistent are Regional Disparities in Employment? The Role of Geographic Mobility," in *OECD Employment Outlook* (Paris: Organisation for Economic Co-operation and Development, 2005).

34. Kelly and Donegan, *City Limits*.

35. Claude Jacquier, "On Relationships between Integrated Policies for Sustainable Urban Development and Urban Governance," *Tijdschrift voor Economische en Sociale Geografie* 96, no. 4 (2005).

36. Jago Dodson, and Neil Sipe, *Shocking the Suburbs: Oil Vulnerability in the Australian City* (Kensington, Australia: UNSW Press, 2008).

37. Katharina Manderscheid, "Integrating Space and Mobilities into the Analysis of Social Inequality," *Distinktion: Scandinavian Journal of Social Theory* 10, no. 1 (2009): 7.

38. Angela T. Ragusa, "Seeking Trees or Escaping Traffic? Socio-cultural Factors and 'Tree-Change' Migration in Australia," in *Demographic Change in Australia's Rural Landscapes*, ed. Gary W. Luck, Digby Race, and Rosemary Black (New York: Springer, 2010).

39. Ibid.

40. Félix Ravaisson, *Of Habit*, trans. Clare Carlisle and Mark Sinclair (London: Continuum, 2008).

41. Sasha Roseneil, "On Not Living with a Partner," *Sociological Research Online* 11, no. 3 (2006).

42. Arlie R. Hochschild, *The Time Bind: When Home Becomes Work and Work Becomes Home* (New York: Metropolitan, 1997).

43. Helen Jarvis, "Moving to London Time: Household Co-ordination and the Infrastructure of Everyday Life," *Time and Society* 14, no. 1 (2005).

44. Ben Anderson, "Preemption, Precaution, Preparedness: Anticipatory Action and Future Geographies," *Progress in Human Geography* 34, no. 6 (2010).

45. See also Scott A. Cohen, Tara Duncan, and Maria Thulemark, "Lifestyle Mobilities: The Crossroads of Travel, Leisure and Migration," *Mobilities* 10, no. 1 (2015).

46. Erika Sandow and Kerstin Westin, "The Persevering Commuter: Duration of Long-Distance Commuting," *Transportation Research Part A: Policy and Practice* 44, no. 6 (2010).

47. Lauren Berlant, "Slow Death (Sovereignty, Obesity, Lateral Agency)," *Critical Inquiry* 33, no. 4 (2007): 754.

48. Ibid., 759.

49. Ibid., 754.

50. A consistent refrain in teleworking; see Sandi Mann and Lynn Holdsworth, "The Psychological Impact of Teleworking: Stress, Emotions and Health," *New Technology, Work and Employment* 18, no. 3 (2003).

51. On the transition from Fordism to post-Fordism, see Ash Amin, ed., *Post-Fordism: A Reader* (Oxford: Blackwell, 2011).

52. On the strained relationships between teleworkers and managers, see Yehuda Baruch, "Teleworking: Benefits and Pitfalls as Perceived by Professionals and Managers," *New Technology, Work and Employment* 15, no. 1 (2000).

53. Susanne Tietze and Gillian Musson, "When 'Work' Meets 'Home': Temporal Flexibility as Lived Experience," *Time and Society* 11, no. 2–3 (2002).

54. John Urry, "Mobility and Proximity," *Sociology* 36, no. 2 (2002).

55. On mobile work and issues of control, see Sven Kesselring, "Corporate Mobilities Regimes: Mobility, Power and the Socio-geographical Structurations of Mobile Work," *Mobilities* 10, no. 4 (2015).

56. Hannah Lewis et al., "Hyper-precarious Lives: Migrants, Work and Forced Labour in the Global North," *Progress in Human Geography* 39, no. 5 (2015).

57. Ibid.

58. Merijn Oudenampsen and Gavin Sullivan, "Precarity and N/European Identity: An Interview with Alex Foti (Chain-Workers)," *Mute* 2, no. 0 (2004), http://www .metamute.org/editorial/articles/precarity-and-neuropean-identity-interview-alex -foti-chainworkers.

4 Experimental Interruptions

1. Michael Wolf, *Tokyo Compression Revisited* (Hong Kong: Asia One Books, 2011).

2. Henri Lefebvre, *The Production of Space*, trans. Donald Nicholson-Smith (Oxford: Blackwell, 1991).

3. Stuart Elden, "There Is a Politics of Space Because Space Is Political: Henri Lefebvre and the Production of Space," *Radical Philosophy Review* 10, no. 2 (2007): 112.

4. Peter Merriman, "Human Geography without Time-Space," *Transactions of the Institute of British Geographers* 37, no. 1 (2012).

5. Ole B. Jensen, "Flows of Meaning, Cultures of Movements: Urban Mobility as Meaningful Everyday Life Practice," *Mobilities* 4, no. 1 (2009).

6. Steven Graham and Nigel Thrift, "Out of Order: Understanding Repair and Maintenance," *Theory, Culture and Society* 24, no. 3 (2007): 1–25.

7. Anna Tsing, *Friction: An Ethnography of Global Connection* (Princeton, NJ: Princeton University Press, 2005).

8. David Bissell and Gillian Fuller, *Stillness in a Mobile World* (London: Routledge, 2011).

9. Jon Shaw and Iain Docherty, *The Transport Debate* (Bristol, UK: Policy Press, 2014).

10. Georg Simmel, "The Metropolis and Mental Life," in *The Blackwell City Reader*, ed. Gavin Bridge and Sophie Watson (Oxford: Blackwell, 2010), 19.

11. Gillian Fuller, "The Arrow—Directional Semiotics: Wayfinding in Transit," *Social Semiotics* 12, no. 3 (2002).

12. Anne Cronin, "Mobility and Market Research: Outdoor Advertising and the Commercial Ontology of the City," *Mobilities* 3, no. 1 (2008): 103.

13. In relation to automobiles, see Mimi Sheller, "Automotive Emotions: Feeling the Car," *Theory, Culture and Society* 21, no. 4–5 (2004).

14. Thomas Davenport and John Beck, *The Attention Economy: Understanding the New Currency of Business* (Cambridge, MA: Harvard Business Press, 2013).

15. Gillian Fuller, "> store > forward >: Architectures of a Future Tense," in *Aeromobilities*, ed. Saulo Cwerner, Sven Kesselring, and John Urry (London: Routledge, 2009).

16. Kurt Iveson, "Branded Cities: Outdoor Advertising, Urban Governance, and the Outdoor Media Landscape," *Antipode* 44, no. 1 (2012).

17. Anthony Elliott and David Radford, "Terminal Experimentation: The Transformation of Experiences, Events and Escapes at Global Airports," *Environment and Planning D: Society and Space* 33, no. 6 (2015).

18. On the relationship between exercise and commuting, see Simon Cook, Jon Shaw, and Paul Simpson, "Jography: Exploring Meanings, Experiences and Spatialities of Recreational Road-Running," *Mobilities* 11, no. 5 (2016).

19. Harold Schweizer, *On Waiting* (London: Routledge, 2008).

20. Ash Amin, "Re-thinking the Urban Social," *City* 11, no. 1 (2007).

21. David Harvey, *The Condition of Postmodernity: An Enquiry into the Origins of Social Change* (Oxford: Basil Blackwell, 1989). Arguably, it is the variable nature of this information that creates this effect. Although the knowledge of a precise location of a bus might "compress" the perceived distance between the vehicle and person, a delayed train or bus might at the same time create an experience of space extending out.

22. Juliet Jain, "Bypassing and WAPing: Reconfiguring Time-Tables for 'Real-Time' Mobility," in *Mobile Technologies of the City*, ed. Mimi Sheller and John Urry (London: Routledge, 2006).

23. Stephen Graham, "Software-Sorted Geographies," *Progress in Human Geography* 29, no. 5 (2005).

24. Kim Sawchuk, "Impaired," in *The Routledge Handbook of Mobilities*, ed. Peter Adey et al. (London: Routledge, 2014).

25. David Bissell, "Conceptualising Differently-Mobile Passengers: Geographies of Everyday Encumbrance in the Railway Station," *Social and Cultural Geography* 10, no. 2 (2009).

26. Rob Imrie, "Disability and Discourses of Mobility and Movement," *Environment and Planning A* 32, no. 9 (2000).

27. The ambivalence of freedom and unfreedom is well articulated in Malene Freudendal-Pedersen, *Mobility in Daily Life: Between Freedom and Unfreedom* (London: Routledge, 2009).

28. Tim Dant, "The Driver-Car," *Theory, Culture and Society* 21, no. 4–5 (2004).

29. Mimi Sheller and John Urry, eds., *Mobile Technologies of the City* (London: Routledge, 2006).

30. Patricia T. Clough, *Autoaffection: Unconscious Thought in the Age of Teletechnology* (Minneapolis: University of Minnesota Press, 2000).

31. Nigel Thrift and Shaun French, "The Automatic Production of Space," *Transactions of the Institute of British Geographers* 27, no. 3 (2002).

32. Graham, "Software-Sorted Geographies." On the complexity of social control in transit spaces, see Kaima Negishi, "From Surveillant Text to Surveilling Device: The Face in Urban Transit Spaces," *Surveillance and Society* 11, no. 3 (2013).

33. Jenni Ryall, "Frugal Opal Card Users 'Beat the System' for Cheaper Fares," *Sydney Morning Herald*, November 25, 2014, http://www.smh.com.au/nsw/frugal-opal-card -users-beat-the-system-for-cheaper-fares-20141124-11t4r0.html#ixzz46zM5Ritt.

34. On how mobility is central to the making and unmaking of intimacy, see Clare Holdsworth, *Family and Intimate Mobilities* (London: Palgrave Macmillan, 2013).

35. Peter Adey, *Mobility* (London: Routledge, 2010), 167.

36. Fuller, "> store > forward >."

37. William H. Whyte, *The Social Life of Small Urban Spaces* (New York: Project for Public Spaces, 1980).

38. Simpson uses time-lapse photography as a method of enacting Henri Lefebvre's rhythmanalysis. Paul Simpson, "Apprehending Everyday Rhythms: Rhythmanalysis, Time-Lapse Photography, and the Space-Times of Street Performance," *Cultural Geographies* 19, no. 4 (2012).

39. Gilles Deleuze, *Difference and Repetition*, trans. Paul Patton (London: Continuum, 2004).

40. As Latham and McCormack note, from this perspective, images are not just a representational snapshot. Instead, they are "resonant blocks of space-time: they have duration, even if they appear still." They describe how the images "simultaneously conjure the singularity of each individual thing, and, through repetition, the set of relations in which this thing is a participant." Alan Latham and Derek McCormack, "Thinking with Images in Non-representational Cities: Vignettes from Berlin," *Area* 41, no. 3 (2009): 253, 256.

41. David Bissell, "Encountering Stressed Bodies: Slow Creep Transformations and Tipping Points of Commuting Mobilities," *Geoforum* 51, no. 1 (2014).

42. As Hannam, Sheller, and Urry point out, aeromobilities, for instance, require vast networks of relatively immobile infrastructures or "moorings" that enable such mobility. Kevin Hannam, Mimi Sheller and John Urry, "Editorial: Mobilities, Immobilities and Moorings," *Mobilities* 1, no. 1 (2006).

43. Doreen Massey, *For Space* (London: Sage, 2005), 9.

44. Bissell, "Encountering Stressed Bodies."

45. This follows Crang and Travlou's contention that "the city produces ruins that bring the past into the present and future." Mike Crang and Pennie S. Travlou, "The City and Topologies of Memory," *Environment and Planning D: Society and Space* 19, no. 2 (2001): 174.

46. Massey, *For Space*, 120.

47. Marc Augé, *In the Metro* (Minneapolis: University of Minnesota Press, 2002), 18.

48. This is a different mode of distancing from Simmel's infamous, although more self-conscious, cultivation of a "blasé attitude." See Paula Jirón, "Mobile Borders in Urban Daily Mobility Practices in Santiago de Chile," *International Political Sociology* 4, no. 1 (2010).

49. Bernard Stiegler, *For a New Critique of Political Economy* (Cambridge: Polity, 2010).

50. Peter Adey, "Airports, Mobility and the Calculative Architecture of Affective Control," *Geoforum* 39, no. 1 (2008).

51. Nigel Thrift, "Driving in the City," *Theory, Culture and Society* 21, no. 4–5 (2004).

52. Rob Kitchin and Martin Dodge, *Code/Space: Software and Everyday Life* (Cambridge, MA: MIT Press, 2011).

53. Cronin, "Mobility and Market Research," 110.

54. Massey, *For Space*.

55. Ole B. Jensen, *Staging Mobilities* (London: Routledge, 2013).

5 Impassioned Voices

1. Phillip Vannini, *Ferry Tales: Mobility, Place, and Time on Canada's West Coast* (London: Routledge, 2012).

2. Helen Wilson, "Passing Propinquities in the Multicultural City: The Everyday Encounters of Bus Passengering," *Environment and Planning A* 43, no. 3 (2011).

3. David Bissell, "Passenger Mobilities: Affective Atmospheres and the Sociality of Public Transport," *Environment and Planning D: Society and Space* 28, no. 2 (2010).

4. Peter Adey, "'May I Have Your Attention': Airport Geographies of Spectatorship, Position, and (Im)mobility," *Environment and Planning D: Society and Space* 25, no. 3 (2007).

5. Katherine Brickell, "Towards Geographies of Speech: Proverbial Utterances of Home in Contemporary Vietnam," *Transactions of the Institute of British Geographers* 38, no. 2 (2013): 207.

6. Different forms of voicing are both a product of our social environments and need to be sustained through repetition. See Judith Butler, *Bodies that Matter: On the Discursive Limits of "Sex"* (London: Routledge, 1993).

7. Vic Lorusso is speaking in a personal capacity, and the views expressed here do not necessarily reflect the views of the company that he works for.

8. Although televised traffic reports in Sydney began in 2002, radio traffic reports have a much longer history.

9. Caren Kaplan, "Mobility and War: the Cosmic View of US 'Air Power,'" *Environment and Planning A* 38, no. 2 (2006).

10. This presents a rather different analysis of the role of the helicopter in urban commuting than that of Cwerner, who focuses on how helicopter travel is the choice of elite business people in São Paulo. Saulo Cwerner, "Vertical Flight and Urban Mobilities: The Promise and Reality of Helicopter Travel," *Mobilities* 1, no. 2 (2006).

11. Paul Simpson, "Falling on Deaf Ears: A Post-phenomenology of Sonorous Presence," *Environment and Planning A* 41, no. 11 (2009).

12. Judy Delin, *The Language of Everyday Life: An Introduction* (London: Sage, 2000), 51.

13. Arlie R. Hochschild, *The Managed Heart: Commercialization of Human Feeling* (Berkeley: University of California Press, 1983).

14. Other sorts of on-the-fly changes to routes are discussed by Laurier and Lorimer, who describe how conversational exchanges between drivers and passengers involve

scanning roadscapes for signals that a different route might be required. Eric Laurier and Hayden Lorimer, "Other Ways: Landscapes of Commuting," *Landscape Research* 37, no. 2 (2012).

15. Sianne Ngai, *Our Aesthetic Categories: Zany, Cute, Interesting* (Cambridge, MA: Harvard University Press, 2012).

16. Daya K. Thussu, *News as Entertainment: The Rise of Global Infotainment* (London: Sage, 2009).

17. This point is lucidly illustrated in Crary's dark polemic analysis of the rise—and debilitating effects—of what he calls *24/7 culture*. Jonathan Crary, *24/7: Late Capitalism and the Ends of Sleep* (London: Verso, 2014).

18. Goode describes citizen journalism as a range of web-based practices by which ordinary users engage in journalistic practices. See Luke Goode, "Social News, Citizen Journalism and Democracy," *New Media and Society* 11, no. 8 (2009): 1288.

19. David Beer, "Public Geography and the Politics of Circulation," *Dialogues in Human Geography* 3, no. 1 (2013).

20. mX "Vent Your Spleen," *mX Newspaper*, December 6, 2013, 16.

21. Dina Al-Kassim, *On Pain of Speech: Fantasies of the First Order and the Literary Rant* (Berkeley: University of California Press, 2010), 3, 18.

22. Mike Michael, "Anecdote," in *Inventive Methods: The Happening of the Social*, ed. Celia Lury and Nina Wakeford (London: Routledge, 2012).

23. Butler, *Bodies that Matter*, xxi.

24. See, for example, Mark Poster, *Information Please: Culture and Politics in the Age of Digital Machines* (Durham, NC: Duke University Press, 2006).

25. Monika Büscher, Lisa Wood and Sung-Yueh Perng, "Altruistic, Augmented, Agile: Public Crisis Response" (paper presented at the Closing Conference of the ZiF Research Group "Communicating Disaster," Bielefeld, Germany, January 26–28, 2012); see also Mimi Sheller, "News Now: Interface, Ambience, Flow, and the Disruptive Spatio-temporalities of Mobile News Media," *Journalism Studies* 16, no. 1 (2015): 12–26.

26. Shaun W. Davenport et al., "Twitter versus Facebook: Exploring the Role of Narcissism in the Motives and Usage of Different Social Media Platforms," *Computers in Human Behavior* 32 (2014).

27. CityRail was the brand for commuter rail in and around Sydney, Newcastle, and Wollongong from 1988 until 2013. It was superseded by Sydney Trains and NSW TrainLink, the former for the suburban network, and the latter for the medium- and long-distance services.

28. The UK comedy *Peep Show* uses this device extensively for comedic effect.

29. Jack Katz, *How Emotions Work* (Chicago: University of Chicago Press, 1999), 18–86.

30. Eric Laurier et al., "Driving and 'Passengering': Notes on the Ordinary Organization of Car Travel," *Mobilities* 3, no 1 (2008).

31. Erving Goffman, *Interaction Ritual: Essays in Face to Face Behaviour* (New Brunswick, NJ: Transaction Publishers, 1967).

32. Denise Riley, *Impersonal Passion: Language as Affect* (Durham NC: Duke University Press, 2005), 20.

33. Ibid.

34. Denise Riley, "'A Voice without a Mouth': Inner Speech," *Que Parle* 14, no. 2 (2004): 73.

35. Riley, *Impersonal Passion*, 23.

36. Ibid., 21.

37. Eckhart Tolle, *The Power of Now* (Sydney: Hachette, 2009).

38. Riley, *Impersonal Passion*, 27.

39. Graeme Turner, "Politics, Radio and Journalism in Australia," *Journalism* 10, no. 4 (2009).

40. Ben Anderson, "Time-Stilled, Space-Slowed: How Boredom Matters," *Geoforum* 35, no. 6 (2004).

41. Richard Sennett, *Flesh and Stone: The Body and the City in Western Civilization* (New York: W. W. Norton, 1994).

42. Turner, "Politics, Radio and Journalism," 422.

43. Ibid., 416.

44. Doreen Massey, *For Space* (London: Sage, 2005), 151.

45. Yi-Fu Tuan, "Language and the Making of Place: A Narrative-Descriptive Approach," *Annals of the Association of American Geographers* 81, no. 4 (1991), 684; emphasis added.

46. Pierre Bourdieu, *The Logic of Practice* (Redwood City, CA: Stanford University Press, 1990), 71.

6   Stranded Expectations

1. Emilio Ferrier, Sean Macken, and Sam Stewart, *Getting Us There: Funding the Transport Infrastructure of Tomorrow* (Sydney: The McKell Institute, 2014), 26.

2. Stephen Graham and Simon Marvin, *Splintering Urbanism: Networked Infrastructures, Technological Mobilities and the Urban Condition* (London: Routledge, 2001), 92.

3. Stephen Graham and Colin McFarlane, eds., *Infrastructural Lives: Urban Infrastructure in Context* (London: Routledge, 2014), 12.

4. Derek McCormack, "Pipes and Cables," in *The Routledge Handbook of Mobilities*, ed. Peter Adey et al. (London: Routledge, 2014), 227.

5. Ibid.

6. Peter Dwyer, "Worlds of Waiting," in *Waiting*, ed. Ghassan Hage (Melbourne: Melbourne University Press, 2009).

7. Ghassan Hage alludes to this duality of waiting as being both situational and existential when he points out that "waiting happens in time, in the sense that time and time frames pre-exist the subjects that are waiting within them. On the other hand, waiting creates time. That is, various modalities of waiting produce their own temporality that may or may not be in tune with other social and natural temporalities." Ghassan Hage, "Introduction," in *Waiting*, ed. Ghassan Hage (Melbourne: Melbourne University Press, 2009), 7.

8. Henri Bergson, *Time and Free Will: An Essay on the Immediate Data of Consciousness*, trans. F. Pogson (London: Dover, 2001).

9. Harold Schweizer, *On Waiting* (London: Routledge, 2008), 16.

10. Ibid., 128.

11. Hage, "Introduction," 2.

12. Peter Adey, *Mobility* (London: Routledge, 2010).

13. Hage, "Introduction," 4.

14. Of particular interest to me in these interviews was the capacity to diagnose public sentiment. I was not performing these interviews to uncover a journalistic scoop; instead, I was interested in hearing how these politicians might articulate some of Sydney's transport challenges and the sorts of discourses they might enact in the process.

15. This interview was conducted in late 2015.

16. Graham Currie et al., "Investigating Links between Transport Disadvantage, Social Exclusion and Well-Being in Melbourne—Preliminary Results," *Transport Policy* 16, no. 3 (2009): 97–105.

17. Tim Cresswell, "Mobilities II: Still," *Progress in Human Geography* 36, no. 5 (2012).

18. See Stephen Graham, ed., *Disrupted Cities: When Infrastructure Fails* (London: Routledge, 2010).

19. Phillip Vannini, *Ferry Tales: Mobility, Place, and Time on Canada's West Coast* (London: Routledge, 2012). A more everyday—but certainly much less desirable—sense of stuckness is central to geographer Craig Jeffrey's ethnography of educated but unemployed men in Meerut, India, who are unable to realize their goals owing to limited opportunities. Craig Jeffrey, *Timepass: Youth, Class, and the Politics of Waiting in India* (Redwood City, CA: Stanford University Press, 2010).

20. Ghassan Hage, "Waiting Out the Crisis: On Stuckedness and Governmentality," in *Waiting*, ed. Ghassan Hage (Melbourne: Melbourne University Press, 2009), 97.

21. Ibid., 102.

22. Ibid.

23. Ibid., 105.

24. Australian Bureau of Statistics, *Regional Population Growth, Australia, 2013–14*, cat no. 3218.0 (Canberra: Australian Bureau of Statistics, 2015).

25. Bob Fagan and Robyn Dowling, "Neoliberalism and Suburban Employment: Western Sydney in the 1990s," *Geographical Research* 43, no. 1 (2005).

26. Peter Thomas, "Railways," in *The Routledge Handbook of Mobilities*, ed. Peter Adey et al. (London: Routledge, 2014).

27. Ibid., 218.

28. Ibid., 222.

29. Nigel Thrift, "Intensities of Feeling: Towards a Spatial Politics of Affect," *Geografiska Annaler: Series B, Human Geography* 86, no. 1 (2004).

30. The problem here is that affect becomes recuperated as yet another terrain in which dominant powers stake their claims—often in the name of security or capital accumulation. To suggest that affect can be successfully manipulated is to overlook how its excessive dimensions limit the effective functioning of power, even when affect is its object. Because affects—understood as transitions in power, rather than secondary effects of power—are in perpetual formation, it is this perpetual formation that generates ongoing variations.

31. Mitch Rose, "Negative Governance: Vulnerability, Biopolitics and the Origins of Government," *Transactions of the Institute of British Geographers* 39, no. 2 (2014): 217.

32. This point in the article refers to the different pricing policies for Sydney's private toll motorways. Although private motorways charge tolls for motorists, the cost of using the M5 (and formerly also M4) motorway in the southwest of the city in NSW is reimbursed for privately registered vehicles by the state government. This rebate stems from an election promise by then NSW opposition leader, Bob Carr, in

1995. The cashback scheme has been in place since 1998, suggesting that politicians deem it too politically risky to remove. However, it has given rise to a geographical unevenness in the city in terms of which residents are reimbursed for their tolls.

33. Bellinda Kontominas, "These Hills Are Alive with Murmurs of Discontent," *Sydney Morning Herald*, March 13, 2007, http://www.smh.com.au/news/state -election-2007/these-hills-are-alive-with-murmurs-of-discontent/2007/03/12/ 1173548110049.html.

34. Sundanda Creagh, "Off the Rails: How the West was Stung," *Sydney Morning Herald*, September 26, 2007, 4.

35. Thomas, "Railways," 223.

36. Ibid., 222.

37. AbdouMaliq Simone, "Relational Infrastructures in Postcolonial Worlds," in *Infrastructural Lives: Politics, Experience and the Urban Fabric*, ed. Stephen Graham and Colin McFarlane (London: Routledge, 2014), 33.

38. Ibid.

39. Ibid.

40. Ilze Paklone, "Conceptualization of Visual Representation in Urban Planning," *Limes: Borderland Studies* 4, no. 2 (2011).

41. Sam Kinsley, "Representing 'Things to Come': Feeling the Visions of Future Technologies," *Environment and Planning A* 42, no. 11 (2010): 2771–2790.

42. Monica Degen, Clare Melhuish, and Gillian Rose, "Producing Place Atmospheres Digitally: Architecture, Digital Visualisation Practices and the Experience Economy," *Journal of Consumer Culture* 17, no. 1 (2017).

43. Kinsley, "Representing 'Things to Come,'" 2772.

44. Brian Massumi, *Politics of Affect* (Cambridge: Polity, 2015).

45. Nigel Thrift, "The Insubstantial Pageant: Producing an Untoward Land," *Cultural Geographies* 19, no. 2 (2012): 153.

46. Massumi, *Politics of Affect*.

47. Ibid., 2.

48. Ibid., 3.

49. Massumi's example is the antiglobalization movement. He says: "It's easy to find weaknesses in it, in its tactics or in its analysis of capitalism. If you wait around for a movement to come along that corresponds to your particular image of the correct approach, you'll be waiting your life away. Nothing is ever that neat." Ibid., 16.

50. The Airport Link railway was built as a public-private partnership. The deal involved a private operator covering the costs of building four of the stations, including the two airport stations. In return, the operator would run those stations for thirty years and have the right to impose a surcharge on fares for their use. Passengers using the two airport stations are currently charged a station access fee of A$13.80.

51. J. K. Gibson-Graham and Gerda Roelvink, "An Economic Ethics for the Anthropocene," *Antipode* 41, no. s1 (2010): 342.

52. Furthermore, such small steps could build momentum for larger changes. The way that the Alliance helps organizations to act in concert has some striking parallels with geographer Ed Soja's account of the importance of networked social movements and coalition building in the pursuit of social justice. Indeed, the first example in his book is the Los Angeles Bus Riders Union, a grassroots advocacy organization that won a historic legal victory in 1996 against the city's transit authority. The resulting consent decree forced the transit authority to reorient the mass transit system to better serve the city's poorest residents rather than the well-served suburban wealthy classes; conventional governance and planning in the United States has typically favored the latter group. See Ed Soja, *Seeking Spatial Justice* (Minneapolis: University of Minnesota Press, 2010).

53. Mimi Sheller, "Sustainable Mobility and Mobility Justice: Towards a Twin Transition," in *Mobilities: New Perspectives on Transport and Society*, ed. Margaret Grieco and John Urry (Aldershot, UK: Ashgate, 2011).

54. As an exemplary story, Ruth played me a short video that profiled Michael, a man with 3–5 percent vision who commutes by bus to volunteer at his local Men's Shed, a nonprofit community organization. His poignant narration described the difficulties that he experienced in reading the numbers and destination of buses, in addition to unsympathetic encounters with transport staff.

55. Bent Flyvbjerg, *Rationality and Power: Democracy in Practice* (Chicago: University of Chicago Press, 1998).

56. Jon Shaw and Iain Docherty, *The Transport Debate* (Bristol, UK: Policy Press, 2014).

57. Ole B. Jensen, *Staging Mobilities* (London: Routledge, 2013).

58. See Bruno Latour's response to the academic habit of critical thinking as perpetuating a kind of conspiracy theory. Bruno Latour, "Why Has Critique Run Out of Steam? From Matters of Fact to Matters of Concern," *Critical Inquiry* 30, no. 2. (2004): 229.

59. Adey, *Mobility*, 119.

60. Maria Hynes, "Reconceptualizing Resistance: Sociology and the Affective Dimension of Resistance," *British Journal of Sociology* 64, no. 4 (2013).

61. Kathleen Stewart, "Road Registers," *Cultural Geographies* 21, no. 4 (2014): 550.

62. Massumi, *Politics of Affect*, 81.

63. Ibid.

64. This is a point that Deleuze reaffirms in his writing with Guattari when they emphasize that "every politics is simultaneously a macropolitics and a micropolitics." Gilles Deleuze and Félix Guattari, *A Thousand Plateaus: Capitalism and Schizophrenia*, trans. Brian Massumi (London: Continuum, 1992), 213.

65. J. K. Gibson-Graham, "Diverse Economies: Performative Practices for Other Worlds," *Progress in Human Geography* 32, no. 5 (2008): 619.

Epilogue

1. Jacques Derrida, "Plato's Pharmacy," *Dissemination*, trans. Barbara Johnson (London: Athlone Press, 1981): 61–172.

2. Brian Massumi, *Politics of Affect* (Cambridge: Polity, 2015), 115.

3. Ash Amin and Nigel Thrift, *Cities: Reimagining the Urban* (Cambridge: Polity, 2002).

4. The North West Rail Link, now renamed Sydney Metro Northwest, is due to open in 2019.

5. See, for example, Hod Lipson and Melba Kurman, *Driverless: Intelligent Cars and the Road Ahead* (Cambridge, MA: MIT Press, 2016).

6. Félix Guattari, "Ecosophical Practices and the Restoration of the 'Subjective City,'" in *Machinic Eros: Writings on Japan*, ed. Gary Genosko and Jay Hetrick (Minneapolis: University of Minnesota Press, 2015), 106.

7. Juliet Jain, "The Classy Coach Commute," *Journal of Transport Geography* 19, no. 5 (2011): 1017–1022.

8. Félix Guattari, *The Three Ecologies* (London: Continuum, 2000).

9. Some of the destructive consequences are described by Franco "Bifo" Berardi, who argues that the most recent post-Fordist mode of production, which characterizes much contemporary employment, is precarious and involves us producing "subjectivities" rather than material goods. Workers in the post-Fordist economy do not leave the workplace at the end of the day, because their subjectivity is tethered to their job—which, for Berardi, results in panic and depression. See Franco "Bifo"

Berardi, *The Soul at Work: From Alienation to Autonomy* (New York: Semiotext[e], 2009).

10. Sikivu Hutchinson, "Waiting for the Bus," *Social Text* 18, no. 2 (2000): 107.

11. Gilles Deleuze and Claire Parnet, *Dialogues II*, trans. Hugh Tomlinson and Barbara Habberjam (London: Continuum, 2002), 126.

12. Paul Harrison, "Making Sense: Embodiment and the Sensibilities of the Everyday," *Environment and Planning D: Society and Space* 18, no. 4 (2000): 498.

Bibliography

Adey, Peter. "'May I Have Your Attention': Airport Geographies of Spectatorship, Position, and (Im)mobility." *Environment and Planning D: Society and Space* 25, no. 3 (2007): 515–536.

Adey, Peter. "Airports, Mobility and the Calculative Architecture of Affective Control." *Geoforum* 39, no. 1 (2008): 438–451.

Adey, Peter. *Mobility*. London: Routledge, 2010.

Agger, Ben. *Speeding Up Fast Capitalism*. Boulder, CO: Paradigm Publishers, 2004.

Ahmed, Sara. *The Cultural Politics of Emotion*. London: Routledge, 2004.

Al-Kassim, Dina. *On Pain of Speech: Fantasies of the First Order and the Literary Rant*. Berkeley: University of California Press, 2010.

Aldred, Rachel. "The Commute." In *The Routledge Handbook of Mobilities*, edited by Peter Adey, David Bissell, Kevin Hannam, Peter Merriman, and Mimi Sheller, 450–459. London: Routledge, 2014.

Aldred, Rachel. "Incompetent or Too Competent? Negotiating Everyday Cycling Identities in a Motor Dominated Society." *Mobilities* 8, no. 2 (2013): 252–271.

Amin, Ash, ed. *Post-Fordism: A Reader*. Oxford: Blackwell, 2011.

Amin, Ash. "Re-thinking the Urban Social." *City* 11, no. 1 (2007): 100–114.

Amin, Ash, and Nigel Thrift. *Cities: Reimagining the Urban*. Cambridge: Polity, 2002.

Anderson, Ben. "Affective Atmospheres." *Emotion, Space and Society* 2, no. 2 (2009): 77–81.

Anderson, Ben. "Preemption, Precaution, Preparedness: Anticipatory Action and Future Geographies." *Progress in Human Geography* 34, no. 6 (2010): 777–798.

Anderson, Ben. "Time Stilled, Space Slowed: How Boredom Matters." *Geoforum* 35, no. 6 (2004): 739–754.

Anderson, Ben, and James Ash. "Atmospheric Methods." In *Non-representational Methodologies: Re-envisioning Research*, edited by Phillip Vannini, 34–51. London: Routledge, 2015.

Anderson, Ben, and Paul Harrison, eds. *Taking-Place: Non-representational Theories and Geography*. Aldershot, UK: Ashgate, 2010.

Augé, Marc. *In the Metro*. Minneapolis: University of Minnesota Press, 2002.

Australian Bureau of Statistics. *Regional Population Growth, Australia, 2013–14*, cat no. 3218.0. Canberra: Australian Bureau of Statistics, 2015.

Baccini, Peter. "A City's Metabolism: Towards the Sustainable Development of Urban Systems." *Journal of Urban Technology* 4, no. 2 (2007): 27–39.

Baker, Tom, and Kristian Ruming. "Making 'Global Sydney': Spatial Imaginaries, Worlding and Strategic Plans." *International Journal of Urban and Regional Research* 39, no. 1 (2015): 62–78.

Bannister, David. *Transport Planning: In the UK, USA and Europe*. London: Spon Press, 2004.

Baruch, Yehuda. "Teleworking: Benefits and Pitfalls as Perceived by Professionals and Managers." *New Technology, Work and Employment* 15, no. 1 (2000): 34–49.

Beer, David. "Public Geography and the Politics of Circulation." *Dialogues in Human Geography* 3, no. 1 (2013): 92–95.

Berardi, Franco "Bifo." *The Soul at Work: From Alienation to Autonomy*. New York: Semiotext(e), 2009.

Bergson, Henri. *Creative Evolution*. Translated by Arthur Mitchell. New York: Modern Library, 1944.

Bergson, Henri. *The Creative Mind*. Translated by Mabelle Andison. New York: Philosophical Library, 1946.

Bergson, Henri. *Matter and Memory*. Translated by Nancy M. Paul and W. Scott Palmer. New York: Zone Books, 1988.

Bergson, Henri. *Time and Free Will: An Essay on the Immediate Data of Consciousness*. Translated by F. Pogson. London: Dover, 2001.

Berlant, Lauren. "Humorless. Serious. Critical." Paper presented at the "Moods of Criticism: Theatrical, Humorless, Prurient, Susceptible, Alacritous" panel of the MLA conference, Philadelphia, Pennsylvania, January 7, 2017.

Berlant, Lauren. "Slow Death (Sovereignty, Obesity, Lateral Agency)." *Critical Inquiry* 33, no. 4 (2007): 754–780.

Bissell, David. "Conceptualising Differently-Mobile Passengers: Geographies of Everyday Encumbrance in the Railway Station." *Social and Cultural Geography* 10, no. 2 (2009): 173–195.

Bissell, David. "Encountering Stressed Bodies: Slow Creep Transformations and Tipping Points of Commuting Mobilities." *Geoforum* 51, no. 1 (2014): 191–201.

Bissell, David. "How Environments Speak: Everyday Mobilities, Impersonal Speech, and the Geographies of Commentary." *Social and Cultural Geography* 16, no. 2 (2015): 146–164

Bissell, David. "Micropolitics of Mobility: Public Transport Commuting and Everyday Encounters with Forces of Enablement and Constraint." *Annals of the Association of American Geographers* 106, no. 2 (2016): 394–403.

Bissell, David. "Passenger Mobilities: Affective Atmospheres and the Sociality of Public Transport." *Environment and Planning D: Society and Space* 28, no. 2 (2010): 270–289.

Bissell, David. "Transforming Commuting Mobilities: The Memory of Practice," *Environment and Planning A* 46, no. 8 (2014): 1946–1965.

Bissell, David. "Travelling Vulnerabilities: Mobile Timespaces of Quiescence." *Cultural Geographies* 16, no. 4 (2009): 427–445.

Bissell, David, and Gillian Fuller. *Stillness in a Mobile World*. London: Routledge, 2011.

Böhme, Gernot. "Atmosphere as the Fundamental Concept of a New Aesthetics." *Thesis Eleven* 36, no. 1 (1993): 113–126.

Bouissou, Julien. "Mumbai's Rail Commuters Pay a High Human Price for Public Transport." *The Guardian*, October 29, 2013. https://www.theguardian.com/world/2013/oct/29/india-mumbai-population-rail-accidents (accessed October 31, 2015).

Bourdieu, Pierre. *The Logic of Practice*. Redwood City, CA: Stanford University Press, 1990.

Brickell, Katherine. "Towards Geographies of Speech: Proverbial Utterances of Home in Contemporary Vietnam." *Transactions of the Institute of British Geographers* 38, no. 2 (2013): 207–220.

Bryant, Levi. "The Ethics of the Event: Deleuze and Ethics without Αρχή." In *Deleuze and Ethics*, edited by Nathan Jun and Daniel Smith, 21–43. Edinburgh: Edinburgh University Press, 2011.

Bryson, Bill. *The Lost Continent: Travels in Small Town America*. London: Secker and Warburg, 1991.

Bull, Michael. *Sound Moves: iPod Culture and Urban Experience.* London: Routledge, 2007.

Bureau of Infrastructure, Transport and Regional Economics. *Australia's Commuting Distance: Cities and Regions: Information Sheet 73.* Canberra: Australian Government Department of Infrastructure and Regional Development, 2015.

Bureau of Infrastructure, Transport and Regional Economics. *Population Growth, Jobs Growth and Commuting Flows in Sydney: Report 132.* Canberra: Australian Government Department of Infrastructure and Regional Development, 2012.

Büscher, Monika, and John Urry. "Mobile Methods and the Empirical." *European Journal of Social Theory* 12, no. 1 (2009): 99–116.

Büscher, Monika, John Urry, and Katian Witchger, eds. *Mobile Methods.* London: Routledge, 2010.

Büscher, Monika, Lisa Wood, and Sung-Yueh Perng. "Altruistic, Augmented, Agile: Public Crisis Response." Paper presented at the Closing Conference of the ZiF Research Group "Communicating Disaster," Bielefeld, Germany, January 26–28, 2012.

Butler, Judith. *Bodies that Matter: On the Discursive Limits of "Sex."* London: Routledge, 1993.

Calfee, John, and Clifford Winston. "The Value of Automobile Travel Time: Implications for Congestion Policy." *Journal of Public Economics* 69, no. 1 (1998): 83–102.

Carey, James W. *Communication as Culture: Essays on Media and Society.* Boston: Unwin Hyman, 1989.

Cebr. *The Future Economic and Environmental Costs of Gridlock in 2030.* London: Cebr, 2014.

Chard, Chloe. *Pleasure and Guilt on the Grand Tour: Travel Writing and Imaginative Geography, 1600–1830.* Manchester: Manchester University Press, 1999.

Clough, Patricia T. *Autoaffection: Unconscious Thought in the Age of Teletechnology.* Minneapolis: University of Minnesota Press, 2000.

Cohen, Scott A., Tara Duncan, and Maria Thulemark. "Lifestyle Mobilities: The Crossroads of Travel, Leisure and Migration." *Mobilities* 10, no. 1 (2015): 155–172.

Conradson, David, and Alan Latham. "The Affective Possibilities of London: Antipodean Transnationals and the Overseas Experience." *Mobilities* 2, no. 2 (2007): 231–254.

Cook, Simon, Jon Shaw, and Paul Simpson. "Jography: Exploring Meanings, Experiences and Spatialities of Recreational Road-Running." *Mobilities* 11, no. 5 (2016): 744–769.

Crang, Mike, and Pennie S. Travlou. "The City and Topologies of Memory." *Environment and Planning D: Society and Space* 19, no. 2 (2001): 161–177.

Crary, Jonathan. *24/7: Late Capitalism and the Ends of Sleep.* London: Verso, 2014.

Creagh, Sundanda. "Off the Rails: How the West Was Stung." *Sydney Morning Herald,* September 26, 2007, 4.

Cresswell, Tim. "Mobilities II: Still." *Progress in Human Geography* 36, no. 5 (2012): 645–653.

Cresswell, Tim. *On the Move: Mobility in the Modern Western World.* London: Routledge, 2006.

Cronin, Anne. "Mobility and Market Research: Outdoor Advertising and the Commercial Ontology of the City." *Mobilities* 3, no. 1 (2008): 95–115.

Currie, Graham, Tony Richardson, Paul Smyth, Dianne Vella-Brodrick, Julian Hine, Karen Lucas, Janet Stanley, Jenny Morris, Ray Kinnear, and John Stanley. "Investigating Links between Transport Disadvantage, Social Exclusion and Well-Being in Melbourne—Preliminary Results." *Transport Policy* 16, no. 3 (2009): 97–105.

Cwerner, Saulo. "Vertical Flight and Urban Mobilities: The Promise and Reality of Helicopter Travel." *Mobilities* 1, no. 2 (2006): 191–215.

Dant, Tim. "The Driver-Car." *Theory, Culture and Society* 21, no. 4–5 (2004): 61–79.

Davenport, Shaun W., Shawn S. Bergman, Jacqueline Z. Bergman, and Matthew E. Fearrington. "Twitter versus Facebook: Exploring the Role of Narcissism in the Motives and Usage of Different Social Media Platforms." *Computers in Human Behavior* 32 (2014): 212–220.

Davenport, Thomas, and John Beck. *The Attention Economy: Understanding the New Currency of Business.* Cambridge, MA: Harvard Business Press, 2013.

Davison, Graeme. "Australia: First Suburban Nation?" *Journal of Urban History* 22, no. 1 (1995): 40–74.

de Certeau, Michel. *The Practice of Everyday Life.* Translated by Steven Rendall. Berkeley: University of California Press, 1984.

DeLillo, Don. *Point Omega: A Novel.* New York: Simon and Schuster, 2010.

de Silva, Hema, Leanne Johnson, and Karen Wade. "Long Distance Commuters in Australia: A Socio-Economic and Demographic Profile." Paper presented at the Australasian Transport Research Forum, Adelaide, Australia, September 28–30, 2011.

Degen, Monica, Clare Melhuish, and Gillian Rose. "Producing Place Atmospheres Digitally: Architecture, Digital Visualisation Practices and the Experience Economy." *Journal of Consumer Culture* 17, no. 1 (2017): 3–24.

Deleuze, Gilles. *Difference and Repetition.* Translated by Paul Patton. London: Continuum, 2004.

Deleuze, Gilles. *Expressionism in Philosophy: Spinoza.* Translated by Martin Joughin. New York: Zone Books, 1990.

Deleuze, Gilles. *Logic of Sense.* Translated by Mark Lester and Charles Stivale. London: Continuum, 2004.

Deleuze, Gilles, and Félix Guattari. *A Thousand Plateaus: Capitalism and Schizophrenia.* Translated by Brian Massumi. London: Continuum, 1992.

Deleuze, Gilles, and Claire Parnet. *Dialogues II.* Translated by Hugh Tomlinson and Barbara Habberjam. London: Continuum, 2002.

Delin, Judy. *The Language of Everyday Life: An Introduction.* London: Sage, 2000.

Derrida, Jacques. "Plato's Pharmacy." In *Dissemination,* trans. Barbara Johnson, 61–172. London: Athlone Press, 1981.

Dewey, John. *Human Nature and Conduct.* London: Dover, 2002.

Dewsbury, J-D, and Paul Cloke. "Spiritual Landscapes: Existence, Performance and Immanence." *Social and Cultural Geography* 10, no. 6 (2009): 695–711.

Dewsbury, J-D, Paul Harrison, Mitch Rose, and John Wylie. "Enacting Geographies." *Geoforum* 33, no. 4 (2002): 437–440.

Diski, Jenny. *Stranger on a Train: Daydreaming and Smoking Around America.* London: Virago, 2002.

Dodson, Jago, and Neil Sipe. *Shocking the Suburbs: Oil Vulnerability in the Australian City.* Kensington, Australia: UNSW Press, 2008.

Dowling, Robyn. "Cultures of Mothering and Car Use in Suburban Sydney: A Preliminary Investigation." *Geoforum* 31, no. 3 (2000): 345–353.

Dreyfus, Hubert. "Intelligence without Representation: Merleau-Ponty's Critique of Mental Representation." *Phenomenology and the Cognitive Sciences* 1, no. 4 (2002): 367–383.

Dwyer, Peter. "Worlds of Waiting." In *Waiting,* edited by Ghassan Hage, 15–26. Melbourne: Melbourne University Press, 2009.

Edensor, Tim. "Commuter." In *Geographies of Mobilities: Practices, Spaces, Subjects,* edited by Tim Cresswell and Peter Merriman, 189–203. Aldershot, UK: Ashgate, 2011.

Edensor, Tim. "Defamiliarizing the Mundane Roadscape." *Space and Culture* 6, no. 2 (2003): 151–168.

Edensor, Tim. "Mundane Mobilities, Performances and Spaces of Tourism." *Social and Cultural Geography* 8, no. 2 (2007): 199–215.

Ehn, Billy, and Orvar Löfgren. "Routines—Made and Unmade." In *Time, Consumption, and Everyday Life: Practice, Materiality and Culture*, edited by Elizabeth Shove, Frank Trentmann, and Richard Wilk, 99–114. Oxford: Berg, 2009.

Elden, Stuart. "There Is a Politics of Space Because Space Is Political: Henri Lefebvre and the Production of Space." *Radical Philosophy Review* 10, no. 2 (2007): 101–116.

Elliott, Anthony, and David Radford. "Terminal Experimentation: The Transformation of Experiences, Events and Escapes at Global Airports." *Environment and Planning D: Society and Space* 33, no. 6 (2015): 1063–1079.

Eriksen, Thomas Hylland. *Tyranny of the Moment: Fast and Slow Time in the Information Age*. London: Pluto Press, 2001.

Fagan, Bob, and Robyn Dowling. "Neoliberalism and Suburban Employment: Western Sydney in the 1990s." *Geographical Research* 43, no. 1 (2005): 71–81.

Falconer, Delia. *Sydney*. Sydney: NewSouth Publishing, 2010.

Feeney, Nolan. "See How Bad Your Commute Is Compared to Other Cities." *TIME*, March 18, 2015. http://time.com/3748746/commute-times/ (accessed October 31, 2015).

Ferrier, Emilio, Sean Macken, and Sam Stewart. *Getting Us There: Funding the Transport Infrastructure of Tomorrow*. Sydney: McKell Institute, 2014.

Fisher, Philip. *The Vehement Passions*. Princeton, NJ: Princeton University Press, 2002.

Flyvbjerg, Bent. *Rationality and Power: Democracy in Practice*. Chicago: University of Chicago Press, 1998.

Foucault, Michel. *The Use of Pleasure*. Vol. 2 of *The History of Sexuality*. Translated by Robert Hurley. Harmondsworth, UK: Penguin, 1984.

Freestone, Robert. "Planning Sydney: Historical Trajectories and Contemporary Debates." In *Sydney: The Emergence of a World City*, edited by John Connell, 119–143. Melbourne: Oxford University Press, 2000.

Freudendal-Pedersen, Malene. *Mobility in Daily Life: Between Freedom and Unfreedom*. London: Routledge, 2009.

Frumkin, Howard. "Urban Sprawl and Public Health." *Public Health Reports* 117, no. 3 (2002): 201–217.

Fuller, Gillian. "The Arrow—Directional Semiotics: Wayfinding in Transit." *Social Semiotics* 12, no. 3 (2002): 231–244.

Fuller, Gillian. "> store > forward >: Architectures of a Future Tense." In *Aeromobilities*, edited by Saulo Cwerner, Sven Kesselring, and John Urry, 63–75. London: Routledge, 2009.

Garfinkel, Harold. *Studies in Ethnomethodology*. Cambridge: Polity, 1991.

Get Living London. "British Workers Will Spend 1 Year 35 Days Commuting 191,760 Miles in Their Lifetime." Get Living London (n.d.). http://www .getlivinglondon.com/pressmedia/british-workers-will-spend-1-year-35-days -commuting-191-760-miles-in-their-lifetime.aspx (accessed July 6, 2016).

Gibson, James J. *The Ecological Approach to Perception*. London: Houghton Mifflin, 1979.

Gibson-Graham, J. K. "Diverse Economies: Performative Practices for Other Worlds." *Progress in Human Geography* 32, no. 5 (2008): 613–632.

Gibson-Graham, J. K., and Gerda Roelvink. "An Economic Ethics for the Anthropocene." *Antipode* 41, no. s1 (2010): 320–346.

Giddens, Anthony. *The Constitution of Society: Outline of the Theory of Structuration*. Cambridge: Polity, 1984.

Goffman, Erving. *Behavior in Public Places: Notes on the Social Organization of Gatherings*. New York: Free Press, 1963.

Goffman, Erving. *Interaction Ritual: Essays in Face to Face Behaviour*. New Brunswick, NJ: Transaction Publishers, 1967.

Goode, Luke. "Social News, Citizen Journalism and Democracy." *New Media and Society* 11, no. 8 (2009): 1287–1305.

Graham, Stephen. "Software-Sorted Geographies." *Progress in Human Geography* 29, no. 5 (2005): 562–580.

Graham, Stephen. *Disrupted Cities: When Infrastructure Fails*. London: Routledge, 2010.

Graham, Stephen, and Simon Marvin. *Splintering Urbanism: Networked Infrastructures, Technological Mobilities and the Urban Condition*. London: Routledge, 2001.

Graham, Stephen, and Colin McFarlane, eds. *Infrastructural Lives: Urban Infrastructure in Context*. London: Routledge, 2014.

Graham, Stephen, and Nigel Thrift. "Out of Order: Understanding Repair and Maintenance." *Theory, Culture and Society* 24, no. 3 (2007): 1–25.

Green, Nicola. "On the Move: Technology, Mobility, and the Mediation of Social Time and Space." *Information Society* 18, no. 4 (2002): 281–292.

Gregg, Melissa. *Work's Intimacy*. Cambridge: Polity, 2011.

Grosz, Elizabeth. "Habit Today: Ravaisson, Bergson, Deleuze and Us." *Body and Society* 19, no. 2–3 (2013): 218–239.

Guattari, Félix. "Ecosophical Practices and the Restoration of the 'Subjective City.'" In *Machinic Eros: Writings on Japan*, edited by Gary Genosko and Jay Hetrick, 97–116. Minneapolis: University of Minnesota Press, 2015.

Guattari, Félix. *The Three Ecologies*. London: Continuum, 2000.

Hage, Ghassan. "Waiting Out the Crisis: On Stuckedness and Governmentality." In *Waiting*, edited by Ghassan Hage, 97–106. Melbourne: Melbourne University Press, 2009.

Hage, Ghassan. "Introduction." In *Waiting*, edited by Ghassan Hage, 1–12. Melbourne: Melbourne University Press, 2009.

Hall, Peter, and Ulrich Pfeiffer. *Urban Future 21: A Global Agenda for Twenty-First Century Cities*. London: Routledge, 2013.

Hannam, Kevin, Mimi Sheller, and John Urry. "Editorial: Mobilities, Immobilities and Moorings." *Mobilities* 1, no. 1 (2006): 1–22.

Harrison, Paul. "Making Sense: Embodiment and the Sensibilities of the Everyday." *Environment and Planning D: Society and Space* 18, no. 4 (2000): 497–517.

Harvey, David. *The Condition of Postmodernity: An Enquiry into the Origins of Social Change*. Oxford: Basil Blackwell, 1989.

Hawkins, John, Catherine Caruana-McManus, Matt English, and Edward Chung. *IBM Australia Commuter Pain Study*. Sydney: IBM, 2011. https://www-03.ibm.com/press/au/en/presskit/33518.wss (accessed June 1, 2012).

Hochschild, Arlie R. *The Managed Heart: Commercialization of Human Feeling*. Berkeley: University of California Press, 1983.

Hochschild, Arlie R. *The Time Bind: When Home Becomes Work and Work Becomes Home*. New York: Metropolitan, 1997.

Holdsworth, Clare. *Family and Intimate Mobilities*. London: Palgrave Macmillan, 2013.

Horton, David. "Fear of Cycling." In *Cycling and Society*, edited by David Horton, Paul Rosen, and Peter Cox, 133–152. Aldershot, UK: Ashgate, 2007.

Hughes, Ainsley, Kathleen Mee, and Adam Tyndall. "'Super Simple Stuff?': Crafting Quiet in Trains between Newcastle and Sydney." *Mobilities* 12, no. 5 (2017): 740–757.

Hutchinson, Sikivu. "Waiting for the Bus." *Social Text* 18, no. 2 (2000): 107–120.

Hynes, Maria. "Reconceptualizing Resistance: Sociology and the Affective Dimension of Resistance." *British Journal of Sociology* 64, no. 4 (2013): 559–577.

Imrie, Rob. "Disability and Discourses of Mobility and Movement." *Environment and Planning A* 32, no. 9 (2000): 1641–1656.

Ingold, Tim. *The Perception of the Environment: Essays in Livelihood, Dwelling and Skill.* London: Routledge, 2000.

Iveson, Kurt. "Branded Cities: Outdoor Advertising, Urban Governance, and the Outdoor Media Landscape." *Antipode* 44, no. 1 (2012): 151–174.

Jacquier, Claude. "On Relationships between Integrated Policies for Sustainable Urban Development and Urban Governance." *Tijdschrift voor Economische en Sociale Geografie* 96, no. 4 (2005): 363–376.

Jain, Juliet. "Bypassing and WAPing: Reconfiguring Time-Tables for 'Real-Time' Mobility." In *Mobile Technologies of the City*, edited by Mimi Sheller and John Urry, 79–101. London: Routledge, 2006.

Jain, Juliet. "The Classy Coach Commute." *Journal of Transport Geography* 19, no. 5 (2011): 1017–1022.

James, William. *The Principles of Psychology.* Cambridge, MA: Harvard University Press, 1983.

Jarvis, Helen. "Moving to London Time: Household Co-ordination and the Infrastructure of Everyday Life." *Time and Society* 14, no. 1 (2005): 133–154.

Jarvis, Helen, Andy Pratt, and Peter Wu. *The Secret Lives of Cities: Social Reproduction of Everyday Life.* Harlow: Prentice Hall, 2001.

Jeffrey, Craig. *Timepass: Youth, Class, and the Politics of Waiting in India.* Redwood City, CA: Stanford University Press, 2010.

Jensen, Ole B. "Flows of Meaning, Cultures of Movements: Urban Mobility as Meaningful Everyday Life Practice." *Mobilities* 4, no. 1 (2009): 139–158.

Jensen, Ole B. *Staging Mobilities.* London: Routledge, 2013.

Jirón, Paula. "Mobile Borders in Urban Daily Mobility Practices in Santiago de Chile." *International Political Sociology* 4, no. 1 (2010): 66–79.

Jones, Caroline, and David Ogilvie. "Motivations for Active Commuting: A Qualitative Investigation of the Period of Home or Work Relocation." *International Journal of Behavioral Nutrition and Physical Activity* 9, no. 109 (2012): 1–12.

José, Francisco Sionil. *Tree.* Manila: Solidaridad Publishing House, 1981.

Kahneman, Douglas, Alan Krueger, David Schkade, Norbert Schwarz, and Arthur Stone. "A Survey Method for Characterizing Daily Life Experience: The Day Reconstruction Method." *Science* 306, no. 5702 (2004): 1776–1780.

Kaplan, Caren. "Mobility and War: The Cosmic View of US 'Air Power.'" *Environment and Planning A* 38, no. 2 (2006): 395–407.

Katz, Jack. *How Emotions Work*. Chicago: University of Chicago Press, 1999.

Kelly, Jane-Frances, and Paul Donegan. *City Limits: Why Australia's Cities Are Broken and How We Can Fix Them*. Melbourne: Melbourne University Press, 2015.

Kesselring, Sven. "Corporate Mobilities Regimes: Mobility, Power and the Socio-geographical Structurations of Mobile Work." *Mobilities* 10, no. 4 (2015): 571–591.

Kinsley, Sam. "Representing 'Things to Come': Feeling the Visions of Future Technologies." *Environment and Planning A* 42, no. 11 (2010): 2771–2790.

Kitchin, Rob, and Martin Dodge. *Code/Space: Software and Everyday Life*. Cambridge, MA: MIT Press, 2011.

Kontominas, Bellinda. "These Hills Are Alive with Murmurs of Discontent." *Sydney Morning Herald*, March 13, 2007. http://www.smh.com.au/news/state-election-2007/these-hills-are-alive-with-murmurs-of-discontent/2007/03/12/1173548110049.html (accessed October 15, 2015).

Kullman, Kim. "Pedagogical Assemblages: Rearranging Children's Traffic Education." *Social and Cultural Geography* 16, no. 3 (2015): 255–275.

Lapoujade, David. "The Normal and the Pathological in Bergson." *MLN* 120, no. 5 (2006): 1146–1155.

Lash, Scott. *Intensive Culture: Social Theory, Religion and Contemporary Capitalism*. London: Sage, 2010.

Latham, Alan, and Derek McCormack. "Thinking with Images in Non-representational Cities: Vignettes from Berlin." *Area* 41, no. 3 (2009): 252–262.

Latour, Bruno. "Why Has Critique Run Out of Steam? From Matters of Fact to Matters of Concern." *Critical Inquiry* 30, no. 2 (2004): 225–248.

Laurier, Eric. "Doing Office Work on the Motorway." *Theory, Culture and Society* 21, no. 4–5 (2004): 261–277.

Laurier, Eric, and Hayden Lorimer. "Other Ways: Landscapes of Commuting." *Landscape Research* 37, no. 2 (2012): 207–224.

Laurier, Eric, Hayden Lorimer, Barry Brown, Owain Jones, Oskar Juhline, Allyson Noble, Mark Perry, D. Pica, Phillipe Sormani, Ignaz Strebel, Laurel Swan, Alex S. Taylor, Laura Watts, and Alexandra Weilenmann. "Driving and 'Passengering': Notes on the Ordinary Organization of Car Travel." *Mobilities* 3, no. 1 (2008): 1–23.

Laurier, Eric, and Chris Philo. "Cold Shoulders and Napkins Handed: Gestures of Responsibility." *Transactions of the Institute of British Geographers* 31, no. 2 (2006): 193–207.

Law, Robin. "Beyond 'Women and Transport': Towards New Geographies of Gender and Daily Mobility." *Progress in Human Geography* 23, no. 4 (1999): 567–588.

Lefebvre, Henri. *Everyday Life in the Modern World.* Translated by Sacha Rabinovitch. London: Transaction Publishers, 1984.

Lefebvre, Henri. *The Production of Space.* Translated by Donald Nicholson-Smith. Oxford: Blackwell, 1991.

Lennon, Scott. *Sydney: Australia's Global City.* Sydney: PricewaterhouseCoopers and NSW Business Chamber, 2010.

Lewis, Hannah, Peter Dwyer, Stuart Hodkinson, and Louise Waite. "Hyper-precarious Lives: Migrants, Work and Forced Labour in the Global North." *Progress in Human Geography* 39, no. 5 (2015): 580–600.

Lin, Weiqiang. "Wasting Time? The Differentiation of Travel Time in Urban Transport." *Environment and Planning A* 44, no. 10 (2012): 2477–2492.

Lipson, Hod, and Melba Kurman. *Driverless: Intelligent Cars and the Road Ahead.* Cambridge, MA: MIT Press, 2016.

Lyons, Glenn. "Transport and Society." *Transport Reviews* 24, no. 4 (2004): 485–509.

Lyons, Glenn, and Kiron Chatterjee. "A Human Perspective on the Daily Commute: Costs, Benefits and Trade-Offs." *Transport Reviews* 28, no. 2 (2008): 181–198.

Lyons, Glenn, and John Urry. "Travel Time Use in the Information Age." *Transportation Research Part A: Policy and Practice* 39, no. 2–3 (2005): 257–276.

Maddrell, Avril. "Moving and Being Moved: More-than-Walking and Talking on Pilgrimage Walks in the Manx Landscape." *Culture and Religion* 14, no. 1 (2013): 63–77.

Maller, Cecily, and Yolande Strengers. "The Global Migration of Everyday Life: Investigating the Practice Memories of Australian Migrants." *Geoforum* 44, no. 1 (2013): 243–252.

Manderscheid, Katharina. "Integrating Space and Mobilities into the Analysis of Social Inequality." *Distinktion: Scandinavian Journal of Social Theory* 10, no. 1 (2009): 7–27.

Mann, Sandi, and Lynn Holdsworth. "The Psychological Impact of Teleworking: Stress, Emotions and Health." *New Technology, Work and Employment* 18, no. 3 (2003): 196–211.

Manning, Erin. *Relationscapes: Movement, Art, Philosophy*. Cambridge, MA: MIT Press, 2009.

Massey, Doreen. *For Space*. London: Sage, 2005.

Massumi, Brian. *Politics of Affect*. Cambridge: Polity, 2015.

Massumi, Brian. *The Power at the End of the Economy*. Durham, NC: Duke University Press, 2014.

McCormack, Derek. "Pipes and Cables." In *The Routledge Handbook of Mobilities*, edited by Peter Adey, David Bissell, Kevin Hannam, Peter Merriman, and Mimi Sheller, 225–232. London: Routledge, 2014.

McGuirk, Pauline, and Phillip O'Neill. "Planning a Prosperous Sydney: The Challenges of Planning Urban Development in the New Urban Context." *Australian Geographer* 33, no. 3 (2002): 301–316.

Merleau-Ponty, Maurice. *Phenomenology of Perception*. London: Routledge, 2002.

Merriman, Peter. *Driving Spaces: A Cultural-Historical Geography of England's M1 Motorway*. Oxford: Blackwell, 2007.

Merriman, Peter. "Human Geography without Time-Space." *Transactions of the Institute of British Geographers* 37, no. 1 (2012): 13–27.

Metz, David. *The Limits to Travel: How Far Will You Go?* London: Routledge, 2012.

Michael, Mike. "Anecdote." In *Inventive Methods: The Happening of the Social*, edited by Celia Lury and Nina Wakeford, 25–35. London: Routledge, 2012.

Middleton, Jennie. "'I'm on Autopilot, I Just Follow the Route': Exploring the Habits, Routines, and Decision-Making Practices of Everyday Urban Mobilities." *Environment and Planning A* 43, no. 12 (2011): 2857–2877.

Moran, Joe. *Reading the Everyday*. London: Routledge, 2005.

mX. "Vent Your Spleen." *mX Newspaper*, December 6, 2013, 16.

Negishi, Kaima. "From Surveillant Text to Surveilling Device: The Face in Urban Transit Spaces." *Surveillance and Society* 11, no. 3 (2013): 324–333.

Ngai, Sianne. *Our Aesthetic Categories: Zany, Cute, Interesting*. Cambridge, MA: Harvard University Press, 2012.

Nippert-Eng, Christena. "Calendars and Keys: The Classification of 'Home' and 'Work.'" *Sociological Forum* 11, no. 3 (1996): 563–582.

Noble, Greg. "Pedagogies of Civic Belonging: Finding One's Way through Social Space." In *Cultural Pedagogies and Human Conduct*, edited by Megan Watkins, Greg Noble, and Catherine Driscoll, 32–44. London: Routledge, 2015.

Noy, Chaim. "Performing Identity: Touristic Narratives of Self-Change." *Text and Performance Quarterly* 24, no. 2 (2004): 115–138.

Organisation for Economic Co-operation and Development. "How Persistent Are Regional Disparities in Employment? The Role of Geographic Mobility." In *OECD Employment Outlook*, 73–123. Paris: Organisation for Economic Co-operation and Development, 2005.

Office of National Statistics. *Commuting and Personal Well-being, 2014*. London: Office of National Statistics, 2014.

Oudenampsen, Merijn, and Gavin Sullivan. "Precarity and N/European Identity: An Interview with Alex Foti (ChainWorkers)." *Mute* 2, no. 0 (2004). http://www .metamute.org/editorial/articles/precarity-and-neuropean-identity-interview-alex -foti-chainworkers (accessed March 1, 2016).

Paklone, Ilze. "Conceptualization of Visual Representation in Urban Planning." *Limes: Borderland Studies* 4, no. 2 (2011): 150–161.

Pooley, Colin, and Jean Turnbull. "Modal Choice and Modal Change: The Journey to Work in Britain since 1890." *Journal of Transport Geography* 8, no. 1 (2000): 11–24.

Poster, Mark. *Information Please: Culture and Politics in the Age of Digital Machines*. Durham, NC: Duke University Press, 2006.

Pred, Allan. *Lost Words and Lost Worlds: Modernity and the Language of Everyday Life in Late Nineteenth-Century Stockholm*. Cambridge: Cambridge University Press, 1990.

Pucher, John, Nisha Korattyswaropam, Neha Mittal, and Neehu Ittyerah. "Urban Transport Crisis in India." *Transport Policy* 12, no. 3 (2005): 185–198.

Rabinbach, Anson. *The Human Motor: Energy, Fatigue, and the Origins of Modernity*. Chicago: University of Chicago Press, 1992.

Ragusa, Angela T. "Seeking Trees or Escaping Traffic? Socio-cultural Factors and 'Tree-Change' Migration in Australia." In *Demographic Change in Australia's Rural Landscapes*, edited by Gary W. Luck, Digby Race, and Rosemary Black, 71–99. New York: Springer, 2010.

Ravaisson, Félix. *Of Habit*. Translated by Clare Carlisle and Mark Sinclair. London: Continuum, 2008.

Richardson, Tim, and Ole B. Jensen. "How Mobility Systems Produce Inequality: Making Mobile Subject Types on the Bangkok Sky Train." *Built Environment* 34, no. 2 (2008): 218–231.

Riley, Denise. *Impersonal Passion: Language as Affect*. Durham, NC: Duke University Press, 2005.

Riley, Denise. "'A Voice without a Mouth': Inner Speech." *Que Parle* 14, no. 2 (2004): 57–104.

Rosa, Hartmut. "Social Acceleration: Ethical and Political Consequences of a Desynchronized High-Speed Society." *Constellations* 10, no. 1 (2003): 3–33.

Rosa, Hartmut. *Social Acceleration: A New Theory of Modernity*. New York: Columbia University Press, 2013.

Rose, Mitch. "Negative Governance: Vulnerability, Biopolitics and the Origins of Government." *Transactions of the Institute of British Geographers* 39, no. 2 (2014): 209–223.

Roseneil, Sasha. "On Not Living with a Partner." *Sociological Research Online* 11, no. 3 (2006): 1–21.

Ryall, Jenni. "Frugal Opal Card Users 'Beat the System' for Cheaper Fares." *Sydney Morning Herald*, November 25, 2014. http://www.smh.com.au/nsw/frugal-opal-card-users-beat-the-system-for-cheaper-fares-20141124-11t4r0.html#ixzz46zM5Ritt (accessed June 5, 2016).

Sandow, Erika, and Kerstin Westin. "The Persevering Commuter: Duration of Long-Distance Commuting." *Transportation Research Part A: Policy and Practice* 44, no. 6 (2010): 433–445.

Sankam, Visarut. "Research Reveals Ugly Side to Bangkok Life." *The Nation*. http://www.nationmultimedia.com/national/Research-reveals-ugly-side-to-Bangkok-life-30271979.html (accessed October 31, 2015).

Savage, Mike, and Roger Burrows. "Some Further Reflections on the Coming Crisis of Empirical Sociology." *Sociology* 43, no. 4 (2009): 762–772.

Sawchuk, Kim. "Impaired." In *The Routledge Handbook of Mobilities*, edited by Peter Adey, David Bissell, Kevin Hannam, Peter Merriman, and Mimi Sheller, 409–420. London: Routledge, 2014.

Schivelbusch, Wolfgang. *The Railway Journey: The Industrialization of Time and Space in the Nineteenth Century*. Berkeley: University of California Press, 1986.

Schweizer, Harold. *On Waiting*. London: Routledge, 2008.

Seamon, David. "Body-Subject, Time-Space Routines, and Place-Ballets." In *The Human Experience of Space and Place*, edited by Anne Buttimer and David Seamon, 146–165. London: Croom Helm, 1980.

Seamon, David. *A Geography of the Lifeworld: Movement, Rest and Encounter*. London: Croom Helm, 1979.

Sennett, Richard. *Flesh and Stone: The Body and the City in Western Civilization*. New York: W. W. Norton, 1994.

Sheets-Johnstone, Maxine. *The Primacy of Movement*. Philadelphia: John Benjamins Publishing, 2011.

Sheller, Mimi. "Automotive Emotions: Feeling the Car." *Theory, Culture and Society* 21, no. 4–5 (2004): 221–242.

Sheller, Mimi. "News Now: Interface, Ambience, Flow, and the Disruptive Spatio-temporalities of Mobile News Media." *Journalism Studies* 16, no. 1 (2015): 12–26.

Sheller, Mimi. "Sustainable Mobility and Mobility Justice: Towards a Twin Transition." In *Mobilities: New Perspectives on Transport and Society*, edited by Margaret Grieco and John Urry, 289–304. Aldershot, UK: Ashgate, 2011.

Sheller, Mimi, and John Urry, eds. *Mobile Technologies of the City*. London: Routledge, 2006.

Sheller, Mimi, and John Urry. "The New Mobilities Paradigm." *Environment and Planning A* 38, no. 2 (2006): 207–226.

Shaw, Jon, and Iain Docherty. *The Transport Debate*. Bristol, UK: Policy Press, 2014.

Shove, Elizabeth, Mika Pantzar, and Matt Watson. *The Dynamics of Social Practice: Everyday Life and How It Changes*. London: Sage, 2012.

Simmel, Georg. "The Metropolis and Mental Life." In *The Blackwell City Reader*, edited by Gavin Bridge and Sophie Watson, 11–19. Oxford: Blackwell, 2010.

Simmons, Jack, ed. *Railway Travellers' Handy Book: Hints, Suggestions and Advice, before the Journey, on the Journey and after the Journey*. London: Old House Books, 1862.

Simone, AbdouMaliq. "Relational Infrastructures in Postcolonial Worlds." In *Infrastructural Lives: Politics, Experience and the Urban Fabric*, edited by Stephen Graham and Colin McFarlane, 17–38. London: Routledge, 2014.

Simpson, Paul. "Apprehending Everyday Rhythms: Rhythmanalysis, Time-Lapse Photography, and the Space-Times of Street Performance." *Cultural Geographies* 19, no. 4 (2012): 423–445.

Simpson, Paul. "Falling on Deaf Ears: A Post-phenomenology of Sonorous Presence." *Environment and Planning A* 41, no. 11 (2009): 2556–2575.

Soja, Edward. *Seeking Spatial Justice*. Minneapolis: University of Minnesota Press, 2010.

Southerton, Dale. "Analysing the Temporal Organization of Daily Life: Social Constraints, Practices and their Allocation." *Sociology* 40, no. 3 (2006): 435–454.

Spinney, Justin. "Cycling the City: Movement, Meaning and Method." *Geography Compass* 3, no. 2 (2009): 817–835.

Stewart, Kathleen. "Regionality." *Geographical Review* 103, no. 2 (2013): 275–284.

Stewart, Kathleen. "Road Registers." *Cultural Geographies* 21, no. 4 (2014): 549–563.

Stiegler, Bernard. *For a New Critique of Political Economy*. Cambridge: Polity, 2010.

Stratford, Elaine. *Geographies, Mobilities, and Rhythms Over the Life-Course: Adventures in the Interval*. London: Routledge, 2015.

Stutzer, Alois, and Bruno Frey. "Stress that Doesn't Pay: The Commuting Paradox." *Scandinavian Journal of Economics* 110, no. 2 (2008): 339–366.

Symes, Colin. "Coaching and Training: An Ethnography of Student Commuting on Sydney's Suburban Trains." *Mobilities* 2, no. 3 (2008): 443–461.

Symes, Colin. "Entr'acte: Mobile Choreography and Sydney Rail Commuters." *Mobilities* 8, no. 4 (2013): 542–559.

Tan, Lara. "Metro Manila Has 'Worst Traffic on Earth,' Longest Commute," CNN Philippines (n.d.). http://cnnphilippines.com/metro/2015/10/01/Metro-Manila -Philippines-worst-traffic-longest-commute-Waze-survey.html (accessed October 31, 2015).

Theroux, Paul. *Last Train to Zona Verde*. London: Penguin, 2013.

Thomas, Peter. "Railways." In *The Routledge Handbook of Mobilities*, edited by Peter Adey, David Bissell, Kevin Hannam, Peter Merriman, and Mimi Sheller, 214–224. London: Routledge, 2014.

Thrift, Nigel. "But Malice Aforethought: Cities and the Natural History of Hatred." *Transactions of the Institute of British Geographers* 30, no. 2 (2005): 133–150.

Thrift, Nigel. "Driving in the City." *Theory, Culture and Society* 21, no. 4–5 (2004): 41–59.

Thrift, Nigel. "The Insubstantial Pageant: Producing an Untoward Land." *Cultural Geographies* 19, no. 2 (2012): 141–168.

Thrift, Nigel. "Intensities of Feeling: Towards a Spatial Politics of Affect." *Geografiska Annaler: Series B, Human Geography* 86, no. 1 (2004): 57–78.

Thrift, Nigel. *Spatial Formations*. London: Sage, 1996.

Thrift, Nigel, and Shaun French. "The Automatic Production of Space." *Transactions of the Institute of British Geographers* 27, no. 3 (2002): 309–335.

Thussu, Daya K. *News as Entertainment: The Rise of Global Infotainment*. London: Sage, 2009.

Tietze, Susanne, and Gillian Musson. "When 'Work' Meets 'Home': Temporal Flexibility as Lived Experience." *Time and Society* 11, no. 2–3 (2002): 315–334.

Tolle, Eckhart. *The Power of Now*. Sydney: Hachette, 2009.

Transport for New South Wales. *Train Statistics 2014*. Sydney: Bureau of Transport Statistics, 2014.

Tsing, Anna. *Friction: An Ethnography of Global Connection*. Princeton, NJ: Princeton University Press, 2005.

Tuan, Yi-Fu. "Language and the Making of Place: A Narrative-Descriptive Approach." *Annals of the Association of American Geographers* 81, no. 4 (1991): 684–696.

Tuan, Yi-Fu. *Space and Place: The Perspective of Experience*. London: Pion, 1977.

Turner, Graeme. "Politics, Radio and Journalism in Australia." *Journalism* 10, no. 4 (2009): 411–430.

Urry, John. *Mobilities*. Cambridge: Polity, 2007.

Urry, John. "Mobility and Proximity." *Sociology* 36, no. 2 (2002): 255–274.

Urry, John. *Sociology beyond Societies: Mobilities for the Twenty-First Century*. London: Routledge, 2000.

Urry, John. "The 'System' of Automobility." *Theory, Culture and Society* 21, no. 4–5 (2004): 25–39.

Vanderbilt, Tom. *Traffic: Why We Drive the Way We Do (and What It Says about Us)*. London: Penguin, 2009.

Vannini, Phillip. *Ferry Tales: Mobility, Place, and Time on Canada's West Coast*. London: Routledge, 2012.

Waitt, Gordon, and Theresa Harada. "Parenting, Care and the Family Car." *Social and Cultural Geography* 18, no. 8 (2016): 1079–1100.

Wajcman, Judy. "Life in the Fast Lane? Towards a Sociology of Technology and Time." *British Journal of Sociology* 59, no. 1 (2008): 59–77.

Walker, Ian, Gregory Thomas, and Bas Verplanken. "Old Habits Die Hard: Travel Habit Formation and Decay during an Office Relocation." *Environment and Behavior* 47, no. 10 (2015): 1089–1106.

Walker, Jared. *Human Transit: How Clearer Thinking about Public Transit Can Enrich Our Communities and Our Lives*. Washington, DC: Island Press, 2012.

Walsh, Arlie. "Sardine Express: Welcome to the Peak Hour Commute on Sydney Trains." *Channel 9 News*, November 11, 2014. http://www.9news.com.au/national/2014/11/11/20/17/sardine-express-for-sydney-trains (accessed March 12, 2016).

Watson, Rod. "Tacit Knowledge." *Theory, Culture and Society* 23, no. 2–3 (2006): 208–210.

White, Elwyn Brooks. *Here Is New York*. New York: Little Book Room, 2011.

Whyte, William H. *The Social Life of Small Urban Spaces*. New York: Project for Public Spaces, 1980.

Williams, Raymond. *Marxism and Literature*. Oxford: Oxford University Press, 1977.

Wilson, Helen. "Passing Propinquities in the Multicultural City: The Everyday Encounters of Bus Passengering." *Environment and Planning A* 43, no. 3 (2011): 634–649.

Wolf, Michael. *Tokyo Compression Revisited*. Hong Kong: Asia One Books, 2011.

Woolgar, Steve, and Daniel Neyland. *Mundane Governance: Ontology and Accountability*. Oxford: Oxford University Press, 2013.

Zerubavel, Eviatar. *Hidden Rhythms: Schedules and Calendars in Social Life*. Berkeley: University of California Press, 1985.

Zerubavel, Eviatar. "Timetables and Scheduling: On the Social Organization of Time." *Sociological Inquiry* 46, no. 2 (1976): 87–94.

Ziegler, Friederike, and Tim Schwanen. "'I Like to Go Out to Be Energised by Different People': An Exploratory Analysis of Mobility and Wellbeing in Later Life." *Ageing and Society* 31, no. 5 (2011): 758–781.

Index

Urban and Industrial Environments

Series editor: Robert Gottlieb, Henry R. Luce Professor of Urban and Environmental Policy, Occidental College